BLACK OPS

The Incredible true story of a British Secret Agent

By

Carlton King

All Rights Reserved

Copyright © Carlton King 2016

This edition first published in 2016 by: Ck

Acknowledgements

None of my activities could have been achieved without the steadfast and capable encouragement of my beautiful and highly accomplished wife. I also thank my children for their understanding of my lengthy and frequent absences throughout their lives. And finally, I thank my parents for their direction and guidance throughout my formative years. Moreover, I thank all those people from whom I've learnt much along the way. I must also add a special thanks to Sky Andrews for believing in the project and Kris Hollington for helping with it.

Content

Foreword 5

List of abbreviations 6

Disclaimer 10

Prologue - Fortitude through Intelligence *'Staying Alive, the Special Branch Way'* 11

Chapter One - Disco Days 22

Chapter Two - Home to the Met 28

Chapter Three - Getting in 33

Chapter Four - Life in the Branch 38

Chapter Five - Guarding the Gateway 49

Chapter Six - Armed and Dangerous 55

Chapter Seven – Dougie 61

Chapter Eight - Stray Dogs 68

Chapter Nine - Any Gunmen? 73

Chapter Ten - China In Our Hands 80

Chapter Eleven - Deutschland: Cold War, Luke Warm Politics 88

Chapter Twelve - Rumble from the Jungle 98

Chapter Thirteen – SDS (The Special Demonstration Squad) 103

Chapter Fourteen - Becoming the Black Bond 118

Chapter Fifteen - From MI6 to Room 1834 via the NPOIU 126

Chapter Sixteen - Royal Flush 138

Chapter Seventeen - When It Goes Wrong…144

Chapter Eighteen - Poison Chalice – Head of Iraqi Special Branch 156

Chapter Nineteen - To Any Length 166

Chapter Twenty - Heads of State 178

Chapter Twenty-One - Dis-integration 195

Images 205

Foreword

The publication of this memoir is a testimony to tenacity and evocative of David's victory over Goliath.

Over the last three and a half years, the British state, particularly Scotland Yard, has utilised every available pretext to prevent Carlton publishing his memoir. Carlton has been accused of violating national security, undermining confidentiality, damaging international security co-operation and endangering his own life, and the lives of his erstwhile colleagues.

During this struggle to gain the authority to publish his sensitively managed memoir, recounting his more than a quarter of a century at the heart of Britain's Secret Intelligence and National Security milieu, Carlton has complied with every reasonable request to protect personal and operational security. Therefore, with due cognisance to national security, Carlton's memoir lifts the lid off Britain's unnecessarily blanket national security net, to sensitively and democratically inform the public of some of the operations he undertook in their name.

Carlton's entertaining and enlightening human story captures the very spirit of endeavour, allowing us to follow the unlikely twists and turns that brought this northern lad of colonial heritage into realms, that as a child, he couldn't even imagine.

Carlton's memoir, **'Black Ops – *The incredible True Story Of A British Secret Agent'*,** should therefore be of interest to all those who wish to be informed and to understand, rightly or wrongly, what the secret state does on their behalf. However, more importantly **'Black Ops .....'** is simply an exhilaratingly good read.

List of utilised abbreviations

2ic … …..Second in Command

AAFES…Army Air Force Exchange Service (USA)

ACSO….. Assistant Commissioner Specialist Operations (MPS)

ACPO…. Association of Chief Police Officers

ATF……. Alcohol Tobacco & Firearms (USA)

ACI……..Central Intelligence Agency (Colombia)

ANO (FRC)… Abu Nidal Organisation (Fatah Revolutionary Council)

BEM….. Black & Ethnic Minority (UK)

BTP…….British Transport Police

BKA……Bundeskriminalamt (German Federal Bureau Investigation (FRG)

CAT…….Counter Assault Team

CBRN….Chemical, biological, radiological and nuclear (Weapons)

CIA…….. Central Intelligence Agency (USA)

CID…… Criminal Investigation Department (UK – Police)

CO11… Specialist Public Order policing unit (MPS)

COBRA… Cabinet Office Briefing Rooms (UK Government).

CCRU….. Covert Counter-reconnaissance Unit (MPSB/SO1)

CPA……Coalition Provisional Authority (US/UK Governing body in Iraq post 2003 invasion)

CP, Prot …. Close Personal Protection

CPI (POTA)….Commission, Preparation, Instigation of terrorism

CRI...... Centrale Recherche Informatiedienst (Netherlands Police Inelligence)

CSS..... Committee for State Security (Bulgarian)

CTC (SO15)..... Counter-Terrorism Command (MPS)

CW...... Chemical Weapons

GCS..... Government Car Service (UK)

Dangle..... Espionage speak for a covert access agent

DC...... Detective Constable

DCI..... Detective Chief Inspector (UK)

DCS.... Detective Chief Superintendent (UK)

DDR (East Germany)..... Democratic Republic of Germany

DEA....Drug Enforcement Administration (USA)

DGI.....Dirección General de Inteligencia (Cuba)

DIA (DIS).....Defence Intelligence Agency (UK MOD)

DI, Governor, Boss...... Detective Inspector

DPM....Deputy Prime Minister

DPG.... Diplomatic Protection Group (MPS)

DNI..... Colombian Security Service

DS, Skipper..... Detective Sergeant

DSU.... District Support Unit (MPS)

DSS (USDSS).... United States Diplomatic Security Service

DST.....Directorate of Territorial Security (French Security Service)

DV...... Developed Vetting (highest security clearance UK)

EOD... Explosive Ordnance Disposal officer (UK Military)

ELS..... European Liaison Section ('E' Squad MPSB)

FBI......Federal Bureau of Investigation (USA)

F&CO..... Foreign & Commonwealth Office (UK)

FSB..... Federal Security Service (Russia- KGB successor)

GCHQ.... Government Communication HQ (UK's Communications Intelligence Service)

GRU..... Soviet Military Intelligence

GID...... General Intelligence Department (Jordan)

HTLI..... High threat Low infrastructure (MPSB/SO1 Prot officer trained for HTLI environments)

HMG.....Her Majesty's Government (UK)

IDF (Military parlance)..... Indiscriminate Fire (artillery)

IDF...... Israeli Defence Force

IO... Intelligence Officer (spy)

I-Corp..... Intelligence Corps (British Military)

JTAC..... Joint Terrorism Analysis Centre (UK)

KGB...... Primary intelligence & security agency (Soviet Union)

MI5, BSS...(British) Security Service (UK)

MOD..... Ministry of Defence (UK)

MPS, The Met, Scotland Yard... The Metropolitan Police Service (London, UK)

MPSB, SB, The Branch, SO12..... Metropolitan Police Special Branch (UK Police Intelligence Service, Scotland Yard)

MP......Military Police (US Army)

MI...... Military Intelligence (US Army)

Mossad...... Israeli Intelligence Service

NCIS....National Criminal Intelligence Service (UK)

NCIS....Naval Criminal Investigative Service (USA)

PPO NCS..... National Crime Squad (UK)

NPOIU...... National Public Order Intelligence Unit (UK)

NSA....National Security Agency (USA's Secret Communications Intelligence Service)

OSA.... Official Secrets Act (UK) (The criminal law governing breaches of UK official Secrets)

OSI......Office of Special Investigation (US Air Force)

PAP......People's Armed Police (China)

PPO.....Principal (close) Protection Officer

PPS (PS)...... Personal Private Secretary (Private Secretary)

PGI......Palestinian General Intelligence (FATAH)

PC....... Police Constable

PS........ Police Sergeant

POTA...The Prevention of Terrorism Acts of 1984, 89 & 2000 (UK)

RMV.....Royalty & Ministerial Visits Committee (UK Governmental body)

RMP.....Royal Military Police (British Army)
RPG..... Rocket propelled Grenade

RP, (SO14)..... Royalty Protection (MPS)

RCMP.......Royal Canadian Mounted Police

RG......Direction Central des Renseignements Généraux (French Police intelligence)

Scotland Yard...... MPS HQ (and location of its major specialist Detective units)

SEG.... Special Escort Group (Specialist Traffic Unit (MPS)

SF...... Special Forces (UK Military - SAS/SBS)

SAU.... Strategic Analysis Unit of the NPOIU (UK)

Shin Bet (SB).....Israeli Special Branch/Security Service

SO19 (previously PT17)...... Specialist Firearms Unit (MPS)

SoSNI...... Secretary of State for Northern Ireland (UK government Minister responsible for NI)

STASI (MfSS)... Security & Intelligence Organisation (of East Germany - DDR)

SoSD...Secretary of State for Defence (UK Minister responsible for the Defence portfolio)

SoSDFID...... Secretary of State for International Development (UK Minister in charge of ID)

SAC..... Special Agent In-Charge (US - governmental rank)

SDS......Special Demonstration Squad (Ultra Deep Cover section of 'C' Squad's MPSB)

SIGINT......Signals Intelligence

SIS, MI6...... Secret Intelligence Service (UK)

SO1..... Specialist Protection (successor to MPSB's 'A' Squad)

SO13, ATB...... Anti-Terrorist Branch (MPS - CID)

Supt..... Superintendent (UK Police)

The Nick...... Police Station (MPS slang)

USSS...... United States Secret Service (USA)

UC...... Under Cover ops

UN...... United Nations

UNGA..... United Nations General Assembly

USMS..... US Marshall Service

Disclaimer

Pseudonyms are utilised for all Special Branch, National Security and Secret intelligence officers throughout this book.

Prologue
Fortitude through Intelligence
'Staying Alive, the Special Branch Way'

....4:30pm, 19 August 2003, United Nations headquarters, Baghdad...

There was nothing unusual about the flatbed truck that approached what had once been the Canal Hotel, now transformed into UN HQ. This transformation had involved a great deal of construction work, including a brick wall that surrounded the compound, and large deliveries were frequent and regular.

Inside the building, overlooking the truck, Sergio Vieira de Mello, the United Nations Secretary-General's Special Representative in Iraq (and expected to take over the post of UN Secretary-General) was hard at work at his desk.

Vieira de Mello had achieved the impossible – he had brought Iraq's many warring factions together — and had also persuaded international critics of the war in Iraq that there was no point in continued gloating; everyone had a duty to help the beleaguered country retain a long lasting stability - and that this was possible.

Times journalist Marie Colvin, killed in a Syrian rocket attack in 2012, once wrote: "He was a man whose smile could light up a ballroom in a blackout and shame men steeped in hatred into the handshake of remorse."

Sergio Vieira de Mello knew the dangers. He had witnessed terror in Ethiopia, Cambodia, Lebanon and Rwanda. But two days earlier he had told a Brazilian daily, *O Estado de Sao Paulo*, that he did not sense any Iraqi hostility towards him or the United Nations in

Baghdad. Asked if terrorists would target his UN compound, de Mello replied, "I don't believe so."

De Mello, who was the UN High Commissioner for Human Rights, was sent to Iraq because, as UN Secretary-General Kofi Annan said, no one could "hit the ground running" like Sergio. Even though, as the UN High Commissioner for Human Rights, de Mello had spoken out publicly about the 'legal black hole' at Guantanamo Bay. US President George Bush agreed with Annan's assessment: this was the best man for an impossible job.

The truck veered, as if looking for the right spot; then drove towards Sergio's window.

*

…Two weeks earlier…

"Heads up!"

The range instructor's voice cut through the gunfire. My hand itched for its Glock 17 semi-automatic pistol in the pancake holster on the right side of my hip.

Steady… I controlled my excitement, slowed my heart rate. Until the targets flipped into view - signifying an immediate and deadly threat - my Glock had to remain holstered.

Ever since an instructor had been hit in the chest by a ricochet (the bullet bounced off a rib and he survived), we were required to wear body armour at all times while on the range. I was therefore wearing my ultra-thin covert body armour, designed to be worn under a shirt, over mine. I was otherwise dressed as always, to fit in with the city's movers and shakers.

My suit had been tailored whilst I was on a mission to Singapore. French navy pin-stripe in lightweight cashmere, it was cut to an Armani design with one simple modification – it concealed the Glock pistol I generally carried in a shoulder holster so that the bulge was much harder to spot.

My pale blue silk shirt came from an area close to the five-star Estelar La Fontana Hotel in downtown Bogota, Colombia; a regular residence when on a mission in that paradoxical nation. My silk tie was a gift from the German Ambassador and my cuff links came from the US Secret Service. My chrome Omega wristwatch was down to my own extravagance.

Okay, so I was a tad overdressed for my bi-monthly reclassification shoot held at this secret range near London's Marble Arch, but I was a Special Branch officer and the Branch liked to do things differently. More importantly, if it ever happened (and it had) I had to fight as I dressed - it paid to have lightweight and perfectly fitted suits.

I enjoyed close-quarter shooting just as much as practising my unconventional mixed martial arts, and today's aim was to shoot a perfect score.

The classification shoot had several parts to it. The particular drill simulated a close quarter multiple assailant attack on my principal. It was fast and furious. As with all protection officer shoots, it would commence spontaneously, with all weapons holstered and concealed. For this shoot my Glock was loaded with a 'light' magazine of five live rounds, which would have to be replaced by another five round mag during the shoot to complete the drill. The three man-sized targets spread out in front of me, were about ten metres away and three to four metres apart from one another. Presently the targets were side on, but once they flipped to '*attack*' me, I'd have to instantly shield my principal from the assassins' bullets, hoping that any incoming rounds would miss or be defeated by my body armour, whilst simultaneously drawing my weapon and responding with deadly force. To heap the maximum amount of pressure on us, when returning fire we had to strike in a specific order. The first two rounds had to be fired into target one, followed by two into two and the remaining round into target three. Then, following the rapid re-load the next round had to be fired into target three again prior to two further rounds each into targets' two and one. Success was measured by an officer completing the whole drill within a maximum of ten seconds and by hitting the targets with *stopping* shots (i.e., no flesh wounds - the targets had to be immobilised). This drill was all about speed, timing, precision and maintaining a cool, clear head in the face of certain death.

Whooosssh. The targets turned.

"Down Minister!" I shouted, stepping in front of the figure whilst flipping my jacket open, drawing my pistol, and in a rapid smooth arc steadying on target one – I fired. BANG-BANG!

Rounds one and two were squeezed off, all within a second or so.

Shots are loud; even when wearing earmuffs and earplugs, the noise can cause you to shoot inaccurately so one has to get used to the sound.

Now controlling my breathing again I redirected my Glock onto targets two and three in quick succession. As the final round spun out of my Glock into target three its mechanism locked back - "OUT!" I screamed; an automatic response from years of training.

As I ejected the spent magazine by pushing down the mag lock with my thumb, I twisted and arched my body dropping my left hand from my Glock and whisking my jacket back to clasp the spare five-round magazine from the mag pouch on the left side of my hip. Never averting my eyes from the targets, my left hand now placed the new mag in my pistol, slamming it home. As it connected, my right hand thumb pushed the slide lever down allowing the mechanism to ratchet forward stripping a new round into the chamber. This familiar mechanical clunking sound told me my Glock was deadly again. "IN!" I shouted as I squeezed the trigger, placing bullet one into target three and then just as swiftly two into both targets two and one again.

Whoosssh, the targets snapped back to the side-on position.

Relieved I'd got them all off, I glanced across at a Branch colleague some way along the firing point. He also appeared satisfied.

Now we had to see whether we'd hit our targets.

On command, we holstered up and moved towards the targets. The instructors peered and counted, mine were all there. All centre mass.

Some training shoots, especially with the MP5, required us to aim solely for the head. This tactic was not used lightly, but if the assassin is wearing body armour then head shots it had to be. Re-evaluation was a maxim of protection, once deployed, 'Protmen' always had to be willing to reassess.

At its starkest, my present Special Branch role was simple. As a member of Scotland Yard's finest, engaged on 'A' Squad personnel protection duties, I was sanctioned to prevent would-be assassins murdering my *principal*, by all means necessary – whether it was the Prime Minister, other senior UK officials or visiting Presidents, Prime Ministers or Foreign Secretaries.

An hour later, having completed the rest of the classification shoot utilising both Glock and the MP5 machine pistol at various longer range quick-turning targets, it was time to clean both weapons, place my covert body armour in my rucksack, rearrange my clothing and reload my Glock with a full mag of seventeen live rounds.

Finally, before leaving the secret range and heading towards the tube I cocked the fully loaded weapon so it was ready to fire and placed it in the shoulder holster under my arm. Now I was ready for work.

*

My office, Room 1834, on the eighteenth floor of New Scotland Yard was the heart of Special Branch's 'A' Squad. We were expecting a sprinkling of Presidents and Prime Ministers from all corners of the globe, all on their own missions to one of the diplomatic centres of the world, full of the hopes of their respective nations.

I had spent half a lifetime monitoring various UK subversive, extremist and terrorist organisations. I'd also secured the lives of leading politicians on countless operations at home and abroad and uniquely, as an MI6 Case Officer, I'd run agents and performed operations against terrorist organisations worldwide. Regardless of my task though, it was all aimed at one thing - to oil the wheels of democracy so that peace, as far as possible, could reign.

The Metropolitan Police Special Branch was different from the rest of the police service. It was practically a force in itself and attracted unusual characters, not least due to the requirement for independent and conceptualised thinking.

I was definitely a Branch man.

Fluent in several languages, I had, like most Branch Officers, a love of history and politics and a respect for worthwhile traditions. Perhaps unlike most I'd never tried drugs or smoked cigarettes. I drank only in moderation and I almost never swore. I was audacious yet ethical, and if I was absolutely truthful I'd have to say that I battled OCD, perhaps created in part by the constant checking and rechecking required during the preparation and execution of my many missions.

Outward signs of this condition were the gleaming chrome taps in my home; the distinct lack of any fat on my body and the fact that I never, ever had a day off work.

As I pulled the numerous sensitive files out of my safe, a glance at the title of one secret pink file *'HRH The Duke of Windsor and Consort'* reminded me that I needed to find time to draft a report of my recommendation in this matter. Amid other duties, I'd been tasked with evaluating whether, in line with the 30-Year Rule, the Branch's Secret files on the Duke could be declassified and placed in the Public Records Office.

Through the years SB officers had gathered intelligence and reported secretly on the Duke's indiscretions along with those of his wife-to-be, Mrs Simpson and her friends and lovers. As a black officer I found it particularly interesting that one of the reporting Branch officers commented on a close, wealthy and extremely high society female confidante of Mrs Simpson who had *'sexual liaisons with Negros in Harlem, the Negro quarter of New York'*. It appeared that reflecting the sensibilities of the era the officer found this action in itself to be sufficient to consider both Mrs Simpson and this confidante subversive.

The files also revealed that Mrs Simpson was conducting an affair, not only with the Prince, but with a handsome Yorkshire *'cad'*. The cad, a mechanic by trade, was apparently a *'whizz'* on the dance floor and often fraudulently gave himself to have been an officer in the Great War. A *'quite unscrupulous fellow'*, the cad's interest in the Prince's consort appeared in the SB officer's opinion to be principally financial. Yet, even more interestingly, the officer surmised that the future King appeared to be aware of the affair and at least acquiesced to its continuance. Having familiarised myself with the files and considered any possible current national security sensitivities, I felt that there was no good reason to withhold this information from the British public for another thirty years.

I was in the midst of writing my report to this effect when my boss, Frank, called me into his office. 'A' Squad's second in command, Detective Superintendent Frank Thompson was one of the newer breed of SB senior management having entered the Branch as a supervisory officer. Until the mid-90s officers selected for MPSB were generally young in police service, had passed the Branch's extremely stringent selection process and held the primary police rank of constable. The aim was to mould these recruits into professional security/secret intelligence officers who, after learning the Branch's unique processes and procedures from the ground-up would remain in the department throughout their police careers. Those subsequently wishing to take up supervisory roles within the Branch had to first pass the general police promotion process before competing with similarly qualified SB colleagues for these senior posts. Gaining promotion in the Branch was therefore a highly competitive and arduous process. Frank had usurped all of this.

Frank had gained his initial promotions in uniform, rising to the rank of Inspector. Then, due to the Met Commissioner's new corporate policy known as 'Tenure', Frank had been selected to join the Branch as a Detective Inspector.

Designed to counter 'elitism' in the MPS the Tenure policy directed that the Branch accept senior uniform and CID officers into the fold. Unfortunately, unlike traditional SB supervisors these officers had no Special Branch grounding, nor allied understanding of the British security and secret intelligence community in which the Branch operated. They were instantly disadvantaged. Many such officers tended to lean heavily on their past uniform experience to deal with SB matters. This 'corporate' MPS one size fits all perspective tended to rub many established SB officers up the wrong way. Secret intelligence and security ops were intrinsically different than general duty uniform tasks. The witch hunt against elitism was compromising what the Branch had crafted for over a century – a free-thinking, self-starting, assured cadre of officers capable of performing complex and sensitive political, security and secret intelligence assignments.

Frank presently oversaw all 'A' Squad's protective security functions, save running the Prime Minister's protection team and 'A' Squad's Security Vetting functions. These elements came under 'A' Squad's other Detective Superintendent, Jim Day.

Traditionally the Branch had always engendered a fierce loyalty in its officers. However the corporate perspective and seeming willingness of many of the newer supervisors to defer to those with influence had weakened this hitherto strong independent stance. Consequently, MPSB was haemorrhaging influence vis-à-vis its secret intelligence, security and police service partners.

I entered Frank's office and took a seat.

"Carlton, I know you've got a lot on with Room 1834 and the various inbound visits, but I've just been contacted by the chair of the RMV with a job that's just been authorized to Iraq, and as you know the layout, I thought you'd be best placed to deal with it."

The Royalty and Ministerial Visits Committee (RMV) is a powerful Cabinet Office committee answerable to the Number 10 machine. The Committee decides if a member of the Royal Family or a Minister of the Crown is authorized to travel abroad on official business and dictates what precautions should be met to ensure their safety. When the committee believes that there is a significant danger to the principal's life, which could be mitigated by Close Protection (CP), the committee authorizes 'A' Squad or Royalty Protection to provide security. Close Protection is a very expensive beast and limits the freedom of Ambassadors, High Commissioners and ministerial private offices' to control a Minister's visit as the lead protection officer has the capacity to intervene in the Minister's programme on security grounds. Consequently, close protection is not lightly invoked.

The RMV sits in one of the Cabinet Office Briefing Rooms (COBRA) and is generally chaired by a Knight of the Realm. The body itself is made up of various interested parties including for the Metropolitan Police Service the Assistant Commissioner for Specialist Operations but more normally his/her delegate (Supt or DCI from 'A' Squad and/or the equivalent from Royalty protection). As head of Room 1834 I occasionally took on this role. Delegates from other organisations varied as required and included: the Chief of the Foreign and Commonwealth Office (F&CO) protocol office, representatives from the agencies (MI5, MI6 and GCHQ), the Military (often Special Forces) and various other civil servants. Additionally, the RMV took soundings from the HM Ambassador/High Commissioner of the country or countries to be visited.

"Good," I said. "I'm ready to get out of the kitchen."

"I thought you'd say that," Frank answered, as though he was doing me a favour. "I thought of you because of our previous operation in Iraq during the war. All your American contacts proved instrumental, not to mention people within, um, other government departments."

This was a euphemism for my contacts in SIS, the Security Service and the MOD. Frank, as a late entrant to the Branch, seemed rather apprehensive when dealing with such agencies and appeared to resent the relatively unfettered access I had to such sources.

"The job is to Prot Foreign Secretary Jack Straw's visit to Baghdad."

"Okay. When do you want me to travel?"

"Soon as."

*

....14:30pm, 12 August 2003, Central Baghdad HQ of the Coalition Provisional Administration...

"But the Foreign Secretary must visit de Mello!"

"I'm sorry Ambassador, it's simply not possible."

I was with Sir Jeremy Greenstock, the British Ambassador to the Coalition Provisional Administration *(CPA),* the administrative body that governed Iraq since the war had been 'won'.

"But not to do so would be akin to stating that Iraq has not been fully pacified, the resistance has a popular mandate, and to admitting there is limited security in country."

Years ago my first boss on 'A Squad had advised me never to call anybody outside *the job* 'Sir'.

"You call him Foreign Secretary or whatever his or her title is," he'd told me. "You are an expert in your role and they in theirs – you are *not* subservient. They are not your boss and you need to be able to tell them no. They mustn't second-guess you. Their safety and survival is more important than any other desire they may have."

I had stuck to that advice ever since, often to the frustration of some of the world's most powerful people.

As part of the preparations for the first visit of Foreign Secretary Jack Straw to 'liberated' Iraq, I'd travelled to Baghdad in advance of his arrival to establish safety and security procedures. The Foreign Secretary would be the most senior Western Official to visit the country and was a prime target for assassination by the many enemies of the coalition.

One of the proposed venues for the visit was the UN HQ in Baghdad, which my advance team and I had recced. I had sought threat intelligence on the site from my various sources and had collated some very worrying threat forecasts so I was confident in my decision.

"Ambassador, my sources tell me that the building is under a real threat of attack. I've also personally been to the building and I do not consider their security to be in any way comprehensive enough."

"But the Foreign Secretary needs to stage a ground-breaking meeting there with Sergio Vieira de Mello."

"They could meet somewhere else that's secure," I said as Sir Jeremy's expression turned from frustration to anger. "Perhaps here at the CPA or the Baghdad Conference centre."

"You appear not to be aware of the political imperative of this meeting!"

"I am perfectly aware but it is not safe. And if the Foreign Secretary is murdered, it will set back any peace process months, if not years."

Sir Jeremy immediately dismissed my concerns and hammered forth with short-term Westminster-centric, media-driven political considerations.

"Consider what the media will say once they find out. Not to mention the war's political opponents. They will take the Foreign Secretary's absence as proof positive that the vast majority of the Iraqi people consider themselves to be occupied rather than liberated."

"I absolutely understand," I sympathised. "Such a view at this time could be politically disastrous for the government. Now that the war has concluded it needs to be seen as a total and unmitigated success."

An ever so slight expression of triumph flickered crossed the Ambassador's face, as though he'd finally made a recalcitrant child see the error of his errant ways.

"Ah. So you'll allow it?"

"No, Ambassador, I will not. It's simply too dangerous."

As the UK's former Ambassador to the UN, Sir Jeremy was a senior diplomat and was used to getting his way. So, although he did not challenge me further, I suspected this would not be the end of the matter.

Some days later, during the actual visit of the Foreign Secretary, Sir Jeremy played his power card. Without my knowledge he reserved a military helicopter to fly the Foreign Secretary to the UN HQ.

I first became aware of this when I checked the day's programme and travel arrangements with the various military organizations.

Stunned, I immediately contacted the aviation logistics' officer and asked who had authorized the proposed 'serial' (movement) to the UN building. Unsurprisingly I was informed that the order had come directly from Sir Jeremy. I cancelled the serial on the spot and sought out the Ambassador.

He knew the moment he saw me that I'd found out what he'd tried to do.

"Jack has to visit the UN," he said. "It's imperative. I checked with the military and they didn't object to the visit."

"Ambassador, *I* am in *sole* charge of the Foreign Secretary's protection, not the military and in my judgment, it is not safe to allow him to visit the UN building."

"You don't understand; you don't get it, do you?"

I did, of course, and I was growing increasingly impatient with Sir Jeremy. I repeated that the meeting could take place elsewhere.

Sir Jeremy remained adamant and stated he would go over my head to achieve his goal.

I attempted to outline the Intelligence I had, from MI6, NSA and the CIA, adding that the war might be won but the fighting continued. Ali Hassan al-Majid, known as "Chemical Ali" for his use of chemical weapons in northern Iraq, had just been captured after a series of bloody firefights, and three British soldiers had just been killed in Basra on Saturday.

Of course Sir Jeremy knew all of this but refused to budge. Oh well, I thought, I've tried to do it the nice way.

"Ambassador, I will personally direct the Foreign Secretary not to attend the venue and if he doesn't comply I will withdraw protection from him and inform the Yard and the RMV in Whitehall the reason why."

*

....4:31pm, 19 August 2003, United Nations headquarters, Baghdad...

Fawzi Sirhan al-Hamdani, who was waiting for a friend outside the building, spotted the driver of the flat-bed truck, a young, clean-shaven man wearing a T-shirt, before he accelerated and drove into a corner of the UN building, detonating the enormous bomb, the blast of which knocked people to the ground up to 200 yards away.

The building's interior was left devastated. Mohammed al-Hakim, a driver with the International Monetary Fund, was in an office on the second floor. "Everything seemed to be collapsing around me," al-Hakim told a reporter in the hours after the explosion. "There was smoke everywhere. I saw a man lying with a bar of metal through his cheek."

Disoriented by the darkness and thick choking dust, survivors left trails of blood on the wall as they felt their way downstairs.

The bomb exploded right below Sergio's office. He was found trapped under the rubble, suffocating. He survived into the night, as the rescuers' klieg lights came on; his last words, spoken to a US soldier trying to free him (and reported by Marie Colvin for *The Times*), were: "Don't let the mission leave."

Recovery of the dead took a week. The building was unsafe and soldiers risked their lives to crawl into the debris to retrieve bodies, which were quickly washed before being identified. The count was 22. Dozens more wounded. It earned the ugly distinction of being the deadliest attack on foreign nationals since the ousting of Saddam Hussein.

The Russian-made lorry had pulled up on an unguarded road directly under de Mello's window. Mortar and artillery shells (imported from the Soviet Union in the 1970s and '80s) had been bundled around a 500-pound bomb, which had been 'shaped' so that the full power of the blast was aimed at de Mello's third-floor office.

An acquaintance of mine, Bernard Kerik, the former New York police commissioner who as interim Iraqi Interior Minister was trying to re-establish law and order in Iraq, said that someone inside the mission had tipped off the driver. Several of the security guards working at the Canal Hotel were former agents of the Mukhabarat (Iraqi Special Branch), Saddam's secret service.

A hitherto unknown body called the Armed Vanguard of Muhammad's Second Army claimed responsibility, but it was simply impossible to know if the group even existed, let alone whether it had carried out the attack. Suspects included Baathists, members of Fedayeen Saddam, the U.N.'s own security guards, Ansar al-Islam, al-

Qaeda, or foreign jihadists. It could have been a combination of any of the above. Ultimately it didn't matter.

Whomever the killers were, they wanted Sergio Vieira de Mello dead because they wanted to kill his vision of peace, to end the suffering of a people who, in his own words, had been "trampled on by those who have shown nothing but disdain for the dignity of the human being". They wanted him dead because he was the person most likely to achieve his goals.

Sergio de Mello believed that the UN's reputation would be its shield and so he had kept security light so that Iraqi people would feel as though the UN headquarters was accessible.

Sir Jeremy had reluctantly acquiesced to my final demand, even though it was clear that he felt as though he had been dictated to by someone whom he considered his subordinate. Now with de Mello's death my decision had been vindicated in the most horrific way. Protection commanders have to be willing to stick to well-founded and researched assessments. Lives depend on it.

I have spent a lifetime in covert operations, all designed to maintain security and peace in the UK. Peace can be fleeting and does not keep itself. Constant vigilance is always required. Industrial and communal strife led to thirty years of 'The Troubles' in Northern Ireland. Keeping the peace was my calling and was something that I had grown to be damn good at. But, of course, like everyone, I had to learn the hard way.

Chapter One - Disco Days

I was born in a village, the middle child of seven on the outskirts of a northern mill town in the mid-1950s. My childhood was frugal but happy and with a sport-loving father, I was encouraged in all athletic pursuits. To this end, I travelled to Manchester to represent the Church Lad's Brigade in the 100, 200 and 400 metres. I won every one of them and was presented with a cup for blitzing the 200. This was despite not owning a pair of spikes, nor indeed running shoes of any description. When I returned home, waving my trophy in triumph, my mother wept - not with pride, but at the one-week-old suede shoes decimated by the wet red cinder track, shoes they couldn't really afford to buy, let alone replace. Similarly, my father - once a professional sportsman - had to check his pride in place of a telling off.

"Why didn't you tell us you were running?" he wanted to know. I couldn't answer. Perhaps I knew they would forbid me from running in my new suede shoes.

One of life's great opportunities was presented to me when, at sixteen, I was offered the chance of an apprenticeship with the local third division club. Choosing between football and A-levels wasn't easy, especially as my dad was so proud but my doubts about the hazards of professional football tipped the scales in favour for the lifelong benefits of education with a safe future as a sports teacher.

I did however harbour secret ambitions of appearing in Kung Fu movies, after seeing the 1973 film *King Boxer*. After some quick experimentation I found I could kick head-high and block and punch superfast and signed up for lessons. I was hooked and spent more and more time training, to the detriment of my studies.

As is so often the case, life had other plans. After brief post-school stints working as a trainee electrical engineer, a salesman and financial advisor, I jumped at the chance to turn another of my great passions into a full-time role – I became a professional DJ.

I'd worked my way up from mobile DJ work to club residency before being offered a role as one of the Bass-Charrington brewery's travelling DJs working throughout the North West in their disco pubs, clubs and working men's clubs, where I compered variety shows introducing top level comedians, dancers and variety acts as well as solo singers and groups, including Ken Dodd, Bernard Manning, Roy Castle, the Hollies and Sweet Sensation. I also worked with most of the Radio 1 DJs, such as Noel Edmonds, Dave Lee Travis and the infamous Jimmy Saville, on their roadshows. Despite my success and despite much effort on my part, however, I couldn't find a way to break through the BBC's colour bar to enter the 'dream palace' of Radio 1.

So with the dream of becoming a Kung Fu actor in Hong Kong being just that, and the BBC being a non-starter, I was all ears when during my regular Manchester University afternoon gig a guy called Neville came to me with a proposition. Although Neville had found chart success as the lead guitarist for Mike Batt's novelty pop group the Wombles, he was a serious musician and wanted to escape the costume. To this end, he had formed his own jazz funk band and had a contract to play in West Germany. He pitched me "a once in a lifetime opportunity" as he put it, to work as his DJ compere. After I confirmed the details with my agent, I signed up to tour the US Military bases in West Germany with Neville's band.

It was spring 1978 and there were up to a million and a half American service personnel and their families in West Germany, securing the West against the Soviet menace, spread out in bases all over the country. That meant that some gigs were five hundred miles apart. My German agent, an elderly, bee-hived and chain-smoking lady by the name of Mrs Hoffmann was supposed to pay my expenses out of her 50% cut of my salary. So, to maximise her earning she 'housed' me in a cheap shared hostel. Most of my fellow residents were Turkish *Gastarbeiter*, the German name for migrant workers who were allowed in their millions to work in West Germany to feed the runaway economy's need for cheap labour.

When I complained to Mrs Hoffmann about having to share a room, shower and toilet with multiple occupants after many hours on the road she replied that I had three options – get used to it, leave her agency or, as a young, good-looking guy, she suggested I take a German prostitute as a girlfriend and live with her.

"Why a prostitute?" I asked. "Is this what you think of me or indeed of white women who go with black guys?" Hoffmann just dragged on her cigarette and looked me coldly in the eye. She spoke not one more word but the look was cutting. I demanded my wages and quit on the spot.

I was only six weeks into to my German adventure and I'd effectively become homeless and unemployed, but most devastating of all, the girl I loved and hoped to marry was arriving to set up home with me in two days. That night as I lay head down to sleep in my car's backseat, it struck me that perhaps I'd been a bit hasty.

My saviour came in the form of John, a keyboard player for the chart-topping bubblegum pop duo Mac and Katie Kassoon who put me in touch with the owners of the best German disco in the city, a high class venue where the wealthy clientele often purchased spirits by the bottle instead of per glass. The club's clientele loved soul, disco and some German new wave music so I had a good knowledge of most of their needs and, during that first night's audition, I had the dance floor pumping. I took up immediate residency as the club's DJ.

Within a week of the Hoffmann debacle, my life had unexpectedly come together. I had a six-month rolling DJ contract paying thousands of Deutschmarks a month and I had set up home in a decent apartment with my girlfriend Angela who had arrived in Germany from Belgium.

I first met Angela almost two years earlier at one of the disco pubs where I was DJ-ing. It was surprising we hadn't met before, as we were born and raised in the same small village but being a Catholic, she went to a different school and then, being particularly bright, she was sent to the regional selective girls' convent school located in a town miles from our village. She was a year younger than me and had a flair for languages and, after we'd been going out for a few months, she took up a gap year starter post in Belgium as an au pair to improve her French. I scuppered Angela's plans when en route to Germany. I rocked up at her employer's house in Brussels and managed to tempt her to change her path, to join me – as I put it - on a fantastic voyage of discovery.

I also found I had a capacity for languages, so after insisting everyone I met (who usually spoke good English) speak to me in German, within several months I could understand, speak, read and - to a lesser extent – write the language quite well.

Life was just one long party for two years until disaster struck during Germany's Fasching (carnival) season. Carnival streamers decorating the club caught fire after the club had closed. The first I heard of the incident was the following day when the owner knocked on my door. The disaster was short-lived though as I was immediately headhunted by another club later that evening.

A friend of mine, Thomas Rheine, had also heard of the fire and to true to form he took the opportunity to press me again about working with him as a 'Haus Detektiv'. Thomas had dreams of owning his own Detective agency but needed a partner to get this venture off the ground. Aware that I had no knowledge of this field, Thomas proposed that I gain experience by working for the detective agency where he was then employed.

I was 23-years-old and earning good money in the entertainment business. "Why would I want to give up all this?" was my stock response to Thomas's repeated suggestion. That said, something about the offer intrigued me and I suppose Thomas was intuitive enough to see this so he never stopped pushing the idea.

"You'll make a great detective," he told me. "You speak perfect Deutsch and as a darker-skinned black man nobody will think you're a detective."

There were, and are, quite a number of mixed race Germans but many fewer with a darker complexion.

"You'd be great. You'd definitely catch a lot of thieves. It'll be fun."

The club fire started me thinking. Although the fire was only a blip in my extremely comfortable life, and I'd received a whopping three months' salary pay-out from the disco as well as receiving a comparable monthly salary from my new club, the incident showed me how precarious the entertainment industry could be. I took up Thomas' suggestion and accompanied him to the Detective Agency the following morning to meet his boss.

The firm was housed in Neu Isenberg, a suburb of Offenbach, close to Frankfurt am Main. As we entered the agency's plush offices I saw why Thomas was intent on opening his own agency. Profits in the security industry were obviously good. Just as importantly, I began to understand why Thomas thought I could assist him in this dream, especially in the initial stages. I would be the asset that could make the agency that little bit different.

Thomas introduced me to one of the agency's directors, Herr Seidel and after a short interview Seidel offered me a job with immediate effect. Flattered and intrigued, I accepted and began training almost immediately. Like Thomas, Seidel also thought that I would make an excellent covert asset who would never be suspected of being in the law enforcement game.

I took up the role offered by Seidel but I'd also continued to DJ. This meant less time with Angela but I thought the money would allow us to save. Throughout, as always, Angela was supportive.

A Haus Detektiv in Germany is akin to a Store Detective in the UK but with police powers of arrest and detention. When a Haus Detektiv arrests a suspect for shoplifting he/she is also responsible for verifying the suspect's identity and drafting any indictment. The Detektiv then submits the papers to the Staatsanwalt (CPS/District Attorney) for assessment. If the individual is subsequently summonsed to attend court for trial, the Haus Detektiv, as the complainant, is then required to provide the prosecution's evidence. These procedures provided me with an excellent education taking me through the whole German legal process, from arrest to prosecution, on many occasions. Something else that proved useful was seeing the offence take place. Uniformed police officers rarely see offences (they're reactive). As a proactive Haus Detektiv, I became well-versed in analysing the expressions and body language of those who were up to no good.

After nine months as a Haus Detektiv I was offered a job as an investigator with the United States Army and Air Force Exchange Service (AAFES). AAFES was the body in the US Military that supplies the US Army and Air Force with its retail and 'comfort' goods, from cars to hi-fi systems to furniture, to clothing to cigarettes and even personal weapons. AAFES was massive in West Germany, supporting the approximately 1.5 million Army, Air Force, civilian contractors and civilian dependents of the US military and its facilities in West Germany.

After six months of training I was put in charge of investigating all crimes emanating from AAFES facilities on five bases in and around my city. Those using AAFES facilities kept me very busy investigating offences ranging from theft, to robbery, to fraud, to violent crime and most prominently customs violations and drugs trafficking.

My boss at AAFES was Frank Anderson, an ex-senior FBI Special Agent during the J Edgar Hoover years. Frank Anderson provided me with the most important advice that anybody connected with law enforcement can ever receive. Leaving the interview room, after just being offered the job, Frank called me back. Peering over the top of his horn rimmed spectacles he looked me in the eye and said:

"Don't forget Carlton, whatever you do in this Job - C-Y-A."

I looked at him blankly. Frank then spelt it out for me.

"Cover Your Ass, Carlton, Cover Your Ass."

Frank liked to regale me with stories of his time in the FBI, along with his thoughts on MI5 and to my surprise, the awe in which he held Scotland Yard's Special Branch. He rated the Branch so much that he'd often say:

"If I were an Englishman I'd have joined the Special Branch."

I decided to take him up on his word. I wrote to the British embassy in Bonn, enclosing my CV and asking them to consider me for a role in Special Branch. Several weeks later I received a letter from the Metropolitan Police. The letter suggested that I should call in to the MPS recruitment centre when I was next in the UK.

A few months later I was interviewed at the Met's recruitment office in London. The interview panel consisted of three uniformed officers - a Constable (PC), a Sergeant and an Inspector. They were not impressed.

"I think you've been used to a very exciting type of policing in Germany," the Inspector told me. "You wouldn't be a detective here like you are there. In fact, you might spend your entire career as a uniform constable. But what is certain is that people don't just walk into Special Branch."

The PC said I needed to understand what British policing was all about and that was an officer "Working his/her beat."

"Here's a reading list," the sergeant said. "These books will give you a better understanding about policing in the UK. If you're still interested about working for the Met after reading these, then come back and see us."

I ordered the books and devoured them. I learnt that British police officers worked for thirty years before being entitled to a ⅔ final salary pension, that the vast majority of officers would remain as constables throughout their career and that most would serve throughout in uniform performing general beat duties. Every officer had to start as a uniform constable. To gain promotion, officers had to pass the police promotion exams and selection processes and, most interesting to me, was that a selection process was also required to gain some specialist posts (Traffic, Dogs, Firearms, Criminal Investigation Department (CID) and Special Branch). Scotland Yard was the headquarters of London's Metropolitan Police and that it housed the Met's main specialist 'CID' units including Special Branch. The Met offered full-time specialist roles in areas like Traffic, CID and Special Branch. Moreover, in the absence of a national police force in the UK, the Met also undertook various responsibilities nationally. And most importantly, with at the time approximately 38,000 employees the Metropolitan Police dwarfed every other police force in Britain. Its closest rivals had less than 8,000 employees. One book contained a fleeting mention of the Metropolitan Police Special Branch (MPSB), and the sensitivity of its role. My mind was made up. I was absolutely convinced, regardless of the odds, I was going to forge a career in Scotland Yard's Special Branch.

Chapter Two - Home to the Met

A year later, in February 1984, I returned to the UK to be sworn in as a Police Constable in the Metropolitan Police Service (aka MPS/The Met). After the obligatory six months training - learning the law and being taught the rudiments of policing at the Peel Centre, the Metropolitan police's renowned police training establishment in Hendon, North London - I was sent to spend my 18 months' probation as a uniformed PC at Rochester Row police station: Rochester Row, I was delighted to learn, was just around the corner from my goal New Scotland Yard, the home of Special Branch.

Part of the purpose of probation was to test your mettle, to see whether you were able to run towards danger (as opposed to away from it) and then were able to cope with whatever you encounter. I did well and was seconded to the CID for more than just a taster day, a great opportunity for a probationer, although for me it felt like home. It was as though I'd returned to AAFES.

My first real baptism of fire came in 1985 when I was attached to the district riot unit, known as the DSU (District Support Unit). The DSU's role was to deal with general criminality on the division and mass public order issues to do with football matches, demonstrations affrays and riots anywhere in the capital.

Later that year I was amongst a large number of officers sent to police a ten thousand strong protest of predominantly black youth. The Met had just ruled out any racial link to the 1981 New Cross Fire that cost the lives of thirteen young black people who had been at a house party celebrating the sixteenth birthday of two friends. At the time of the fire racial tensions in the area had been running high so many black Londoners believed the fire was racially motivated. Two inquests had been held and on both occasions the coroner had reached an inconclusive verdict. For many in the local black community these verdicts simply reinforced their belief that there'd been an establishment cover-up. A number of left wing extremist organisations aimed to exploit this volatile situation for their own ends. They hoped to stir up anti-state racial violence. So it was with the assistance of the Socialist Workers Party, along other left wing groups, that the grieving victims' families and their supporters had organised a large demonstration to demand justice from the police and the Establishment.

In the normal British policing style the officers controlling the demonstration walked alongside the demo in their unprotected general duty uniforms. As the demonstration moved along its route to rally at the site of the fire, various anti-police and anti-British state slogans were chanted with increasing anger. Suddenly, I noticed a group of roughnecks congregating around me – they'd clearly registered that I was black. I was soon in no doubt that these brothers saw me as their enemy and were intent on causing physical harm to me should the slightest opportunity arise. As I assessed my situation, bandanas and scarves began to conceal the faces of those closest to me.

Out of the hundreds of officers on the march that day, I seemed to be the only black officer. One agitator grasped this opportunity and set off what became an infectious chant: "Judas, Judas, Judas!" It spread like wildfire throughout the crowd. Soon it was at fever pitch, with practically the entire demo joining in, menacingly pointing in my direction. Large sections of the demo began to veer towards me.

Luckily at least one of my colleagues from Rochester Row had already perceived the danger and unbeknown to me, had already reported the looming situation to our sergeant. The sergeant had radioed an inspector who having made his way to me, beckoned me to follow him to the front of the demo where reserves were bolstering police lines. I instinctively kicked against this direction and informed him that I intended to hold the line along with my colleagues. I would not retreat!

By now my presence was caustic. Left-wing activists and roughnecks had intensified this mood to a frenzy with the now hysterical shouts and sneers of "Judas, Judas," ringing out like a thunderclap. Elements in the demo began to surge towards me. In return my fellow officers reacted by linking arms in an effort to hold them back the tide. It was becoming ugly. By now, the Chief Superintendent in-charge of the demo had arrived at my location and addressed me directly.

"PC King, isn't it?"

"Yes, Sir."

"I know you don't want to leave your colleagues and I know it must be humiliating but the demo is starting to get out of hand and a lot of people including your colleagues may well be injured today if you stay. I don't want to order you to leave the demonstration but I think you know what's right."

The Chief Supt, who didn't know me from Adam, could have simply ordered me directly to leave but he was handing me the dignified option of leaving of my own accord. Missiles began to fly through the air. The Chief Supt's primary duty was obvious, he had to maintain the safety of the demo, uphold the Queen's peace and where at all possible keep his officers safe – my pride was not a factor.

I learned two lessons that day: Sometimes retreat is a more valiant option and unique is not always positive.

As I left the scene to wait with those officers still left in reserve, a ten-thousand strong jeer went up. Shortly thereafter, we regained control of the crowd.

On October 6, 1985, I was working on the DSU deployed in Peckham South London on a troublesome estate holding a strategic bridge between two stairwells separating two rival gangs, who'd decided to put their differences aside and joined forces to attack the police. Dressed in full riot gear - flame proof overalls, helmets and long shields - we looked a bit like Roman centurions guarding Hadrian's Wall.

At about 8pm our carrier's radio crackled "Alpha 31, Alpha 31, go to channel 8 for instructions MP over". The driver immediately answered the radio in the affirmative and went to get the sergeant in charge, who was having a cheeky fag leaning against the carrier's metal windscreen grills, which are used as protection against bricks, stones and petrol bombs.

The sergeant spoke to the command centre and we could hear his voice growing more and more serious. By the time he stepped out of the carrier's cab, we knew something big was up.

"Let's go guys, it's on." He said. "Broadwater Farm housing estate in Tottenham is up in flames and the rioters aren't playing".

As we travelled across London from South to North, sirens screeching and lights flashing we were joined by more and more carriers (a carrier is an armoured police van that carries eleven riot control officers, including a sergeant supervisor). Our apprehension grew as it became clear that we were headed for a massive riot. We sat in silence listening to the melee over the main-set radio. Continual shouts for "urgent assistance," the most serious cry for help that an officer can make, littered the airwaves. As we arrived at the Farm, the rumour that an officer had been killed was confirmed. The other rumour - that the mob had decapitated him - remained unanswered.

The victim was PC Keith Blakelock. Keith and several other local beat officers had been deployed to protect firefighters as they attempted to tackle fires on the estate. Ambushed and overwhelmed on a stairwell by between thirty to fifty rioters, the eleven-strong team retreated. Keith, who was 39 and the father of three sons, tripped and fell as the team ran for their lives. When Keith's body was finally recovered, the pathologist established that he had suffered over forty serious injuries many inflicted by machetes and knives. A six-inch-long knife had been left buried in his neck, up to the hilt.

We left the carrier at the Farm's entrance as the skipper (Sergeant) ordered us to draw truncheons and we took up a defensive line with long shields. The sight of burning buildings, vehicles and bins and the acrid smell of smoke, petrol and fumes was unnerving to say the least.

As we made our way deeper into the Farm to relieve stranded units surrounded by rioters, I noticed many people, old and young, were just watching the spectacle, each no doubt with their own thoughts of sympathy, bewilderment or perhaps hatred. The riot's trigger had been the death of a black woman during a recent police search on the estate, coupled with tensions caused by the death of a suspect in a police shooting in Brixton a week earlier. However, beneath the surface lay the deeper issues of poverty and social exclusion. London's estates were filled with people who were fed images of the "you-can-have-it-all" society, yet were unable to fulfil any of the wild dreams these images fostered. The message some of the young people on these estates took from the media and their peers who worked the streets, was that crime pays. It was the lore of easy money.

So when police cracked-down on drug dealing on these estates they upset a lot of angry young people who were only too ready to vent their fury. After all, this was the 'only way' they would share in the wealth of the nation.

Later - as a Branch officer – I'd get to experience this world first-hand. I'd observe how idealistic yet callous middle-class revolutionaries welcomed the Broadwater Farm riot and other such *uprisings* as a precursor to their revolution. These activists made no attempt to understand the debilitating effects on the residents of the almost inevitable sense of failure these estates engender. Their only aim was to cynically agitate for disorder by directing the 'lumpen' underclass of Britain's sink estates to become the unwitting vanguard of their revolutionary zeal.

As the riot continued that evening with unabated ferocity we moved from protecting colleagues cut off at one location to supporting the Fire Brigade putting out fires on another part of the estate, prior to coming under sustained Molotov cocktail bombardment and retreating at what seemed to be the sound of incoming gun fire. That night affirmed my suspicions that during public disorder there were other even stronger drivers at play than race, class and poverty. These other factors, primeval in nature, affected the police and rioters alike. It's a dynamic that plays heavily into the psyche of rioting and is often underplayed by State organs or not acknowledged at all. These emotions lie deep in our brains and dictate how we react to conflict. They are responses that all too often heighten our sense of being, as they reaffirm the joy and precious nature of life most noticeably when we are simultaneously engaged in activity where the possibility of death flashes before us.

Consequently, for both the police and protesters, rioting can be exciting and enjoyable. In my experience it's one of the main elements that leads many to conflict. Politicians - whose careers are one long battle - often feel the same emotions. I would feel this excitement/enjoyment often in my career. I'd feel it most readily on the streets of London when targeted to be killed, or on deniable spying missions abroad for Queen & Country, or when meeting an agent who I didn't quite trust in foreign lands from whence I could simply disappear. It would be there when leading protection operations in the enemy's back yard in Afghanistan, Columbia, the Yemen, Iraq, Pakistan, The Lebanon or Gaza where those who wanted to kill me and my charge had home advantage. But although this activity was undoubtedly exciting as well as risky, I knew that I was no adrenaline junkie. I would always try to remain measured and calculated in my clandestine actions.

I could see how some people, if not most, joined The Job (the police) for the excitement. They'd get to drive fast cars, control dangerous situations, take charge of the public and use their powers of detention in a life where (at least in the Met) no two days are the same. My reasons were slightly different. The thrill, I felt, would come from life as a secret police officer who operated in the shadows to prevent crimes against the State. To do this, I had to find a way into the Branch.

Chapter Three - Getting in

My chance came a few months after I'd completed my probation, when the Met's 'Police Notices' (a weekly internal newspaper the size of a pamphlet) pronounced 'Applications are sought from constables wishing to be considered for selection to Special Branch'. My heart leapt. It listed the desired requirements as: a good grasp of English, a fluent writing style, a good understanding of politics, history and current affairs, foreign language skills, shorthand, Morse code and an ability to work unsupervised and throughout all strata of society. It also explained that applicants had to submit a report along with their application, stating why they should be considered as candidates and this should be backed up by - and this was only if the Relief/Divisional Inspector approved - a recommendation of suitability from their superintendent *(the day-to-day head of a police station)*.

Any candidates lucky enough to be recommended would then be invited to sit various *Special Branch* examinations at Peel Centre. The best would then be interviewed in front of a Special Branch selection board, at which point the top candidates from throughout the process would be informed that they had been selected to join the Branch, subject of course to the officer being granted positive developed vetting (DV) status. The application explained that the DV process would not be undertaken by Special Branch, but was performed by government (Ministry of Defence *(MOD)* vetting officers in line with the developed vetting programme for unfettered access to sensitive material. It was made clear that the DV process would involve intrusive investigation into an applicant's past, as well as the lives of their extended family, including partners and grandparents.

Once I'd finished reading the application, a cold rush of fear passed through me. No other section in the Metropolitan Police or in fact in any UK police force had such a stringent application process. The fifty six other force SBs in the UK had no such examination procedure. Even the RUC Special Branch in Northern Ireland (based on MPSB) didn't come close. I guess this was down to the fact that MPSB was in reality more akin to a secret Intelligence or security service than a police entity.

For a split second the doubts crept in. Had I given up a promising career in a country that had been good to me and Angela for the pipe dream of joining the Branch – which now seemed a near impossibility? I certainly didn't fulfil all the desired criteria. I didn't know short-hand or Moss code and I'd be competing against hundreds of well-educated applicants many of whom were probably undertaking the process for the second or third time. Applicants often failed on their first selection attempt. However, more importantly, everybody in the job knew that the Branch only ever selected a very small number of officers. The enormity of the challenge was well and truly hitting home. I resolved to push these fears aside and let nothing hold me back. Consequently, from that moment on, I'd think of nothing but the application process.

First stop was my inspector.

"You've only just completed your probation," he said, "It's too soon for you to apply to the Branch. You'd be better off getting some more experience of general duty policing under your belt. Perhaps apply in a year's time."

Trying to stay calm, and knowing that the Branch did not necessarily seek candidates yearly, I respectfully declined the inspector's suggestion, adding that prior to joining the Met I'd amassed several years of comparatively relevant experience with AAFES.

"To be perfectly honest Sir, the reason I joined the Met was because of Special Branch," I said. "I'd like to apply immediately," I added before quickly tagging on, "If you agree, of course."

He said he'd consider my request with the job's and my best interest at heart. Two days later I was summoned to the Superintendent's office. Like many senior officers the Supt seemed to dislike the Branch's insularity, yet nevertheless revered its capacity. I had had little contact with the Supt thanks to his lofty position, but he knew about me because of my declared ambition to join the Branch. When I was first posted to the nick, along with two other officers eighteen months earlier, the Supt's welcome speech had extoled the virtues of uniform beat policing whilst, now and then, casting a withering eye over me. He'd clearly read my personal file containing the letter I'd sent to the Embassy seeking to join the Branch. Clearly he'd thought that I wished to run before I could walk.

So as I settled myself into the chair in front of the Supt's desk, I wasn't quite sure what to expect. He kicked off by noting that my inspector was strongly backing my application. He then explained that he'd also be supporting me. He'd kept an eye on me since my arrival at the station and had heard good things about my work on the DSU and during my CID attachment. So he had no reason to think that I wouldn't make an excellent candidate for Special Branch. He was therefore strongly supporting my application.

After a further few minutes of small talk we shook hands and I left his office supressing the urge to punch the air with joy. The Supt's strong recommendation, coupled with my application would get me through the initial paper-sift and gain me an invitation to sit the Branch examinations. So, no more than twenty months after passing out of Hendon Police College, I returned to the Peel Centre one Saturday to face my day of reckoning.

The Branch had taken over the Cadet school's Simpson Hall for the day and had decked it out with rows of individual desks and chairs to accommodate the five-hundred-plus hopefuls who had made it to this stage.

The SB Detective Sergeant invigilator introduced himself as Roger Jackson. He then said: "Congratulations, you have already defeated half of your opposition. One final word of note before you begin. If there's anybody here who wants to be the Commissioner, leave now. We only promote from within the Branch so if you're selected your rise through the ranks in the Branch will be slow in comparison to your uniform peers. If it's rapid promotion that you're after I suggest you go and seek your career in uniform or the CID. If you're successful today and you're selected for interview, you will have been chosen against some of the most talented officers in the Metropolitan Police. Good luck!"

I'd done my homework so I had some idea of what to expect. The main preparation I'd undertaken was natural for me, it was what I'd been doing all my life, keeping abreast of political affairs. I listened to the BBC World Service, Radio Four and sometimes Radio Moscow. I read The Times, The Guardian, Der Spiegel, Newsweek and Africa Confidential. And I watched TV news and political commentary programmes such as John Pilger's exposes, ARD's Weltspiegel, CBS' 60 Minutes, Panorama and other informative political programmes. What I didn't know though was what the essays would entail.

The first timed paper was designed to test our English comprehension, easy enough. The next was given over to the infamous SB current affairs paper, which consisted of a hundred questions on politics, history and culture. They included questions like:

What are the six counties of Northern Ireland?

What is the NUT?

What is the capital of Brazil?

Who wrote A Tale of Two Cities?

What is the INLA?

Papers three and four were one-hour essays. The first concerned The Troubles, the Branch's bread and butter: "Should Ireland be united? Discuss."

The second tested an officer's ability to sensibly draft a proposal or a discussion paper: "Provide the Foreign and Commonwealth Office with a paper on how to reorganise the police service in an African Commonwealth country that suffers from acts of terrorism, has porous ports and borders, suffers high levels of insurgency and subversion and has had several leading politicians assassinated."

I'd always been interested in politics so it was just a matter of composure, thinking things through logically and that little personal matter of conquering my dyslexia and putting it coherently on paper. I'd always had problems with deciphering the written word. It wasn't a matter of simply sounding phonemes out, for me the sounds didn't necessarily make sense. It was a matter for me of memorising words or letter strings. As I grew I'd developed coping strategies to overcome this problem although at school those systems were not fully in place, so I never reached my full potential. By now though having learnt German and begun to understand grammar better I knew I could crack the exam, even though I knew that the spelling aid book, and handy pocket-sized machine that I habitually carried, wouldn't be permitted in the exam hall.

I thought I'd done well but my heart was pounding when some weeks later the results arrived. I'd made the cut out of about thousand original applicants. I was over the moon. Now all I had to do was to battle against the fifty-nine other dedicated, talented and ambitious officers who had made it so far, for one of the ten places up for grabs. So for the final stage, which was held at Scotland Yard, I had twenty minutes to convince three senior SB officers that I was better than the rest. They grilled me about the pressing political situations of the day; Angola, Colombia, Northern Ireland, South Africa and UK labour relations. They asked me several personal questions, continually testing my skills. Could I speak a second language? Yes, several. Did I know Morse code or shorthand? No. They asked me to describe my work in Germany and quizzed me on it in great detail.

I left the room befuddled but strangely happy. I knew the subjects and I'd done my best. I couldn't have done more. I had a seven-day wait for the news. When it came I was called into my Inspector's office at Rochester Row. I'd made it! I was one of the ten chosen ones. I was overjoyed but had little time to rest on my laurels. There was still one more hurdle to jump: Developed Vetting.

The MOD officer who vetted me did a thorough job. He travelled to Germany and spoke with some of my friends and employers. He researched and interviewed both mine and Angela's families. He then summonsed me for an interview. He grilled me on my past, including my disco days. Although potential drug use was clearly one of his concerns, I was able to allay his fears by explaining that my sporty and Kung Fu upbringing had prevented this, consequently I'd never taken a narcotic in my life, never smoked a cigarette and as for drinking to excess, up until I was 26 I didn't even drink. In the security/intelligence domain where the drinking culture was pervasive, I'm not so sure if my last declaration wasn't perceived with a degree of suspicion. Nevertheless, aged 28, I received my DV and became a fully-fledged Scotland Yard, Special Branch officer. I was not the youngest officer in my intake, as I had joined the police late in years; but I was by far the one with the shortest police service. I had just over two years in the *job*. I'd later find out that the ten of us selected that year were an eclectic bunch. At least one candidate had attended Harrow Public School whilst a few others were alumni of less celebrated public and grammar schools. Several had university degrees. One had been a Barrister; another a ship's navigator. There was a pilot, an aero-space engineer, a medic and two commissioned Army officers, one from the Intelligence Corps.

I've never forgotten how it felt to sit in the examination room at Peel Centre with those five or six hundred other Branch hopefuls. I can still hear Sergeant Roger Jackson enjoying his preparatory speech to us, his captive and attentive audience. He said: "If in the end you make it into the Branch, you will embark on a service-long career in the most fascinating part of the British Police bar none."

He wasn't wrong.

Chapter Four - Life in the Branch

The sixteenth to nineteenth floors of New Scotland Yard were home to the detectives of Special Branch, officially known as The Metropolitan Police Special Branch (aka MPSB, SB or SO12). To nearly everyone in the Yard, however, it was known simply as The Branch.

The Branch was formed in 1883 as 'The Metropolitan Police Special Irish Branch' *(SIB)* to combat a wave of terrorism on the British mainland by a group of determined Irish nationalists known as the 'Irish Republican Brotherhood,' commonly known as the Fenians. The Fenians had brought their struggle for Irish self-rule to the streets of the British mainland in the form of a bombing and shooting campaign.

The Metropolitan Police Commissioner authorised the recruitment of police officers from the Royal Irish Constabulary directly into the Metropolitan Police's fledgling detective force housed at Old Scotland Yard (a set of buildings bordering London's Whitehall), and tasked them with hunting down the Fenians. Using the new Pinkerton and French secret police methods of surveillance, infiltration and collation, the SIB successfully penetrated and cajoled the British Irish community into ending their support for the Fenians, although the terrorists nevertheless managed, on May 30 1884, to blow a hole in the wall of Scotland Yard. Through penetration and the careful collecting of evidence, the SIB soon brought the bombers to justice.

The defeat of the Fenians on the mainland was total and impressive, but the desire among the Irish for self-rule would not die, and the Fenians' successors, the IRA, came to wreak havoc on the UK mainland for much of the 20th Century, testing MPSB to its limits.

The early successes of the Special Irish Branch were not lost on Britain's wealthy ruling establishment. The UK, a society divided by class, was ruled by a small elite fearful of a French-style revolution as well as the growth of anarchist agitation among the large urban poor. So, in the summer of 1883 the Special Branch, Britain's Secret Police, was quietly born.

At the time MPSB was the sole defender of the realm, acting as the political police for the whole of the United Kingdom with the men from the Yard being called to deal with any kind of political intrigue.

Between the late 1880s and the outbreak of the First World War the MPSB continued its surveillance of Irish Republican activity in the UK, continued to provide close armed personal protection of Britain's leading politicians, undertook observations at ports in Britain, France and even the USA of passengers wishing to travel to Britain and put more resources into keeping tabs on Russian revolutionaries and potential German spies - the greatest threat to Britain's world supremacy. By the beginning of World War I in 1914 the Branch's 114 officers were absolutely overwhelmed. When more than a dozen French speaking SB officers were seconded to Military Intelligence and posted to France, the MPSB requested that the Home Office authorise additional recruitment. By the end of the Great War the Branch had doubled in size.

By the time of the Great War MPSB's boast of being the only 'official' political intelligence/security service in the United Kingdom had been usurped by two newcomers, the Security Service *(MI5)*, dealing with domestic security, established in 1909, and the Secret Intelligence Service *(MI6)*, tasked with obtaining foreign secret intelligence, formed in 1911.

Interestingly, it had been an SB officer who was instrumental in the creation of both of these agencies. Ex-Superintendent William Melville, known as 'M'. Melville, the former Chief of MPSB, had upon his retirement from the Branch in November 1903 lobbied government for the Home Office's blessing to create a counter espionage organisation, *a la* Special Branch, but independent of the Metropolitan Police. Obtaining this authority 'M' created MO3 and MO2 later renamed MO5. In MO3/5 Melville utilised the techniques he had helped systemise in MPSB, including agent recruitment and intelligence/information collation and analysis. By the outbreak of World War I 'M's unit had been incorporated lock stock and barrel into the fledgling MI5 under its first Director General, Sir Vernon Kell. M's operatives provided vital intelligence with regard to Germany's military intentions and by the start of WWI M's use of tried and tested Special Branch techniques had enabled MI5 to successfully identify many, if not all, of the German spies secreted into Britain. Of course this was achieved with the Branch/police assistance, who surveilled and arrested the spies, as MI5 have no 'Powers of Arrest'. The successes of World War I ensured the growth of the MI5. This success, which was built on the foundations of Special Branch, would in the end cost the Branch its supremacy.

Nevertheless, by 1919 the Branch's wartime duties under the Defence of the Realm Act (DORA) had kept it at the heart of the UK's security apparatus, not only on the streets, but in Whitehall where it was still able to rival the Security Service. Indeed by 1920 MI5 had been forced to shed over 600 officers from its wartime peak of approximately 850 and some legislators even asked why it was still required. The police (MPSB), it was argued, had shown they could do the job. Other politicians considered amalgamating both bodies. Finally, a compromise was found and drafted into the 1931 Treaty of Westminster legislation, which cemented both organisations' existence in a co-operative 'standoff'.

The Security Service would go on to have a 'good' Second World War, as would, in the shadows, Special Branch. The Branch and the

Security Service worked relatively well together after the end of WWII, as the Cold War provided MI5 a seemingly inexhaustible and unassailable niche. Consequently, until the fall of the Soviet Union in the early 1990's, The Security Service would have no need to challenge the Branch for its roles.

Between 1964 and the early 70's the British policing system underwent massive change. Government reduced the hundred-plus separate police forces in England and Wales to forty two and down to eight in Scotland. In line with this mood of rationalisation, Metropolitan Police Commissioner Sir John Waldron questioned why his officers should continue to be the sole purveyors of Special Branch work throughout the UK. Consequently, MPSB became the parent Special Branch to the new local constabulary Special Branch units in every police force in England, Wales, Scotland, The Channel Islands and Gibraltar. 'Ulster' had long since had its own SB which continued to work closely with MPSB.

Most of these provincial SBs usually consisted of less than ten full-time SB officers, generally posted for two to three years from their force CIDs. They generally had no exam process, nor was Special Branch a career stream in these forces – it was just another CID posting. Many of these provincial SB officers were not DV'd but received a lesser SC (Security Check) vetting level. Provincial SB officers did receive limited training from MPSB and, after the Cold War, from the Security Service. These training courses taught the provincial officers basic SB concepts and directed them to seek assistance from MPSB on any matter with an effect outside their police area or when they required expert assistance or more resources.

Throughout these years MPSB would continue to act as the central repository for UK police intelligence, the de facto co-ordinator for all British Special Branches on the mainland, as well as the primary body for exploiting all police political intelligence. MPSB also continued to provide armed personal protection to the Prime Minister, senior officials and visiting foreign dignitaries nationally. Moreover, MPSB's 'S' squad surveillance teams also worked nationally on political targets.

When I first worked with the Security Service in the 1980's I could still discern the SB legacy in MI5's procedures, its use of terminology such as 'Desk Officers', and its basic modes of operation.

The MPSB's structure changed over the years I was there but, generally speaking, it was divided into the following sections:

'A' Squad - was tasked with providing armed VIP personal protection and Security Vetting. To achieve this 'A' Squad had a fleet of high performance armoured vehicles, Glock 17 semi-automatic pistols, Heckler & Koch MP5A3 submachine guns & MP5K (Kurz - short) submachine pistols.

'B' Squad - had responsibility for exploiting Irish Republican extremist/terrorists intelligence on mainland Britain, in tandem with the Security Service (MI5) and 'Loyalist' terrorists intelligence regionally.

'C' Squad – was tasked with observing, assessing and combating domestic extremism and subversive activity by extreme right or left wing groupings, Anti- Capitalist, Animal Rights, Anarchist and Environmentalist extremists. 'C' Squad officers investigated election and voting offences, politically orientated racial incitement and racially inspired extremism as well as domestic terrorism, Espionage and Official Secrets Act offences. An extremely small number of SB officers worked under ultra-deep cover in 'C' Squad's 'Special Demonstration Squad' (SDS), infiltrating political extremist organisations (SDS had at one time been under 'S' squad's management).

'E' Squad – was responsible for the monitoring of non-indigenous extremism, terrorism, religiously inspired extremism and Foreign Intelligence officer activity in the capital and that emanating from the London to the rest of the UK. This entailed a great degree of liaison with the Security Service who had primacy in these areas and liaison with the Branch's European and world partners. A specially trained team of 'E' Squad officers also had national responsibility for investigating terrorist finances.

'P' Squad – was tasked with performing SB duties at London's ports of entry and departure into and out of the UK including on-board checks on Eurostar trains on route to Paris or Brussels. P-Squad officers sought out and controlled these air, sea and international rail borders for would-be terrorists, agitators, major criminals and foreign spies/intelligence officers attempting to enter or leave the UK. 'P' Squad officers were also tasked with preventing child abductions through ports in the UK.

'S' Squad - officers were tasked with providing technical coverage, eavesdropping, photography, computer analysis and armed surveillance teams on the Branch's, and when requested the Security Service's political targets within the UK. 'S' squad also provided the embedded intelligence cell in SO13 (the Met's Anti-Terrorist Branch).

'R' Squad – Dealt with the Branch's general administration, technical analysis, SB officer vetting, training & development, Special Branch Reserve, Finances and SB Records. It also dealt with SB officer secondments to NPOIU (National Police Order Intelligence Unit), NCIS (National Criminal Intelligence Service) and the Security Service etc.

All MPSB squads had contacts or worked closely with the Security Service, the National Public Order Intelligence Unit (NPOIU), National Criminal Intelligence Service (NCIS), the National Crime

Squad (NCS), the Military and other organisations where their remits overlapped.

Right up into the 21st Century, the MPSB remained the only intelligence or security body that could keep tabs on all of the vulnerable parts of UK society from ports of entry to the streets of the inner city within its own structure – without going anywhere else for help. With its own armed surveillance teams, technical & eavesdropping capacity, analytical desk officers, deep-cover operatives and protection unit, the Branch could, if necessary, deal with any investigation in total isolation and hence secrecy. With no authority to detain, arrest or question suspects the Security Service (MI5) would never be able to replicate the Branch's legal and lawful capacity. MPSB was in effect the most potent law enforcement body in the UK.

*

At 10am on that Monday morning in the summer of 1986 I was buzzed into this closed world of Special Branch along with the nine other successful applicants. Our first two weeks were given over to the MPSB Induction Course. Led by a Detective Sergeant and her team, this programme officially commenced with a welcome to the Branch speech by Special Branch's most senior officer, Deputy Assistant Commissioner Crawshaw.

In common with all British police officers we'd all signed the Official Secrets Act (OSA), and having been DV'd - the highest security clearance in the UK - we were now (on a need-to-know basis) authorised to see all of Britain's secrets.

The concept of secrecy and need-to-know was hammered home to us. We were left with no misunderstanding that this was the most important principal of the Branch. We were introduced to the various categories of security classification – *Restricted, Confidential, Secret and Top Secret* and the damage unauthorised disclosure of such information/documentation might cause. *'Restricted'* information/documentation if disclosed improperly could have an adverse effect on individuals or organisations, *'Confidential'* information/documentation would "damage" national security, police or judicial operations if publicly disclosed without proper authorisation. Information/documentation classified as *'Secret'* would be likely to cause "serious damage" to national security and potentially cause danger, serious injury or death to individuals or damage nation's reputation if disclosed in an unauthorised manner. Finally, there was *'Top Secret'* Information/documentation. Its unauthorised disclosure could reasonably be expected to cause exceptionally grave damage to national security, serious injury or death, undermine public confidence or the nation's standing internationally.

We also discussed the penalties for breaking the OSA as one of 'C' Squad's sections' jobs was to bring OSA transgressors to court, be they spies, traitors or those who had accidentally fallen foul of this draconian Act. I'd soon begin to realise that Britain was one of the most secretive states in the Western world and that the OSA was its cornerstone. The OSA is very easy to transgress, which in turn makes it extremely difficult for individuals even for sound reasons, to publicise any matters that have previously been categorised as classified.

Most of the Branch's work and the information and documentation that its officers handled, was generally classed as Secret, although the handling of Confidential and Top Secret classified documentation and intelligence data was by no means uncommon. Interestingly, we were made aware that in considering what security category a document/intelligence data should obtain, it is as important not to over-classify as it is not to under-classify. Over-classifying a document/intelligence could markedly reduce its significance as the higher the classification, the fewer people are authorised access to it, thereby limiting its utility. Generally, intelligence is most valuable when it can be acted upon so, one skill all MPSB officers were taught was the trick of 'sanitising' intelligence (removing sensitive material) to make it actionable.

After the documentation and intelligence classification lectures we spent several days overviewing all Special Branch squads and receiving in-depth lectures by officers from some of the larger sections and desks. 'C' Squad officers lectured us on the Communist Party of Great Britain (CPGB) and other extreme Communist/Socialist organisations; the extreme right-wing in the UK (National Front, British National Party & various white supremacists organisations) and the OSA prosecution section spoke of its responsibilities for investigating spying and The Offences Against the People's Act – voting irregularity offences. 'B' Squad lectured on the Irish conflict and extreme Republican and Loyalist organisations such as – the Provisional Irish Republican Army (PIRA), the Irish National Liberation Army (INLA), the Ulster Defence Association (UDA) & Red Hand Commands etc. 'E' Squad officers from the Indian, Iranian and Libyan sections amongst others provided in-depth information on these countries political outlooks and the wash-back for London and the UK. We also heard from 'E' Squad officers attached to ELS (European Liaison Section) as well as the foreign police/intelligence liaison officers on secondment to FI3 from organisations such as the French RG (Direction Central des Renseignements Généraux) and the German BKA (Bundeskriminalamt). To learn about 'P' Squad we visited Heathrow for the day receiving lectures from HM Immigration and HM Customs & Excise as well as 'P' squad officers regarding Special Branch ports work. We also spent two days at the Security Service's HQ, which in those days was Century House in Westminster Bridge Road, Lambeth. We were addressed by Security Service desk officers from various sections including the counter-espionage section, counter-subversion, counter-Soviet & Warsaw pact operations and their Records Bureau, etc. These desk officers continually stressed the need for cooperation and joint operations between the Branch and MI5.

We were shown, through the use of organo-grams, how the relationship between the MPSB and MI6 operated as well as that with GCHQ. We were also informed how we could assist these organisations.

We visited 'S' squads' surveillance teams and photographic unit. 'S' squad did not work out of the Yard for covert reasons. Lectures were given by 'A' Squad officers who also proudly showed us their substantial array of big boys' toys.

Most important of all, we spent a day in Special Branch's immaculate and enormous records department, which took up the whole of one of the Branch's floors. The specially trained and vetted Special Branch civil staff taught us basic file categorisations and indexing as well as the use of safes, and safe file keeping.

Every day was a revelation.

At this time there were approximately 340 Special Branch officers in MPSB, three black officers (including me), two officers of Asian descent and perhaps twenty-five women. For the mid-1980s, the Branch was quite diverse.

In support were approximately two hundred civilian Special Branch staff who managed the extensive records systems, Human Resources, documentation, typing pool, secretariat facilities and the budget as well as Special Branch Reserve's office flows. Most of the civilian members of the Branch were involved in administrative work, although there were some specialist technical experts. Perhaps three-quarters of the civilian staff were women.

Each Squad had many different sections, units and desks and was headed by a single Detective Chief Superintendent (DCS). For example, amongst many other sections 'E' Squad boasted Libyan, Palestinian, Iraqi, Iranian & North African desks. A section was generally headed up by a Detective Sergeant (DS) who controlled the section's Detective Constables (DCs). The DS and the DCs were the section's Desk Officers. A Desk Officer's job was to know everything about his/her area of expertise on the section (e.g., on 'C' Squad - The Communist Party of Great Britain section had a desk officer with years of CPGB experience running the show). Detective Inspectors (DI) oversaw large clusters of sections or units, which meant they had to be knowledgeable about a huge swathe of activity. Detective Chief Inspectors (DCIs) strategically oversaw the work of a number of the squad's DIs whilst, Detective Superintendents (Supts) controlled several units or strategically sensitive operations of his or her Squad, and decided strategies with his/her Security Service equivalents, national police leaders and/or government officials. Supts also deputised for the Squad's DCS. When I joined the Branch there were two Special Branch Commanders (the equivalent to Assistant Chief Constables in provincial police forces). One of the Commanders oversaw 'A' 'P' and 'R' Squad activities whilst the other ran 'B', 'C', 'E' and 'S' squads. At the time of my selection to the Branch its day-to-day chief was an officer of the rank of Deputy Assistant Commissioner (DAC), a rank easily equivalent to a Chief Constable in any of the provincial police forces outside London.

Although the Branch was organised in a fairly traditional hierarchical structure, it was unusual in that officers addressed each other by their first names, regardless of rank. This was thanks to the culture of longevity in the organisation, internal promotion, the weight placed on expertise and the trust put in the recruitment and development processes and procedures. In the British police as many as sixty per cent of officers remain a constable throughout their career, the Branch was no different. However, experienced Branch DCs were accorded the respect their know-how deserved. Of course, there was a time and a place for ranks and surnames and new officers had to quickly learn the nuances of this aspect of Branch life.

Branch officers of all ranks were given great power to achieve their objectives, so missions were, depending on scale and sensitivity, run from the Desk Officer level upwards. Due to the sensitive nature of MPSB's enquiries, all Branch officers - regardless of rank - automatically had a lot of clout when dealing with other police colleagues, even those of very senior rank. The Branch used this imbalance astutely and the ability to accomplish this was considered when selecting and training new officers.

After our two-week initial induction, my new colleagues and I were assigned desks. This was where the real intensive one to one training and tutoring began. With Britain still embroiled in the Cold War with the Soviet Union and its Warsaw Pact allies I was set to work on 'C' Squad observing the Trotskyist left in the UK under the tutelage of an experienced skipper (police slang for a DS). For years I'd been interested in world politics, but as a Branch desk officer one had to gain far greater depth than casual interest, one had to try to become an expert in the field assigned. The whole point was that an officer should try to establish what effect the group he or she was observing had on the citizenry of the capital and the nation as a whole. We were not surveilling people and organisations for fun, but to assess any potential danger to the State and its citizens. It was exhilarating.

In the Branch, particularly on 'C' Squad, the main skill I needed to acquire was to be able to perform my enquiries in the shadows. In Britain every citizen has a right to believe in what they want and to live their life as they feel fit. However, the organs of the state have a duty to remain vigilant. So the trick was to surveil and assess, but not prevent a citizen's freedom of movement, thought or actions until those actions became a threat to the state.

In the field of subversion, at the request of the Security Service or as a result of our own observations, we'd produce in-depth reports (known as Fully Comprehensives) on activists who had crossed the line into actions that were designed to destabilise the Queen's Peace or were calculated to undermine the defence of the realm. The skipper taught me how to perform these extremely comprehensive investigations, which at their conclusion would be documented in a 'Branch Note' fully detailing the individual's life from birth to the date of the report's completion. What was absolutely imperative was that throughout the investigation the subject should never know that they'd been under scrutiny.

The difference between the Branch and other secret police around the world was that the Branch didn't aim to disappear people, even if they were hell bent on causing problems for the safe and secure running of the State. The Branch's aim was to make sure that such extremists were kept in check, whilst the tranquillity of the State was upheld with the least possible unpleasantness.

Although the Branch maintained a meticulous observation of those who were bent on undermining the peace, we were careful not to let the observation lead to actual harmful consequences for the observed. It was a typically British compromise that allowed UK citizens to live in a secure, free and democratic state. Our work was very much conducted behind the scenes, with very rare prudent actions taken to maintain public safety.

However, for no discernible reason, some politicians would subsequently state -particularly in relation to the Branch's 'Special Demonstration Squad (SDS)' - that the Branch's proactive measures against such potential extremists were underhand and even un-British, even though the most senior of politicians had secretly sanctioned these operational tactics. This politically-induced charade would grow from the 1980s onwards and would eventually undermine the reputation of the Branch, and the police in general. Part of the problem, as you will read, was that the Met's leadership failed to challenge the politicians on their complicity in what was a reasonable, authorised and proportionate policy to prevent communal strife and conflict.

For over a hundred years, reports such as my Fully Comprehensives were screened and collated by the Branch's records section and were stored on index cards in huge and atmospheric filing rooms, where one could almost feel the century's worth of carefully-won intelligence (computerisation of these files began to kick in not long after I joined).

To become a proficient SB officer one needed to understand data mining and the use to which such records could be put. For any Branch enquiry the initial and primary source of intelligence was SB records, followed by general police indices, Security Service records and those of other public agencies. To assist me with this learning my skipper had organised further familiarisation sessions with the civilian head of SB records.

I was surprised when this manager said she wanted to show me something peculiar to me and beckoned me to follow her. We halted at the 'K' section of the card index. As she opened one of the many index 'K' card index drawers she informed me - to my amazement - that as far as she knew I was the only SB officer to have an SB index card record. She then proceeded to look me up by my full name and *'factors'* thereof. Factors are important when a subject's full name is unknown or not to hand and we can check and search entries in several different ways.

Finally, she removed my card. It noted: *'Individual contacted HM Embassy in Bonn, West Germany seeking recruitment to Special Branch. Report by E' squad annexed, showing original letter to the British Embassy in West Germany.' File number../......*

We left the index card room and entered the room known as subject index. Expertly the manager fingered a row of files classified *Secret* and drew out a multiple Secret Pink file. Looking down the index she found the desired folio – my entry. I was no activist, I wasn't deemed important enough to have my own personal file, but I did manage to do something that warranted an entry.

It was the Cold War and my request had been abnormal. I suppose I could have been suspected of being a Soviet dangle. I read the mention. It noted that I'd applied to the embassy to join the Branch as well as referring to an annexed report. The report outlined the result of an investigation performed by the Branch's ELS officer stationed with the Bundeskriminalamt in Wiesbaden, West Germany. The officer had checked my bona fides with German colleagues who had given me a clean bill of health. A more cursory check had also been made of the Americans. The Branch was nothing but thorough.

In these early months I would also learn that Branch officers very rarely arrested anyone, except in cases of espionage or voter irregularities, or perhaps cases were no other unit was willing or able to take a case on and it was politically motivated, such as a racially-inspired group who were planning quasi-terroristic actions. Quite simply the aim was to keep Branch officers covert and out of the limelight. When Branch officers did go to court they were seldom revealed to the public as such. In fact many of the cases actually investigated by Special Branch, such as OSA jobs, were so sensitive that when they made it to court, the trials (or parts thereof) were held in-camera *(closed court sessions held in secret)*.

To retain this anonymity and obtain the most current investigative practices in terrorist related cases, SO13 *(the Anti-Terrorist Branch)* had been created in the CID in 1972. Previously this role had been performed by X-Squad the Branch's own investigative wing. The Anti-Terrorist Branch was staffed by seasoned CID officers on a rotational basis, generally over three years. The officers selected to SO13 were generally amongst the best CID investigators in the Met and would procedurally deal with terrorist related investigations like any other crimes. What laws had been broken, what evidence was required to prove the offence, what forensics needed to be collected and what case papers where required to be submitted to the CPS. The methodical and precise SO13 detectives often relied on Special Branch for 'sanitised' intelligence to prosecute there cases and in return the Branch's 'S' squad cell in SO13 handled and collated any secret intelligence garnered by the ATB during its investigations. Such intelligence was then packaged for retention in SB records or further operationally exploited by the Branch. Any secret intelligence provided by the 'S' squad cell to SO13 colleagues was sanitised to a level where it could be safely utilised by the ATB to investigate and convict terrorists without undermining or compromising the safety of agents or other sources of Branch intelligence. Once again, this all kept SB officers covert and out of the limelight.

Amongst many other Branch related training courses and knowledge transfers that I underwent in those early months was the

'Espionage Search Course'. One of 'C' Squad's roles was to investigate and gather evidence to arrest and prosecute spies. For this reason a number of SB officers were trained to find spy paraphernalia such as one time pads, micro-dot film, covert communication systems, secret writing tools, etc. In those early years of my Branch career I was deployed on several Cold War espionage-related operations where I'd put these skills to good use.

Gradually, the Branch used its massive resources to turn me into an investigator with an intelligence-centric mind-set that sought out connections to crimes and intelligence that went far beyond the most obvious perpetrator(s) and to understand the psychology and/or political thought that drove them. This expansive intelligence-driven view allowed the Branch to forgo easy arrests to gather a more explicit understanding of a cause or organisation. Consequently, this sometimes put the Branch at odds with its more risk-averse Uniform and CID colleagues, as the gauge used to measure these departments is the speed and frequency at which they can put bodies behind bars.

Throughout my Branch career I'd never stop learning, but this was at its most intense in those early weeks and months after joining. I soaked up my training and the Branch's development system kept giving me more. Eventually, I was deemed ready to be sent into the field.

Chapter Five - Guarding the Gateway

My first Branch posting was to P-Squad, at Heathrow Airport. The IRA was at its most active and the Branch's port role was crucial. At ports the Branch was responsible for administering counter-terrorism legislation. The main legislation was the Prevention of Terrorism Act of 1984 (Temporary Provisions), known to all who used it as - *POTA*. POTA allowed SB officers at port to detain any person entering or leaving the UK for the purpose of examining them to ascertain whether they were involved in the Commission, Preparation or Instigation of acts of terrorism, regardless of from whence this terrorism emanated. Originally the act had only pertained to terrorism stemming from the Northern Irish conflict but it had been extended by Parliament to cover any form of terrorism. No suspicion of any actual wrongdoing was required for an SB officer to examine an individual at port under POTA. Moreover, the act allowed for a subject to be examined for an initial period of up to twelve hours without legal representation, unless the person was actually arrested, at which point a lawyer could be sought. All examinations lasting over an hour had to be recorded, whereas no record was required for examinations under that time period. In fact subjects *detained* for less than an hour were not legally entitled to know why they were being examined. During examination subjects had to submit to any search of their person, articles, documents or goods as required by the SB officer in his or her efforts to establish whether they were involved in the CPI of terrorism.

POTA was a temporary act which Parliament had to vote to re-authorise yearly. It had been hastily placed on the statute books in 1974, shortly after the two Birmingham pub bombings took the lives of 21 people and injured 182.

POTA was an act that no SB officer wished to abuse. We utilised its powers diligently and fairly and it proved to be an excellent tool in preventing, arresting or surveilling the movements of terrorist or terrorist suspects through British ports. I personally was able to provide much information on Northern Irish and International terrorists or terrorist sympathisers' movements and actions that no doubt saved lives in the UK or probably beyond. The same was also true of my colleagues.

In addition to POTA, 'P' squad officers were the first and last line of defence for the UK on all policing matters. We notified police forces about major criminals and extremists entering or leaving the UK and also managed the Child Abduction Act at port. We also questioned refugees fleeing despotic regimes, in our own interests and those of our colleagues in UK's Security and Intelligence agencies. During the Iran – Iraq war I witnessed the disfiguring results of Saddam Hussein's chemical weapons (CW) systems when some victims of such weapons arrived at Heathrow en route to various British hospitals.

A prime example of such attacks was the Halabja massacre which took place on March 16, 1988, right at the end of the Iran–Iraq War (1980-1988) in the Kurdish city of Halabja in Southern Kurdistan. Halabja remains the largest chemical weapons attack against civilians in history - resulting in between 3,200 and 5,000 deaths and up to 10,000 injured (many thousands more died of complications from the poisonous gas in the years that followed).

Donald Rumsfeld, then a civilian but previously the US Secretary of State for Defence in President Gerald Ford's Administration, had been dispatched by US president Ronald Reagan to Baghdad to open diplomatic relations with Saddam's Baathist regime. The Reagan government wished to prevent an Iranian victory in the war and to ensure US oil interests in the region. The war, which would turn out to be the 20th Century's longest conventional conflict, was going so poorly for Saddam's Iraq *(who had started it in the first place)*, that in an attempt turn the tide the Iraqi regime had resorted to the almost daily use of battlefield chemical weapons. Iraq had been much-criticised for this tactic in the UN, although this had little diplomatic effect due to the US, supported by the UK, being comparatively lukewarm on the issue - citing a position of diplomatic neutrality. This was arguably a strange position as Iraq's action was a clear breech of international law because CW in warfare had been banned since the 1925 Geneva Conventions.

A state's political policy is a living organism, if one is involved in foreign affairs long enough one will appreciate how allegiances ebb and flow with changes in the national interest. US records *(which Rumsfeld contests)* now suggest that Rumsfeld's diplomatic efforts during the Iran–Iraq war had helped Saddam to increase the potency of Iraq's CW payloads and delivery systems. What is irrefutable however is that throughout the Iran-Iraq war Donald Rumsfeld never publicly denounced Iraq's use of CW. This occurred only when US policy changed towards Saddam, at which point Rumsfeld became outraged about Saddam's prior use of CW. Consequently, in his second tour as US Secretary of State for Defence, this time under President George Bush Jr., Rumsfeld continually attacked Saddam for his prior use of CW and cited this as indisputable evidence of Saddam's barbarity and the need for regime change. It's strange how expediency seems to cloud politicians' memories.

'P' squad's work brought me into close proximity with the people who were of most interest to the Branch: extremists and terrorists and their supporters from around the world, be they Basques,

Germans, Palestinians, Irish Republicans or Northern Irish or Scottish Loyalists, etc. Moreover, the world's number one international airport was a location traversed by travelling guerrillas and revolutionaries from Africa, Asia and South America as well as numerous potential or actual Soviet Bloc intelligence officers from every communist state including the Soviet Union's KGB or GRU, Cuba's DGI and Bulgaria's CSS. Branch officers were simply the 'go to guys' for all politically orientated issues. If HM Immigration Service or HM Customs and Excise realised that they had somebody political in front of them who potentially posed a threat to the UK, they'd call for the Branch. This 'suspect' would simply see a well-dressed individual enter the room who'd politely set about questioning him or her, which for many was a disorientating situation.

Sometimes we'd simply stop passengers entering or leaving the UK ourselves whilst standing next to the Immigration officer. Our work was impactive, positive and secured the borders of the UK in a joined up manner. Consequently our reports flowed to all of the Branch's squads, to the Security Service and to a plethora of the Branch's European, Commonwealth and American partners, such as the US Federal Bureau of Investigation (FBI), Germany's Bundeskriminalamt, France's Direction Central des Renseignements Généraux (RG) and the Royal Canadian Mounted Police (RCMP) to name but a few. I would not forget the potential offered by 'P' squad's information flows and opportunity for intelligence and source operations.

In years to come I'd recall this potential for agent (source) recruitment in 'P' squad and utilise it to bring an ingenious plan into operation. Seconded to SIS (MI6) as a case officer I was at the time planning an operation against a terrorist financier who we'd been secretly chasing around the world. To assist in setting up the operation I'd instructed one of my SIS team to search for an SB port report on the financier, which contained information that could assist my operational plan. Prior to joining MI6 I'd been reposted to Heathrow as the SB Detective Inspector in-charge of Terminal One (Internationals) and Terminal Two. Part of my role as the terminals DI was to read all my officers' reports and to decide which squads or agencies to copy in. I had requested the port report on the financier as I knew one of my ports officers had stopped the financier whilst he was transiting through Heathrow on route to a third country. At the time the officer questioned the financier under POTA and subsequently produced an excellent detailed dossier which I classified as SECRET and disseminated to both 'E' Squad and the Security Service for theirs and SIS' attention. The Security Service was tasked with disseminating relevant port reports to SIS. My first shock was that none of the four SIS officers in my team knew what an SB port report was - they'd never seen one. The fact that my guys were researchers and analysts was even more disturbing, as they were exactly the people who needed to data mine such intelligence. Okay, I thought, maybe SB port reports are repackaged by the Security Service as their own intelligence after cannibalising the reports' content. Therefore with this in mind I had one of my SIS team check Security Service records for the name and details of the financier. Although the name was there, none of the original port report details where included. My subsequent research showed that this was not a one-off, port reports were simply not getting through to SIS with any consistency. The UK's intelligence community was missing a potentially big trick and I was determined to change this.

I decided to create a system where SB Ports officers throughout the UK would seek out potential terrorist agents on behalf of SIS. My concepts methodology was such that the plan and the procedures I'd devised would ensure a smooth and secure flow of intelligence and information exchange between SB ports officers nationally, P Squad's Headquarters unit at Heathrow and 'E' Squad's 'sensitive' office at the Yard. This left very little risk for compromise making the agent recruitment process as safe and secure as possible. I outlined my plan to my main boss, the head of SIS' counter-terrorism section and he agreed it was a goer. Unfortunately though, the concept would hit a major organisational barrier when my boss took the idea to 'C' *(the Chief of SIS)*, at the time Sir Richard Dearlove. Sir Richard was happy with the proposed concept, as he knew better than most that gaining agents in terrorist organisations is a very difficult and expensive process and that anything that helped ease this procedure was to be welcomed. However, C's enthusiasm was tempered by the Security Service Deputy Director General's *(DDG)* strong objections to my concept. In her note to the head of SIS' counter-terrorism section the DDG mentioned that my proposal impetuously breached MI5's domain, which would undermine the hitherto excellent relations between SIS and the Security Service. Indeed, the note went on to mention that when her service agreed to my secondment it was on the understanding that my deployments would be exclusively aimed at overseas operations, not stepping on their toes here in the UK. The effect of this note was that my ports concept was put on the back burner.

    A month or so later, Jack Straw, the then the Home Secretary was touring MI6's iconic HQ at Vauxhall Cross with other senior politicians and members of the Intelligence Services Committee. The Security Service DDG was also in attendance. When they entered the Counter-Terrorist Section 'C' brought the committee over to my desk and introduced me to Mr Straw and the other committee members stating that I was an extremely rare animal, an SIS case officer on long term secondment from Special Branch. 'C' knew that my presence in his organisation as a relatively senior SIS officer showed his Service's progressive nature. When Jack Straw asked me what I was working on I explained that I was the lead case officer combating various major international terrorist organisations. Seizing my opportunity, I swiftly added that I was also attempting to introduce a new and much cheaper method of potentially gaining human sources of intelligence by enlisting the aid of Special Branch ports officers from throughout the UK – with of course the necessary safeguards. Mr Straw found this interesting and asked me to expand on my concept – how did I see it actually working and what were the safeguards? I explained quickly yet in some detail, focusing on the joined up nature of the plan. The plan foresaw a structured and centralised working relationship between Police Special Branches, the Security Service and SIS. Based on SIS's needs, 'P' squad would orchestrate Special Branch ports work nationally whilst 'E' Squad would scrutinise proposed recruitment leads prior to dissemination to my team in SIS for evaluation and possible action. Various members of the committee murmured their approval. Jack then turned to 'C' and the DDG and provided them with one of those understated directions that politicians articulate as requests, but functionaries quite rightly decode as directives:

"I'm sure we're looking at this favourably aren't we? As Carlton says, it's perfectly joined up, isn't it Eliza?"

As a political animal the DDG, Elizabeth Manningham-Buller, who would later became MI5's next Director General, didn't need to be 'directed' twice. She agreed that my ports concept had "tremendous merit". Some days later I was provided with a senior Security Service officer to help dovetail my concept into MI5's ports liaison procedures with Special Branches. Jack Straw was no fool; he knew where the bottleneck lay, even though I hadn't actually alluded to any such problem. Jack's intervention meant that my ports recruitment scheme was reborn that very day.

My manoeuvres that day had allowed me to steer a great concept towards implementation. However, although the concept did what it said on the tin, recruiting agents more easily, cheaply and thereby no doubt saving lives, I had nevertheless made powerful enemies. The welcomed and calculated by-product of my concept, which Eliza no-doubt immediately comprehended, was that it would bring SIS and Special Branches closer together under MPSB's auspices. In the lead up to the millennium MI5's position as the sole gate keeper between the provincial Special Branches and MI6 had become unassailable. Yet, with just one fell swoop, my ports scheme had just challenged this situation, kicking that gate wide open and stimulating greater inter-operability between the UK's intelligence and security agencies. This better free-flow of intelligence would enhance agent recruitment opportunities as well as steer SB ports officers towards more fruitful lines of investigation. It was a great legacy.

However, back in 1987, after just a year on 'P' squad, I was asked if I would be willing to undergo bodyguard training to become a Protection Officer on 'A' Squad. The threat of IRA assassination was greater than ever. It was the Branch's responsibility, through the intelligence exploitation activities of 'B' Squad and the protective security measures of 'A' Squad to ensure that the British Government was able remain in a continuous state of business as usual.

I had enjoyed my work on 'P' squad but joining 'A' Squad would mean worldwide travel, much danger and the chance to brush shoulders with the world's most powerful people - the offer was too good to resist.

Chapter Six - Armed and Dangerous

In late spring of 1987 I reported to the Met's specialist firearms training establishment in Epping Forest. I'd been trained to handle guns while working in Germany but the MPS liked to train you their way, no matter what your experience was. This allowed the ironing out of any faults, or bad habits and most importantly of all, if you ever had to shoot someone, or God forbid, made a mistake, the Met could stand-up and say that from day one you were taught the right way - in other words any mistakes would not be down to a lack of training. Throughout training, as this gun-philosophy was drummed into us, I kept hearing the words of my old FBI boss - Cover Your Ass.

I was joined on this initial course by three other SB officers, two females and a male. We were all destined for 'A' Squad. It sounds strange perhaps, especially considering that we were all police officers, but Branch officers were treated differently by other police officers, in particular uniform. We were seen as outsiders. Consequently, on the course, the four of us stuck together supporting one another in a sea of uniforms the majority of course's participants.

The progression from basic beginners' course to advanced training was, if at all, normally progressed over several months or years. The Branch, however, as in so many areas was able to fast-track us through the whole process. This did not go down well with other officers especially the course instructors. We knew from the outset that we pretty much had to end up top of the class from day one; the smallest mistake might be seized upon by our trainers to send us back to the Yard unqualified.

The initial firearms course, which was designed to take total firearms novices to a good general standard of firearms proficiency and tactics, lasted two-and-a-half weeks. Of the other officers on the course, the majority by far, were general duty uniform officers plus a couple of CID flying squad detectives. All of these officers were issued with the black coloured model '10' Smith and Wesson .38 revolver. It held six rounds and had a standard 6" inch barrel for greater accuracy. The Branch officers on the course were issued with the Branch's weapon of the era, a silver coloured model 64 snub nosed .38 Smith and Wesson revolver. This weapon had a much smaller 2" barrel but was ideal for covert carriage. Uniformed officers generally carried their weapons overtly, so the larger sized weapon was not a problem for them.

The course was intense; it had to be. After all, correct weapons handling was paramount. Although I had learnt other methods, there was only one way to do everything - the Met's way. Basic tactics were also taught, including armed stops, cordons, searches and, most important of all, the clear identification of targets, warning commands and talk-downs. If possible the aim was to end an incident without shots being fired. Once an officer became a *'shot'*, (Met slang for being an authorised firearms officer), these tactics would be honed on the quarterly training and re-classification shoots that basic shots had to undergo to keep their *'ticket'* (their firearms authorisation card was also known as a pink card in the Met because of its colour at the time). Royalty and Special Branch Protection Officers had to retrain or reclassify every two months, in addition to attending quarterly two-day tactical meets.

On this initial course most of the shoots we'd undertake were from the drawn weapons position. This meant that the weapon had already been drawn from the holster and positioned in what was termed the low ready carriage, about stomach-high facing the target with a finger just off the trigger. A warning shout would be given before the necessary shots were fired at the turning man sized target. After firing the first shot, each subsequent shot had to be re-evaluated until the target was 'stopped'. All of the shoots were commenced from the double-action position. That meant that the trigger was fully squeezed and released each time you shot a bullet; there was no holding the trigger half-depressed for a subsequent shot as one would later learn during the bodyguard training.

Safety and precision were the course's watch words. Reloading a six-shot revolver could be fiddly but - after substantial practice - speed could be achieved with the aid of a strip loader. Once the weapon was empty, *'out'*, we were taught to drop to the kneeling position in order to reload. If we were shooting on an open-air range with simulated loads we were taught to find 'cover', wherever possible, before reloading as this was clearly a vulnerable time for an officer in a firefight. So the reloading procedure was drilled into our minds by practice, turning it into muscle memory.

Our instructors told us a salutary tale about the dangers of muscle memory. A New York City patrol officer got into a firefight with some gangsters. From the moment the firefight started his training kicked in. He had sought cover behind the hard parts of his vehicle and had returned fire with six well-aimed shots from his 10' Smith & Wesson. Out of rounds he had to reload. He opened the cylinder of his model 10' and dumped the empty bullet casing into his hand. Still on auto-pilot, he broke cover by reaching over to put the empty cases into a *bucket*. The moment he exposed himself this way, the gangsters shot him in the head, killing him immediately.

The officer, a fifteen-year veteran of the NYPD, had acted in response to his muscle memory. On NYPD ranges, officers were taught that once all their rounds had been expended that they should drop the brass casings into their supporting hand and place them directly into a bucket situated by each officer's shooting position. The NYPD sold the brass for scrap. In the heat of the firefight the officer had acted totally from muscle and it cost him his life. Muscle memory is excellent but it must be consciously controlled.

My SB colleagues and I passed the basic firearms course with flying colours and after a weekend off we returned to Epping Forest for another three weeks of shooting, tactics and unarmed combat as part of the MPS's renowned bodyguard course. This bodyguard course was a massive step up from basic firearms course.

The shoots were faster, utilised turning targets as part of the drill and required us to draw from the holster, which had the added complication of being concealed under a jacket. The advanced shooting tactics also required officers to utilise single-action techniques. This meant that whilst drawing our weapons from the holster we cocked the hammer whilst simultaneously bringing the weapon up into the aim. This procedure created a smooth trigger action which allowed for better accuracy and, naturally, greater speed. The drawback was that this procedure could be dangerous, if one cocked the hammer back too far, it could spring forward letting off a round into your thigh. This had happened on a few occasions in the past.

For an even quicker response, many of the close-quarter shoots (seven to ten metres or closer) were timed to take account of sense-of-direction shooting. When shooting at speed and with the extreme movement of drawing a weapon from the holster within a split second, one doesn't always have time to aim. Sense-of-direction shooting takes this into account. It removes the need to close one eye and zero into the target. Hence it saves precious time. At brake neck speed one simply has the presence of one's convictions and points the weapon, with both eyes open looking at the area where you want the round to hit. Done correctly, smoothly and most important of all, with conviction, it works, but it takes a great deal of practice. Action will always beat reaction, so to have any chance at staying alive at all Protection officers have to return fire almost without thinking. Bodyguard shoots, which are always reactive to an assassin's action, account for this, meaning one has to be bloody quick to pass the shoots. In real life if you're not quick you and your principal will mostly certainly die. Most close quarter assassination attempts are fast and furious and Protection officers have to react accordingly, so we don't waste time with verbal warnings. Due to the expected speed, determined intent and generally close proximity of any attack, we had to make sure that we stopped any attacker dead - literally.

Double-tapping (firing two rounds within tenths of a second) was a sound means to this end but it took a lot of practice to bring our speed and dexterity to the optimum. We took on multiple targets at close and long ranges and we'd shoot sitting at a table, kneeling and lying prone. We also undertook many vehicle drills including shooting through the windscreens from inside the car, the tactical use of smoke grenades, cover and withdrawal tactics, vehicle cross-decking tactics, driving through ambushes, anti-vehicle IED attacks, reversing out of ambushes, exiting vehicles under fire, spreading the arcs of fire, retreating to cover, advance and backup car drills as well as multiple-fire and movement-to-cover drills.

In those days, quite rightly, SB officers did not drive protection vehicles. The Branch selected experienced advanced police drivers from Traffic Patrol or the Diplomatic Protection Group (DPG, the Met's armed uniformed unit that protects diplomatic premises in London) to drive for 'A' Squad. Prior to undertaking the bodyguards course 'A' Squad drivers had all completed the Met's world-renowned six week advanced driving course, plus 'A' Squad's armoured vehicle course as well as the protection driver's course. These guys were easily amongst the best drivers in the UK. Hence, as a general rule during the bodyguard course, drivers generally acted as drivers and SB officers as

Protection Officers. That said, all on the BG course be they SB, Royalty or Special Escort Group (SEG, the Met police's armed specialist escort and motorcycle unit) officers were all trained to the same high technical standard of body guarding.

The instructors placed us under increasing pressure during the course. We were sent on three- to five-mile runs, carried logs that required six people to lift through the assault course and were then ordered to the range. Fatigue deadens the body's fine motor skills. On one shoot after a five-mile run, the instructor started firing a shotgun over our heads as we tried to deal with multiple targets - it was all about the pressure.

The unarmed combat elements of the course were adequate, as far as I - a Kung-Fu enthusiast - was concerned, but if one wasn't already acquainted with some form of martial art - Judo, boxing, foot-fighting or Kung Fu, it would have been difficult to build up the required proficiency in the time allotted. Despite my expertise, I still learned a lot of new and excellent techniques for disarming gun-toting enemies as well as ways one could retain hold of one's own weapon while under physical assault. Losing your weapon would almost certainly prove deadly.

In addition to the four of us who joined the Bodyguard Course straight from the Initial Firearms Course there were eight others on the course who were already shots. The eight were split between Special Branch, Royalty Protection and SEG officers. Upon completion of the course, all of us except for the male officer who started the Initial Course with me, passed with flying colours. He never got to grips with the speed required to complete the shoots, he found it all too fast. In addition to the Smith & Wesson model 64 we were also trained on various Heckler & Koch machine pistols and assault rifles.

The Bodyguard course made no attempt to keep the cold reality of protection work from us. The instructors didn't spare our feelings as they explained the damage various projectiles do to the human body when propelled from diverse weapons systems: handguns, shotguns, high velocity weapons and explosive devices. Then we honed in on the thrusting and slashing wounds caused by knives with a variety of edges, points and hooks. It was with such injuries in mind, that the course expanded on the basic first aid knowledge we'd received as regular police officers by providing us with advanced techniques concerning the 'primary care' to stabilise gunshot and flesh piercing wounds. Last but not least the instructors explained that the right mental attitude was just as important as first aid. If one was unlucky enough to be shot the individual's mind-set, particularly his or her will to stay alive can be crucial to their survival in the initial stages. Shock and resignation can kill.

It had taken many weeks, but I returned to the Yard a trained Protection Officer - at least in the 'hard skills'. It would take weeks, if not months before I was totally comfortable employing many of the 'soft skills'. These were the day-in-day-out imponderables that revolved around organising, checking and establishing what was or was not feasible, making measured decisions and of course telling some of the most powerful people in the world what they could or could not do. I found addressing the concepts, procedures and calculations surrounding the decision making elements of VVIP protection to be far more demanding than the physical aspects of 'body-guarding'. It all revolved around timing, steadfastness, flexibility, knowledge and organisation - booking restaurants, hotels, trains, planes and theatre tickets all with security first and foremost in my mind. Planning routes, timings, upholding secrecy and negotiating with the rich and powerful were all par-of-the-course. I also had to learn how to bring in additional security - uniform or plain clothes as well as to estimate the number of officers required to cover an event and to 'bid' for additional 'A' Squad prot officers or other specialist resources when I deemed them necessary.

I directed and requested resources from uniform Commanders from across the UK to secure residences, hotels and facilities where a principal might stay overnight. To assist with static protection I'd learn how to organise and deploy armed coverage from the DPG in London or in the provinces, from provincial armed Special Branch officers or local police firearms units. I'd learn to recce and organise operations in other police areas, to request dog searches for explosives or, in various locations in the UK where dogs weren't available, fingertip (POLSA) searches by numerous police officers. Noting when and how to seek an SEG motorbike escort was also something I learnt over those first few weeks and months. And of course I learnt that everything came with a price attached to it. Our resources were not infinite. Budgets had to be met and that meant using resources in a rational manner. Like so much in Special Branch, I'd learn these skills on the job by watching those talented SB officers who had climbed the mountain before me.

Some of the trickiest decisions were those that if it went wrong you'd be on your own, such as decisions as to when to 'circumvent' the law for official reasons. This is extremely difficult because, as the protection officer, you make numerous instantaneous decisions under pressure, but your judgement will be questioned in the broad light of day by those who have all the time in the world to calmly deliberate them. This is the case even if your decision to 'override' the law can be proved to have been done in an effort to safeguard a principal - or uphold national security. Even simple decisions such as authorising the driver to utilise the covert two's and blues (lights and siren) built into our normal-looking armoured protection vehicles to proceed through congestion, red lights or to circumvent other traffic restrictions could land the Prot officer in hot water. So, just because the principal was going to miss an important vote in the houses of parliament if he was late, didn't automatically justify the use of blue lights and sirens to get him there on the hurry up, no matter how much he pleaded. That said, the pressure exerted on a young inexperience SB Prot officer, such as myself in those early months, to bow to the senior minister's urgent wishes were immense. Fortunately, MPSB's excellent training, my character and the fact that I knew I could count on my supervisor's support, meant that I didn't.

Travelling on flights with weapons was invariably problematic and a variety of authorisations had to be attained. MPSB officers had full police powers in England and Wales, however, in common with all other police officers in England and Wales our powers were limited in Scotland, the Channel Islands and Northern Ireland. Due to the different laws in these parts of the UK, so this was covered by MPSB officers often being sworn in as special constables for the duration of any operation in these locations, be they protection or intelligence in orientation.

Then there were the many problems thrown up by travelling abroad. What authority, if any, would I have when working in X or Y country? How would I get permission to carry firearms? Who at the Foreign and Commonwealth Office (F&CO) in the UK and/or at our Embassy in the country would support me? On top of this, of course, was the need to consult with the agencies of foreign powers and to find ways to work in tandem with their protection, security and intelligence agencies.

I'd also be assigned to 'A' Squad operations to protect various heads of state, heads of government or Foreign Secretaries visiting the UK. On these occasions I could act as the lead UK protection officer, especially on single officer prots. This role would also require me to control that nation's accompanying protection team operatives as well as organising and directing any UK police, military or other assets. Foreign protection teams visiting the UK would almost certainly be refused authority to carry firearms, so they tended to be critical and meticulously assess our proposed protection packages. All arrangements rested on the SB Prot officer's shoulders.

Running protection involved dealing with a constant stream of crucial decisions, all day, everyday. We could break the law to get the job done but we had to make sure we had damn good reasons for doing so – it was CYA on steroids. That's why as an 'A' Squad Prot officer you quickly learnt to say "No!"

Chapter Seven - Dougie

When I returned to the Yard as a trained protection officer I was assigned to the then Home Secretary Douglas Hurd's *(aka "Dougie")* protection team. The team was headed by a charismatic Detective Chief Inspector (DCI), Jonathan Winterton. Jonathan was a suave Roger Moore-type character in his early 50s. He was a Lloyd's name, independently wealthy and, like Dougie, had gone to Eton. 'A' Squad's offices were situated on the sixteenth Floor of the Yard where the boss Detective Chief Superintendent (DCS) Jack Greenham and the rest of the squad's senior management team had their offices. I'd put my best suit on to make an impression as I was ushered into the DCS' plush office along with Johnathan. DCS Greenham broke the ice, explaining that 'A' Squad had needed additional officers to combat the potential for more Mountbatten's, Brighton's or Airey Neave type Republican operations. The Branch couldn't take anything for granted it had to combat these Irish ops one way or another. I had been in the Branch long enough to know that what Greenham really meant was that 'B' Squad had possibly obtained some chatter about upcoming assassination attempts.

"I know you're new to the firearms game," Jack said with a slight smile. "We don't want any accidents. We can deal with all problems here but for 'accidents' with firearms. Firearms frighten everybody on the fifth floor."

By the fifth floor he meant the Commissioner's office. The Commissioner tended to leave the Branch be - as long as Home Secretary Dougie Hurd, his direct political boss, wasn't troubled by any of our actions.

"So listen, take your gun home tonight and get used to it," Jack continued. "Get the fear out of your system, become happy with it. That way we'll have no problems."

"Okay, Sir." I replied expectantly.

"You've not got kids have you?" Jack asked. "Your wife's reliable isn't she? She doesn't have a fear of weapons does she? I'm assuming she's a safe pair of hands?"

Angela and I got married not long after I'd finished police training school and set up home in a police flat in Ealing. After a stint working for McAlpine's she moved to an international drinks company where her French and German put her in good stead in the wines department. Angela announced she was pregnant not long after I'd joined the Branch and once our first child was born, she gave up work to do the most important job in the world – be a mum.

After I confirmed that Angela would be able to cope with a gun in the house, Jack told me to speak to Jonathan who would take me through the procedures for the Home Secretary.

"Don't give him any cause for concern," he added, as I was about to leave. "And welcome aboard, Carlton."

Something had clearly gone wrong with an officer's firearm that had caused Jack some considerable angst. I'd never know what it was.

In the Branch's Armoury I signed for my own personal snub-nosed model 64, a speed loader and thirty rounds of ammunition. I loaded the weapon and placed the remaining rounds in the speedloader and ammo pouches and placed the weapon in a small holster on my hip underneath my jacket. Jonathan and I then left the Yard to walk the short distance to the Home Office where the team had an office on the ground floor.

"In this game, Carlton," Jonathan said, "You never call anybody, outside the *Job,* 'Sir'. For example, Dougie is the Secretary of State for the Home Office. So you should address him by that title. He's not your boss. Well, as Home Secretary he's theoretically the boss of all of us, but he's your subject when it comes to protection. Understand? He's not in the *Job* and you need to able to tell him 'no' when you think it's necessary."

"I understand."

"As in most things in life it's all about perception and the general public perception of the police, including politicians, is either *Dixon of Dock Green* or *The Sweeney*, neither of which are true or flattering. The Branch is a professional organisation and as professionals we demand equal status. This is important Carlton, as with status comes respect, even if it's begrudging. But most importantly it means your advice will carry weight. *He* should look to *you* for your permission. Nothing should be done to undermine this."

I never forgot Jonathan's words. We were professionals who sometimes had to dominate people who were used to controlling others, and if the worst happened there was no time to be second-guessed by them. In years to come, in addition to the CYA concept, I'd also pass this advice onto my subordinates as an important aspect of their tutelage.

We entered the Home Office.

'A' Squad's Home Secretary's protection team consisted of Jonathan, a DI, two DS's, myself and two PC 'A' Squad specialist protection drivers. In those days there was one more member of the team: a government service driver. GCS drivers are the unarmed civilian drivers who drive government ministers' vehicles. Not particularly well-trained or versed in any special techniques, GCS drivers would nevertheless still hold their posts, even though the

Secretary of State or indeed the Prime Minister they were assigned to drive received protection. This massive weak link in our protection packages was driven by tradition and vested interest. The vested interest was primarily that of the Government Car Service, who didn't want to lose jobs – even though the world had changed around them – with security and potential assassination a daily threat. That said, their position was supported by politicians. The politicians might not be able to control the Branch but they could control the GCS. The GCS were more relevant to a politician's day-to-day life, in that the GCS would run errands for them, which obviously the Branch would not.

For the first few weeks I learned on the job and was soon put in charge of running various protection operations for the Home Secretary. It quickly became clear to me just how different the Branch was from the rest of the MPS. On a practical level 'A' Squad officers were allowed to carry up to thirty rounds of ammunition and to keep their weapons with them at all times. General 'Shots' (firearms officers) carried twelve rounds of ammunition and turned their guns in at the end of their shift.

Unless it went wrong, Branch officers' decisions were rarely questioned – even by the most senior of non-Branch officers. If we required police resources we generally got them, regardless of the area we were working in and, to some extent, irrespective of the costs to that force. That said, most if not all Branch officers were sensible and only broke the bank when it was absolutely necessary.

One of the first jobs I was in charge of whilst on Dougie's team was an operation to Liverpool. We were scheduled to travel to a black-tie function in the city on a Friday night but due to Dougie's official commitments we couldn't leave London until the early evening. This meant that the train was the only option to get us there on time. My plan necessitated me sending my team and our vehicles ahead so that when Dougie and I arrived at Liverpool Lime Street the team would have thoroughly checked out the venue, confirmed a route and would be waiting at the station to ferry us to the function.

With my team heading to Liverpool by road I'd arranged to replace them whilst we were in London with a stand in GCS driver and an 'A' Squad back-up team and vehicle. Once at Euston I'd arranged for Dougie and I to travel first class to our destination. A further complication was that to save time we'd have to make the journey to Liverpool in dinner suits so we could drive straight to the function without detouring to the hotel to get changed once we'd arrived in the city. The timings were tight. On Prot one has to think of everything that could possibly affect the principal's security and on this occasion I thought that our black tie outfits might draw attention to us on the train, so I wanted to make sure that we could isolate a first class carriage if the need arose.

This was the 1980's and Mrs Thatcher's policies had devastated the North leaving many with no choice but to take the Tory advice to "get on their bikes" and work on the building sites of London and the south east during the week. These Northern invaders would then typically travel back to Manchester and Liverpool on Friday evenings often somewhat worse for wear and bearing a pathological dislike of the soft Southern bastards they'd had to take orders from during the week. Of course these guys didn't travel first-class but there was always the chance that they might spy us out as we boarded the train and wish to make Dougie aware of their displeasure. As one doesn't want to get stuck on a train without assistance as there is nowhere to hide, I decided to ask the British Transport Police (BTP) to supply some officers to accompany us on the train to deal with any public order issues.

I walked the short distance from the Yard to the BTP's main office at Victoria Station a few days before the proposed operation. As I entered the reception and walked towards the PC behind the counter, his eyes widened in alarm as I reached for my warrant card which was in my jacket pocket. I now realise he caught sight of my model 64 in its shoulder holster which induced tunnel vision in the officer so, in a sudden panic he didn't hear what I was saying. From my perspective I had simply opened the door of the police station saw a uniformed PC behind the counter, pulled out my warrant card and introduced myself.

"Hi there, I'm DC King from the Yard's Special Branch, can I have a word about some assistance we require........"

I didn't get to finish my question.

With hindsight I can only imagine that the PC thought: 'Black man with a gun, this can't be right!' The officer stood there as if frozen, blood draining from his face. Taking no notice of anything I said, the officer rushed out of the room urgently hissing "Sarge, Sarge!"

To be fair to the BTP officer, in the mid 1980's there were very few black police officers, very, very few officers of any colour who carried firearms and fewer still who carried weapons in plain clothes. In fact the BTP as a police force didn't possess a single firearm.

Moments later the PC's sergeant gingerly poked his head around the door frame, the PC somewhere behind him. The sergeant was weighing me up. By now the penny had dropped and I quickly tried to put the hapless PC and his unfortunate sergeant out of their misery.

"Hi there, Sarge. As I said to your PC, I'm DC Carlton King from the Met's Special Branch and I wondered if I could have a word with your Inspector?"

The sergeant saw my warrant card, glanced at my suited and booted appearance, and looked at his PC with an 'I'll-deal-with-you-later expression' on his face. Then the red-faced sergeant apologetically asked if he could help in *any way*, with *anything* at all. Needless to say, from that moment on, I knew I'd get all the BTP officers I required to secure the train for my journey. My Liverpool op passed off without further incident.

Throughout the years of my service the uniqueness of my 'identity' as a British secret intelligence/national security or law enforcement officer, of one type or another, has been 'interesting' in many ways. Some of these situations have been comical, others explosive and some at a level where they could have led to full blown diplomatic incidents.

An amusing but revealing incident that taught me a great deal about human perception took place not long after the train incident, when I was sitting in the front seat of the back-up vehicle, a top-of-the-range Rover Sterling, on a mission protecting the then Secretary of State for Northern Ireland *(SoSNI)*. One of our drivers, John, was cruising along a winding B-road in deepest, darkest Wiltshire, as we made our way steadily to the principal's house. It had been raining so the road surface was slippery and John was driving with due caution when he pointed out that a Range Rover behind us was driving erratically. The vehicles' lights began to flash us as it closed up on our bumper. Then, just as suddenly it dropped back. Seconds later, breaking a number of laws and risking all our lives, the Range Rover accelerated and blasted by.

Although an 'A' Squad veteran of twelve years, John had previously been a member of the Met's traffic patrol. There is a saying in the Job, 'once a trafpol always trafpol' and John was no exception. He flicked on the covert blue lights and switched the vehicle's police siren on twice. The driver of the Range Rover got the message and slowed down, allowing John to overtake. John switched on the *'Police – Follow Me'* matrix system secreted into the rear parcel shelf on our back up vehicle. The other driver complied with the command. We pulled into a nearby lay-by and John went to administer a warning. When he returned to the car he could barely contain his laughter and let out a belly laugh as soon as the door closed.

"What's so funny John?" I asked.

"The driver was a member of the blue rinse brigade, a woman in her late 50's. I showed her my warrant card and she told me she was running late for a WI (Women's Institute) meeting where she was expected to judge a cake competition. She said she'd flashed her lights because she wanted to overtake us. However, when she did, she thought she saw the words *'Police'* in the black panel in the rear window (She'd seen our dot matrix sign). That's why she backed off.

"She then said: 'But then I saw that darkie in the front seat and I thought, you can't be police as we don't have any of them in the police here. If he was in the back seat I'd have known you were the police, as on programmes you always put criminals in the back seat never in the front.'"

John explained that he lectured the blue rinser about her driving, telling her to drive safely in future, adding: "By the way, the guy in the front seat is my colleague, a Scotland Yard detective." He said that the blue rinser looked suitably embarrassed as he wished her good day and walked back to the car.

Mikhail Gorbachev had met Mrs Thatcher in the early 1980s, when he was still heir-apparent to Soviet throne. They appeared to get on well. So, when in December 1987 General Secretary Gorbachev was scheduled to meet US President Reagan in Washington, he was happy to accept the Iron Lady's invitation to a two-hour mini UK – USSR summit at RAF Brize Norton. Due to its rather hasty arrangement, No10 provided the Branch with little notice. Fortunately, as the meet would be wholly contained at RAF Brize Norton, we were able to make our plan simple. Whilst their aircraft was refuelled, the main bulk of the Soviet party would alight, leaving some KGB officers on board to secure the aircraft against any British attempts at espionage, a sensible Cold War precaution.

Those dignitaries who had alighted plus KGB *'prot'* would be shepherded to waiting GCS vehicles by 'A' Squad officers and driven to the base's officers mess. There the parties would be met by Mrs Thatcher and a substantial part of the UK cabinet for a working lunch. Upon conclusion of the luncheon, the RAF police motorcyclist would escort the convoy back to the flight pan where they'd board the aircraft for Washington. 'A' Squad and KGB Prot officers would be given the nod of the principals' intention to return to the aircraft by RAF staff waiting on them at the luncheon. Those involved in the op were detailed an individual Soviet dignitary, I got the Soviet Defence Minister.

The first part of the operation went to plan. We dropped our charges off at the officer's mess and, due to a shortage of space, we moved to an adjacent room to await the nod. The PM's team and Gorbachev's KGB Prot officers remained with their principals in the luncheon.

The meeting ran over. We waited, and waited. Nothing came over the radio. Suddenly, someone noticed the RAF motorcyclists moving off ahead of the convoy. No nod had been given. Our principals were leaving without us! MPSB and KGB Protmen were suddenly engaged in an undignified sprint towards the departing convoy. The DI running this part of the job, realising it had turned pear-shaped, yelled at us to jump in any vehicle not covered by a Prot officer.

So, after a quick and fruitless look for the Soviet Defence Minister, I jumped in the first vehicle I could.

My entry into the vehicle in this manner must have come as some surprise to the much bemedalled general in full Soviet uniform who was in the back seat and, not expecting anyone to enter the vehicle, let alone a black man, looked at me in terror. I can only imagine that he'd thought I'd come to murder him. The GCS driver was similarly shaken as he swerved the car momentarily leaving the convoy. The driver was clearly also petrified.

"Special Branch, Mate," I said, trying to sound as friendly as possible to calm the driver down. "It's all under control."

Composed, I straightened my tie and ordered the driver to keep his vehicle in line with the slow moving convoy. I then turned to the heavily-decorated hero of the Great Patriot War *(with more than 25 million Soviet deaths this was the name given to the Second World War by the Soviet Union)* cowering deep back in his seat behind me as I said: "Dobryy den Tavarich" *(Good day comrade)*.

This seemed to settle our guest somewhat, as his facial expression returned to that befitting of an old warrior of such seemingly evident bravery. Back in control of his emotions our driver began to gain a little speed. Out of the corner of my eye I saw my Soviet colleague, the KGB officer assigned to the Defence Minister who was trying to run with dignity next to the car (still picking up speed) while still looking for his charge the Soviet Defence Secretary. I felt sorry for this fellow professional and motioned for him to enter the vehicle. Finally, with much reluctance, he gave up the ghost, before our speed became too great for him to keep up his charade. He opened the rear door and jumped in the back of the vehicle with the unknown Soviet General. The KGB man obviously knew who the General was and still panting, immediately apologised for the intrusion. Five awkward minutes later we arrived at the aircraft. I stepped out and professionally opened the door for my new principal who sheepishly glanced at me before raising and taking on the stature of a straight backed hero of the Great Patriotic War and senior officer of one of the world's two superpowers. Straightening his tunic, medals jingling, he then strode off towards the waiting aircraft. My KGB colleague exited the vehicle through the off side door and scuttled off behind him without another word. It was not our finest hour.

If nothing else, I was learning that people's perceptions can have an extremely powerful influence on their behaviour - and this applied to politics also. Unlike most other protection agencies, we in the Branch would not shy away from engaging our principals in discussion if addressed. US Secret Service agents assigned to President Bush were said to never look him in the eye. From my first principal onwards I would often converse with my protectee, these discussions were frequently enlightening and educational. I remember challenging Dougie Hurd on our lack of an independent foreign policy vis-à-vis the United States. His reply taught me a lot about British realpolitik: "In terms of Foreign Policy, Carlton, no competent government would embark on any policy that would lessen its ability to punch above its weight." He said.

After spending around 18 months on 'A' Squad, an 'E' Squad skipper took me aside one day and asked if I'd like to enter the worlds of counter-espionage and counter-terrorism, although I was only half way through the normal 'A' Squad tour, I immediately said yes. This was exactly what I'd joined the Branch to do.

Chapter Eight - Stray Dogs

So it was that after just less than half my 'A' Squad tour, I now entered the shadowy world of political crime prevention - as a Desk Officer on the Libyan Section of 'E' Squad. This was during Colonel Muammar Gaddafi's 'Stray Dogs Campaign' in which Libyan Intelligence Service assassination cells were liquidating Libyan counter-revolutionaries throughout the world - many of whom were in London. This was 'proper' Branch work, and I learned to move in the shadows.

As was expected of a desk officer, I read all the intelligence and information I could, open source and secret (Security Service, GCHQ, Foreign Office, Customs, foreign police services, etc.) on Libya, the Gaddafi regime and its adversaries. MI6 was off-limits, at least to start with. Generally we didn't speak to SIS unless we had the all-clear from our Commander.

Colonel Muammar Gaddafi had been a thorn in the US and the UK's side ever since he took power from the pro-Western and conservative King Idris in 1969 after demanding a greater share of the revenues created by the Western-operated oil fields of Libya. Colonel Gaddafi and his fellow coup members had observed how distant Libya's urban elite, along with King Idris, were from the majority of the country's citizens - who could only wonder why the nation's abundant natural resources were not being used to benefit them. This would be the key to Gaddafi's undoubted initial popularity as he and his fellow conspirators seized their chance to oust the King Idris when he left the country on 1 September 1969 for medical treatment in Greece and Turkey. Almost overnight Libya was transformed from a Western orientated Arab traditionalist state to a land of radical nationalists with, as viewed from the US, potential Soviet leanings.

From the outset Gaddafi radically overhauled how Libya was ruled. His popularly-elected Revolutionary People's Committees (RPCs) made up on '*normal*' citizens, were overseen by the 'Basic People's Congresses' (BPC), also made up of citizens not generally from the political class, and then finally, the collective body, the 'General People's Congress' (GPC), which was in turn overseen by Gaddafi as the head of the nation, aka, the *'Brotherly Leader'*. These bodies ruled Libya at the local, regional and national level as a form of collective bringing to fruition Gaddafi's concept of - *Third Universal Way* - not capitalism, not communism nor Islam, but a radical bottom-up system led by the people for the people. While this approach undoubtedly benefited poorer Libyans, it led to resentment and opposition among Libya's well-heeled citizens, who had previously benefited from the petty-cronyism of the Idris era. These Libyans had voted with their feet, many moving abroad. By 1982 somewhere between 50,000 - 100,000 Libyans had left the country. Many of these emigrants were well-educated entrepreneurs, students, intellectuals and prominent members of the Islamic community (who objected to Gaddafi's unorthodox interpretations of the scriptures). Losing them proved significant for both economic and social reasons, and some of these exiles, with Western Intelligence Service assistance, went on to form active anti-Gaddafi opposition groups. In 1979, Gaddafi demanded that these émigrés should return home immediately or face "liquidation," a threat he'd repeat in 1982.

A wave of assassinations of the prominent Libyan *refuseniks* followed, mostly in Western Europe. These state sponsored actions would become known as Gaddafi's *'Stray Dogs'* campaign referring to a speech in which he named such individuals as *"Dogs"*.. Early in 1980, the Branch obtained 'conclusive evidence' that the Libyan People's Bureau in London *(Embassies were renamed 'People's Bureaus' by the*

Libyans) was targeting such dissidents in the UK, when on 11 April 1980 Libyan journalist Mohamed Mustafa Ramadan, a radio reporter and announcer for the Voice of London, was shot dead by two assassins as he left London's Regent Park Mosque after Friday prayers. A few days later Ramadan's killing was followed by another murder in the capital, that of Libyan lawyer Mahmoud Abduassalam Nafe. MPS murder squad officers would later arrested two suspected Libyan 'agents' for both murders. At their trail in September 1980, both were found guilty and sentenced to life imprisonment.

Life on 'E' squad's Libyan Section was as interesting as it was expansive. We worked to thwart further 'Stray Dogs' activity by Libyan Intelligence Officers, helped keep safe Libyan dissidents from groups at the greatest threat from the Libyan Intelligence Service monitoring, such as the US and Saudi-sponsored Anti-Qadhafi organisation - *'The National Front for The Salvation of Libya'* - many of whose high-ranking representatives lived in London. We gained information on Libya's quest for weapons of mass destruction *(nuclear, chemical and biological)*, as well as enlisting the assistance of 'E' Squad's Terrorist Financial Investigative Unit (FISAC) to try and halt Libyan wire transfers embargoed under US President Reagan's economic sanctions in addition to seeking out Libyan terrorist funding. Consequently, I found myself drawn into the huge investigation of the Bank of Credit and Commerce International *(BCCI)* -dubbed by the press as the Bank of Crooks and Cocaine International - after it emerged in 1989 that the bank had engaged in drugs money-laundering for General Noriega of Panama, trafficked in arms for Abu Nidal *(the world's most wanted terrorist)* and assisted in funnelling Libyan terrorist seed money around the world.

It was fascinating work, with the Branch's Libyan desk monitoring and interviewing dissidents, gaining intelligence provided by paid MPSB agents connected in some way to the Libyan regime here in the UK and liaising with foreign police/Security Service contacts to gather intelligence from agents based in their countries and Libya.

I also gathered intelligence in relation to the murder of WPC Yvonne Fletcher, shot dead on 17 April 1984 by machine gun fire whilst helping keep control of a small anti-Gaddafi demonstration outside the Libyan People's Bureau *(LPB)* in London's St James's Square. The fatal shots had been fired from one of the LPB window's and led to the building being besieged by armed Met officers in an attempt to arrest the culprit(s).

As the attack came from within the Embassy, had any relevant intelligence/information about the attack been available prior to it happening, this would most likely have been gained by the Security Service and not Special Branch. Desk Officers from the Security Services' Libyan Desk would have been monitoring the chatter and behaviour of those in the LPB. Such intelligence would have come from any agents MI5 might have had in the LPB, or who had access to it, or to other Libyan facilities. Police and Security Services from around the world were very aware that LPBs in various countries tended to act as arms supply centres for terrorist groups. Weapons were transported to LPBs in diplomatic pouches, whilst Libyan IOs, under diplomat cover, supplied terrorists with intelligence regarding possible targets, as well as logistics such as forged documents and arrangements for safe-houses in target countries.

Security Service desk officers could have also acquired information from its many international Security Service, police and intelligence service allies and partners in various parts of the world. Additionally, MI5 Libyan desk officers might have had the ability to interrogate any 'in-house' technical devices directed at the Embassy or other official Libyan facilities. Had there been any sigint *(signals intelligence)* relating to the attack that would in time lead to WPC Fletcher's murder from Libyan official sources or elsewhere, then GCHQ should made this available to Security Service. As Libyan sigint, should have been routinely scoured for any abnormal aggressive official Libyan directives to undertake 'special measures' – such as shooting at demonstrators under the 'Stray Dogs' policy. Finally, SIS's Libyan or counter-terrorist sections role in monitoring Libyan activity against the UK or UK interests should have - amongst other actions – been engaged in gaining and analysing any intelligence regarding Libya's intentions towards dissidents living in the UK from its agents in Libya, as well as Libyan-centric agents across the world. MI6 would also have been able to garner intelligence from its various world-wide Intelligence, Security Service, Police or Military sources that reported on the activities of the Libyan diaspora.

Consequently, if the Branch, MI5, MI6 and GCHQ were effectively sharing their Libyan-orientated intelligence with each other, and the shooting was a sanctioned act planned by the Libyan State; then a sanitised notification of the intent of Libyan officials to fire on demonstrators outside the LPB that day, could/should have been made available to uniform police colleagues via the Branch. If this intelligence flow had occurred, then it is possible that WPC Fletcher's murder could have been prevented.

However, if the shooting was the random act of a single hot-headed revolutionary Libyan official with no advanced notice or direction provided by the Libyan state, then no procedure could have prevented the shooting's regrettable outcome.

By the mid to late 80's Libya's known or suspected involvement in terrorism was long and extensive. Gaddafi had granted his country's sponsorship to many revolutionary groups fighting *'Western*

Imperialism'. The regime flowed arms to various terrorist organizations, and granted asylum to innumerable 'wanted' terrorists including Carlos the Jackal. Moreover, in November 1976, Libyan and Algerian officials concluded a secret pact to arm, finance and train Spanish Basques, as well as French Breton and Corsican terrorists. The Gaddafi regime also transferred considerable sums of money to the Sandinistas in Nicaragua and groups in El Salvador as well as large quantities of arms to Colombia's M19 revolutionary guerrillas. Other terrorist groups supported by Libya included the Red Brigades in Italy and extremists in Japan, Turkey and Thailand as well as Palestinian groups such as the Abu Nidal Organisation (ANO) and of course the IRA. Libya also offered assistance to non-terrorist organisations which it believed could also cause problems for the western states attempting to topple him, such as Arthur Scargill's National Union of Minerworkers *(NUM)* during the strike of 1984-1985.

Some 'Libyan' terrorist attacks were performed via 'surrogate' terrorist groups on behalf of Libya in return for generous financial reward. In 1989, a French airliner exploded over the Saharan Desert, killing 170 passengers and crew. The French Investigating Magistrate appointed to investigate the attack issued an international warrant for the arrest of a number of Libyan Intelligence Service (Jamahiriya el Mukhabarat *(JeM)* officers suspected of having caused the explosion. These officers included Abdallah Sanoussi, *(Gaddafi's nephew)* and JeM's number-two, Mussa Koussa, the former head of JeM *(who was expelled from the United Kingdom in 1980, after publicly stating that his government intended to murder two political opponents of the Libyan government. Koussa would go on to become the Libyan Foreign Secretary)* and finally one time Deputy Foreign Minister Abdallah Salem Zadma, JeM's number-three.

Economic sanctions against Libya and the freezing of Libyan assets in the USA were ordered by President Ronald Reagan in January 1986 after the Libyan-backed, near-simultaneous attacks at El Al Airline counters at Vienna and Rome airports in 1985 *(carried out by ANO)*. The attackers shot and killed 19 people and wounded over a hundred more. In apparent revenge for subsequent US sanctions, in March 1986, American targets were struck in Lebanon, Italy and Germany. The most severe was the bombing of the La Belle discotheque in Berlin, which killed two U.S. servicemen and injured dozens more. At the time ex US Army Special Agent colleagues of mine in the Army CID were drafted in to assist with the investigation.

In April 1986 President Reagan ordered retaliatory air strikes and targeted Libyan government and military installations in Benghazi and Tripoli. In support of these attacks, the Iron Lady, UK Prime Minister Margaret Thatcher, allowed the US Air Force to launch its planes from US bases in the UK. Thirty Libyans were killed in the US attacks, including Gaddafi's fifteen-month-old adopted daughter, Hannah. Two years later, in December 1988, a Pan American airliner was destroyed by a bomb over the Scottish town of Lockerbie. Two hundred and eighty people were killed in the explosion, including eleven residents of Lockerbie. A Libyan intelligence officer was subsequently found guilty of the attack. The Branch, SO13 and the FBI had assisted Dumfries & Galloway police with the investigation.

Gaddafi's primary revenge on Britain, for its support to the US raids on Libya, was to increase arms shipments to the IRA including Semtex plastic explosives. We knew the Gaddafi regime had no shortage of Semtex but by March 1990, Václav Havel, President of Czechoslovakia, publicly revealed the level of these supplies. Havel explained that the former Czech communist regime had provided Libyan authorities with 1,000 tons of the explosive.

The UK's security-intelligence apparatus including 'B' and 'E' Squad would have a great success when they intercepted the MV Eksund, en route to rendezvous with the IRA. The ship was carrying large quantities of Semtex and crates of assault rifles to the terrorist organisation from the Brotherly leader. Although the Eksund didn't get through, an unknown number of previous shipments had unfortunately evaded us!

I was still serving on 'E' Squad's Libyan section when the Eksund's case became even more personal to me – as with few hours' notice - I found myself lying in wait to ambush an IRA assassination team, who I knew could well be armed with some of those assault rifles supplied by the Brotherly Leader.

Chapter Nine - Any Gunmen?

It was evening and I was hard at work drafting a report when the unmistakeable voice of 'B' Squad's legendary DI, Sean O'Connor, crackled through the silent office.

"Any gunmen? Any gunmen?" he demanded.

It was about 1900 hours and most of the Squad had already made their way home. As a Desk Officer assessing and surveilling the Libyan communities in London and the UK, my hours of work, in keeping with most 'Desk Officers' were generally 10:00 to 18:00hrs Monday to Friday. So normally I would have left the Yard too. On this particular evening however I was working late as I had been out in the city earlier that day attempting to positively identify a potential Libyan Intelligence Officer (IO). We knew Libyan IO's were tasked with keeping tabs on Libyan dissidents in the UK who were scheming to overthrow the Gaddafi regime. I'd stayed late to finish my report so that it would be ready for my DS first thing the following morning. He would then discuss my conclusions with the North Africa and Middle East section DI, before the DS and I attended a meeting on the issue with the Security Service.

I looked around the long open plan 'E' Squad office and saw that the only other officer with me was another DC, an ex-Royal Marine Commando who was on the Indian section and had just returned from Southall in West London where he'd been meeting one of his agents, a member of a radical Indian movement. Tim was one of the few SB officers who, before passing the SB exams and joining the Branch, had been an officer on the Met's specialist firearms unit, at the time named PT17. Consequently, Tim had been trained on most weapons in the Met's arsenal. We both stood up.

"Follow me, Gentlemen," Sean said. "Something urgent has just come in and we need your help."

Sean was an excitable man, insofar as he appeared full of nervous energy, always active, always moving and ever ready to serve the cause. As we turned right towards the door and left into the corridor, past the double doors leading to the central lift shaft we entered the 'B' Squad quadrant of the Yard's seventeenth floor. My heart was already pounding; this was, after all, the late eighties and 'B' Squad was up to its ears in Irish extremist activity, mainly Republican and mainly perpetrated by the IRA. We followed Sean into the 'B' Squad DIs' office where several senior officers were present. The highest ranking man there was 'B' Squad's Detective Chief Superintendent (DCS), Richie Blackmore. Richie was in charge of 'B' Squad. He spoke first.

"Thanks for volunteering gentlemen; you'll be doing the Branch a great service. We'll explain all as we go along, but suffice to say although you'll be on your own in the first instance we'll try and get assistance to you immediately it all happens."

Tim and I shared a glance. On our own? When what happens?

"Okay guys, this is ultra-sensitive," Sean said, speaking quickly. "We just got this in from out West." By 'out West' he meant GCHQ. "The boys are coming in tonight to do some business on a target, and we know the object of their interest. We even know the location, but we just don't know exactly when. So, we propose to covertly pick up the target and give him to 'A' Squad who will covertly prot him."

"So, you don't want us to do that then?" I stated, wondering what on earth they could want us for.

"No," Sean replied, looking me in the eye, "We want you to confront them."

It sunk in as Sean quickly continued to explain, barely giving us time to think. We were going to stealthily ambush an IRA Active Service Unit (ASU). Sean believed the ASU would have no reason to suspect our presence and would therefore be as bold as brass. Consequently, they'd most likely just knock on the door of the senior official's home and 'off him' in the name of the struggle. In essence, our job was to wait in the would-be victim's residence until the ASU knocked on the door or breeched the house in some way and then - within the realms of the law - give them the good news.

Tim was the first to break the silence.

"Okay, Sir. I think this would be a good operation to carry an MP5 Kurtz, or possibly even a shotgun, if Carlton has the Kurtz."

"Err, we thought that pistols would suffice," interjected DCS Blackmore.

DS, Jack McCaskill, a long term 'B' Squad officer and stalwart representative of 'B' Squad's Top Secret analytical intelligence cell - Room 1817 - nodded in agreement. Jack had probably received the intelligence in the first place.

"What will they be using though?" I asked. "Our snub nose model 64's will be no match for AKs or Armalites."

"That's *not* a great match," Tim added emphatically.

I was not a 'B' Squad officer but as an 'E' Squad Libyan desk officer I was only too aware of the potential firepower available to the IRA as a result of my investigations into MV Eksund. I knew this ASU wouldn't be turning up to the target's door with pop guns *(like our model 64 revolvers)*.

"You're the gunmen," Sean conceded. "I guess you know what you need, but I'd just say that we've got no time to get machine guns signed off. More importantly, if we go down that route we'll have every man and his dog crawling over us wanting to know why we need machine guns and what the intelligence is to warrant this decision. Big guns cause big problems."

Sean was determined to protect the sensitivity of the operation and the source of the intelligence. He was right of course, this needed to be a tight Branch op with no outside interference causing delays or even worse, potentially by dilly-dallying alerting the enemy.

The Metropolitan Police and even its elite Scotland Yard units have always played down the use of firearms. Indeed, the British policing system has taken on a distinctly anti-firearms approach, which, in a country where armed crime and terrorism is prevalent is seen by many - myself included - as ludicrous. This dislike or even loathing of guns by many in the police has compromised the efficiency and professionalism of British policing as the vast majority of officers do not have the tools to spontaneously deal with any type of armed incident, be that utilising a knife, gun or any other weapon of offence especially in an active shooter situation. Frankly this state of affairs is dangerous and unfortunately, in the not too distant future, it will cost many British citizens their lives! With 98% of police in England, Wales and Scotland having no access to firearms and not even being trained to use them, the British police have no chance of quickly ending a Paris style active shooter situation. Only the Police Service of Northern Ireland (PSNI) in the UK, whose officers all routinely carry firearms, are capable of dealing with a Paris style suicide shooting spree quickly. Dealing with suicide shootings quickly is extremely important, as every second that such a shooter is not naturalised, innocent men, women and children will lose their lives! Back in the late 80's the situation concerning the police deployment of firearms was no different and the Branch, was in no way immune to this general anti-firearms malaise. The success of our anti-IRA operation - not to mention our survival - was being hampered by the unnecessarily high authority levels for weapons deployments.

It wasn't as if I didn't know that the IRA would be armed and dangerous. Two British tourists had recently been mistaken by the IRA for military personnel and were shot dead in front of their girlfriends in the Netherlands. A Sergeant Major had been shot dead at Ostend in Belgium, a soldier killed in Hanover, and the German wife of a British soldier had been shot dead in Unna, Germany - another mistake by the IRA. The six month daughter of another UK soldier was killed, along with the soldier, in another gun attack. As a result of my fluency in German and Dutch, I'd worked on these cases in 'E' Squad's ELS. And, thanks to the Brotherly Leader and others, I knew trigger-happy IRA terrorists were in possession of some excellent weapons.

For the good of the Branch, to prevent the compromise of its intelligence streams and the expansion of the need-to-know circle, Tim and I chose to take the route of least resistance. So it was, that we arrived at the ambush point *(the large house of a would-be IRA assassination target in an upscale part of London)* some fifty minutes later, armed only with the Branch's pre-authorised weapon of the time, the six-shot, point 36 calibre Smith and Wesson model 64, snub nose revolver.

Having stealthily entered the house Tim and I sat with the TV on and lamps lit in various parts of the otherwise empty building, simulating the target's normal habits. As evening rolled into late night, we switched off the TV, turned on the main bedroom and bathroom lights, and then in due course extinguished both as we settled in to await our fate. To anybody observing from the outside in, it must have looked as if the occupants had turned in for the night.

All locked up, Tim and I waited in the downstairs living room facing the front door. We'd placed an overturned sofa at an angle before us, ballasted by various household articles to provide at least some limited cover in case of a full-frontal attack through the main door. We also attempted to make sure that a multi-pronged attack would be less likely to succeed by locking and bolting rear doors and securing them with furniture. Finally, we'd attempted to cover potential arcs of fire by funnelling furniture to keep us out of view.

It was the small hours when I heard the tiniest scraping sound coming from the front door. Someone, it seemed, was trying to open the door with a set of jigglers. We knew that the target and his family had been swept up by 'A' Squad colleagues and been placed safely under wraps at a secret location. So this could be only one thing. The ASU had arrived and were trying to silently defeat the lock to shoot the official as he slept.

Tim and I simultaneously drew our silver snub-nosed Smith and Wessons and quietly took cover behind our barricade. I aimed just above the latch, believing that to be at about upper chest to head height of the average man. My heart thudded in my chest and echoed in my ears as I considered the woeful inadequacy of our defences.

It took an eternity for the lock to actually tumble. The door began to slowly open. I squeezed the trigger to the single action point, promising myself that if I got out of this alive I'd never be under-gunned again. My heart jumped as the door opened and I don't know why but my first reaction was to yell "POLICE!" at the top of my voice. I don't know why I - or Tim for that matter - didn't shoot immediately. The first figure we saw was a woman but we both knew that the IRA was an equal opportunities employer – women terrorist were just as welcome on killing operations. In the next split second, the lack of a visible weapon calmed my ardour. And I do mean a split second. The pressure I required to pull my trigger on 'single action' was practically zero. Unbelievably, the people entering the house were the official's daughter and her German boyfriend. Their reactions were most puzzling until we realised the daughter was blind and the boyfriend was deaf – one saw us, the other heard our commands. Tim and I, our hearts pounding like rubber balls in a washing machine on spin, practically collapsed with relief. We had come so close to shooting these guys. The fact that we'd waited had saved the day.

Later, in the cold light of day, I considered mine and Tim's actions. The fact we'd waited to shoot and called out the potential ASU assassins, could, possibly would, have cost Tim and I our lives had the actual ASU visited us that night. We'd saved the day by doing things by the book, but we had to be aware that this very tendency was a potential weakness in the split second world of counter-terrorism. We were straddling the line between life and death. Would we have been wrong had we reacted differently?

Neither the girl's parents - nor anybody in the Branch - had known that the couple were returning from Germany that night, she had intended to surprise her parents when they woke in the morning.

We stayed on in the house for another two nights, on rotation with other Branch officers who'd been covertly infiltrated into the house, this time with better weapons *(the daughter and boyfriend were relocated elsewhere)*. When the operation began to slide into its fourth day, 'B' Squad handed the ambush element of the operation over to the Met's firearms unit, PT17. Two weeks later the operation now massive in scale - with all of the Met's facilities in play, high grade assault weapons and technical and medical equipment in place – the op was stood down. Sean was right about one thing, once the correct amount of firepower was brought to bear *(after those on the fifth floor had been provided with a sanitised version of the intelligence)* the operation had spun out of the Branch's control. It had grown into a bit of a circus. As for the official, he retained 'A' Squad protection for some several months. And, the *'boys'*, as Sean had described them, never did manage to 'visit' him.

*

Every day in the Branch was different. I arrived at work one morning to be called into help solve an active robbery/kidnap job, as they needed a fluent German speaker. The head of big German supermarket chain had been kidnapped with the ransom to be paid in bonds in the City of London. I simultaneously translated the comings, goings and demands of the British gangsters to the German police and those of the German gangsters to the City of London police. After about twelve hours, the job was brought to a successful conclusion with the four kidnappers banged up in Germany, the victim returned home safe and sound in Frankfurt and the bonds back in a City bank. My role, small but crucial, was tremendously satisfying.

The Branch liked to keep its officers rotating and, after the Libyan Section, I was posted to a number of 'E' Squad sections over the coming years, including Chinese, Palestinian and Middle Eastern and The Rest of the World, where I covered the Sub-Saharan African desks and the Americas.

On the Americas section I undertook several investigations on behalf of the US Secret Service concerned about the validity of a number of assassination threats to President Ronald Reagan. I was involved in Cold War espionage investigations with the US Military's NCIS (Naval Criminal Investigative Service) and the US Air Forces' OSI (Office of Special Investigation). I was also brought in to assist in investigations into and operations against Colombian narco-terrorists at the height of the 'Cocaine Wars'.

Whilst I was on the Americas desk in 1988 there was a short lived Islamic coup in Trinidad. A short time later, acting as a disaffected West Indian youth, I monitored a meeting of young British West Indians/Africans and Asians who had been drawn to a radical Middle Eastern Islamic organisation that was espousing a dangerous fundamentalist doctrine. The intent was to re-invigorate and then radicalise lapsed Muslims or to convert anyone who might have the potential to join the Jihadi movement.

The leaders of the group, 'Sheik Ibrahim' and 'Faisal' greeted me warmly as I explained that I was looking for a path to follow that allowed me to be a man of truth, honour and modesty, and that I did not wish to be judged by a system that had hijacked an Afro-Asiatic religion for its own ends and corrupted its origins to such an extent that Margaret Thatcher believed that somehow Christianity was British and not African-Asiatic in origin.

"Brother, we understand your pain," the Sheik told me. "Christianity is a religion with one aim. To enslave you, as it had always done, as it did to your ancestors."

I said to the Sheikh and Faisal that Christianity had honourable roots in Ethiopia and Palestine, so not all Christians could be held guilty for the Slave Trade.

"Brother, this might have been the case once, but the righteous religion was usurped by European bigotry and avarice."

Testing them further, I asked about the existence of a slave trade in the East that was controlled by men of the Islamic faith.

"Brother, those who perpetrated this were not true believers, the prophet has all shades in his family and coterie. The true path sees no colour."

Over the course of several meetings I could see that the aim was to bring potential converts into the fold, although the Sheikh and Faisal were too sophisticated to try and convert individuals rashly or overtly. Their aim was to win converts with polemic and friendship until one begged to be converted and to join the brotherhood. The Brotherhood promise to an individual was something bigger than one's self. It was an engaging and seductive approach.

The Sheik and Faisal explained that the true way forward was Jihad, Jihad aimed at recreating the caliphate and returning all those one time Islamic lands back to the faith – which would include all those countries in Africa, Asia and Europe that were once Islamic: Spain, Portugal, Italy, France, the Balkans, Russia, Nigeria, Senegal, Thailand, etc. But first and most importantly, those lands which are Islamic in name but run by apostates would need to be overrun, such as Saudi Arabia and all of the Middle Eastern and North African states. As for the 'State' of Israel, the West's buffer against Islam, it had to be eradicated.

I had successfully monitored what has since become a well-known Islamic radical group when it was still in its infancy. The message it espoused was as potent as it was simple: "Islam loves all people of colour whereas Christianity is colour conscious and has enslaved, colonialized or oppressed you." I was monitoring them at a time when racist Christian radicals ruled South Africa and others still appeared to hold sway in many parts of the Southern United States. Consequently, the organisation's message was explicit and powerful and I assessed that, over time, it would come to create substantial new racial fissures in our society. I therefore reported that the organisation should be continually monitored.

When I provided the Branch with my analysis of the organisation's potential threat, my warning seemed so unusual that the Section's Detective Inspector jokingly asked whether I'd concocted the group from thin air. This was at a time when radical Islam was not felt to be a specific threat to the UK's domestic extremist scene and was not on the radar of any other UK intelligence/security agency (except for the relatively small number of religiously inspired 'Afghan Veterans' being monitored by the Branch and MI5 upon their return to the UK from that Cold War struggle). Although internationally, the mid 80's had seen the French intelligence agencies DST *(Directorate of Territorial Security)* and RG *(General Intelligence Directorate)* engage in combat with joint French left-wing, and *'Arab'* nationalist Islamic terrorists groupings, wreaking explosive havoc on the streets of the French capital over several weeks, the UK had not yet felt the wrath of such organisations.

My reports on the organisation at the time were amongst the first in Britain. When three years later the organisation's leader swore a Fatwa against Prime Minister Sir John Major, due to Britain's involvement in the First Gulf war, my first-hand knowledge of the group was in demand. Although I'd moved desks in the interim I was still available to brief those from the rest of the world desk and the SB cell in SO13 of the organisation's personalities, its ideology and the Fatwa's potential for exploitation. Unfortunately in the intervening years the Branch hadn't taken my advice of keeping tabs on the organisation, so we were having to play catch-up.

Desk Officer Investigations are not necessarily time-sensitive. The intelligence gained can either diminish or intensify in value with time. That's the secret of secret intelligence, the ability to access it when required. The Branch was able to provide this capacity, even when it wasn't at its best.

Chapter Ten - China In Our Hands

On June 3, 1982 Shlomo Argov, 52, Israel's Ambassador to Britain, had accepted an invitation to a reception of ambassadors given that evening at the Dorchester Hotel on Park Lane. As he left his residence near Kensington Palace, three London-based members of the Fatah Revolutionary Council (FRC), also known as the Abu Nidal Organisation (ANO) after its founder, also travelled to the Dorchester intent on his assassination.

Abu Nidal *(meaning 'Father of Struggle')* the nom de guerre of Sabri Khalil al-Bana was, in 1982, the deadliest man alive. He was also incredibly hard to find, bragging that "not even my eight-year-old son Bissam knows exactly who I am." In 1981 alone, his group was responsible for 33 terrifying assaults, ranging from the September 16 bombing of Rome's Café de Paris (40 injured) to the November 23 hijacking of an EgyptAir jetliner (59 dead) to the slaughter of innocent travellers at airports in Rome and Vienna (19 dead, 112 injured). Initially a committed senior member of the Palestinian Liberation Organisation (PLO), Abu Nidal split from Yasser Arafat's FATAH group in 1971 and by 1974 he ran his own terror operations from bases in Iraq, Libya and Syria. Abu Nidal accused Arafat of cowardice; for not using terror against their many enemies, in particular Israel and Jordan. His gunmen tried and failed to assassinate Arafat on numerous occasions. In reply, the FATAH and the PLO sentenced Abu Nidal to death.

Shlomo Argov's assassination had been ordered by Abu Nidal to provoke an Israeli assault on Arafat's bases in Lebanon, creating a war that would weaken his two worst enemies. Naif Rosan, the FRC's man in London who had been with Abu Nidal since 1973, decided to eliminate Argov as he left the Dorchester. Two FRC 'sleepers' Marwan al-Banna *(a second cousin of Abu Nidal)* and Ghassan Said, 23, who were in London as students, were activated two hours before the assassination; an effective practice which gives young terrorists no time to dwell on what they are about to do and aids cellular security. Al-Banna, who stored weapons for the FRC in his flat, brought with him a Polish-made 'Skorpion' wz63 sub-machine pistol. Said was to be the gunman. Rosan didn't tell him who his target was only that he would point him out and that Said should shoot him before he could reach his vehicle.

Shortly after 11pm, Argov left the dinner via the Ballroom exit. Just behind him was the publishing magnate Robert Maxwell. Argov was protected that night by 'A' Squad's DC Colin Simpson; I'd work with Colin a few years later when I was first posted to 'P' squad. As the ambassador neared the vehicle Said quickly drew his Skorpion from a sports bag, rushed forward and shot Argov twice in the face as he entered the vehicle. The deed done, Said turned and ran down Park Lane as Colin gave chase. Running into South Street Colin neared on Said who turned and fired at him. One shot rang out from Said's Skorpion which seemingly jammed as he continued to squeeze the trigger. Colin returned fire hitting Said in the neck with a single shot from his snub nosed Smith & Wesson model 64. Said fell bleeding to the ground.

After hearing the gunfire, al-Banna ran back to his car. A security guard named Trevor Willis who worked for the Hilton Hotel, close by the Dorchester, saw him running and wrote down the car's license plate number. The conspirators were soon captured and both the ambassador and the assassin survived their bullet wounds – although Argov woke up from a three month coma to find he was permanently paralysed.

Israel ignored the fact that the PLO had not committed the hit and ignored the fact that the next name on the FRC's death list, discovered by E-squad, was Nabil Ramlawi, the PLO representative in London. Instead, the then Israeli defence minister Ariel Sharon finally had a pretext for his long-planned campaign to eliminate the PLO and its headquarters in the Lebanese capital, Beirut. In his memoirs, Sharon wrote that the Dorchester ambush was 'the spark that lit the fuse'. The Israeli Prime Minister Menachen Begin gave Sharon the go-ahead for what became 'Operation Peace for Galilee'.

The war lasted for eleven months and Israeli forces did not begin to withdraw from Lebanon until June 1985. By the end, more than 6,000 PLO fighters and Palestinian civilians were killed by the Israelis. Syria lost 600 troops and 468 Lebanese civilians were killed while Israel lost 368 of its soldiers. On September 19, Israel began to withdraw from Beirut, eventually falling back to a four-mile-deep zone of occupation in southern Lebanon, which they didn't leave for another 18 years. In this zone, constant battles were fought between Israeli troops and the Hizbullah (Party of God), an organisation formed explicitly to drive Israel from Lebanon. With hundreds killed on both sides the shooting of the Israeli Ambassador in London that night and the ensuing war it caused, ensured that peace between Arabs and Israelis would not come to pass for at least three decades. The three assassins were convicted of the attempted murder of the envoy and were sentenced to life in prison in March 1983. Argov died in 2003, a consequence of the injuries sustained in the assassination attempt.

From my perspective, one thing was clear: sometimes, Protection Officers can determine the course of history. Many years after the Argov hit, when I took over the de facto day-to-day running of 'A' Squad in Room 1834, I used the Argov shooting to illustrate the inability of a single protection officer to control both the environment and the principal. I argued for the end of all single-officer protections. Banning single-officer protection operations meshed perfectly with my idea of creating *counter-reconnaissance team(s)* to covertly envelope overt protection operations. To my mind, it was unacceptable that in the intervening years since the Argov attempt, nothing had been done to banish the single-officer protection model. The tactic was simply not resilient.

It was with some trepidation then, when in 1988, on E-squad's Chinese Desk, I was assigned to perform the single-handed 'liaison' protection of one of the most powerful people in the world. 'A' Squad were swamped with IRA work and asked if I could protect the General Secretary of the Central Committee of the Communist Party of China, Zhao Ziyang (the de-facto ruler of China). I had a few days to prepare as Zhao was due to arrive in Britain on the forthcoming coming Sunday. I knew my *'liaison'* role was bound to be problematic. Zhao had previously visited Britain when he held the post of Premier of the People's Republic of China and as such he had received a full protection package consisting of lead and back-up vehicles and a Special Escort Group (SEG) motorcycle escort in addition to various Chinese supplied vehicles that were encased by the SEG within the protection bubble. Now Zhao was General Secretary and not the Premier *(the distinction between the two is 'actual ruler' versus 'figurehead,' respectively)*, the Foreign & Commonwealth Office (F&CO) had decided that they would not ask 'A' Squad to provide *any* protection.

'A' Squad's management, uneasy with the F&CO's decision, performed a crude CYA tactic by assigning me as the Yard's lone Protman, which 'A' Squad designated as a liaison protection officer to the Chinese. The Branch knew that if anything security related happened to the Chinese during the visit, that even though both the F&CO and the Home Office didn't request 'A' Squad protection, they would never the less place the blame firmly and squarely at the Met's door. It would not have mattered one iota that the lack of protection was a result of these other departments not asking for it. So now if anything went wrong, I would be the fall guy for the UK government and the Met's senior leadership.

Even though I knew this was a CYA job, it would have been hard for me to say no to the job for a number of reasons. Firstly, 'A' Squad were extremely busy with the Irish Republican threat to our senior ministers. Secondly, the visit would commence on a weekend, a busy period for protection. Thirdly, 'A' Squad management knew I was on the Chinese Desk which was clearly advantageous to the Branch, not least because I'd have a good understanding of the politics surrounding the visit. And finally, I was a trained protection officer and, as a Desk Officer, I generally worked Monday to Friday, meaning I was available at weekends.

When 'A' Squad's DI Arthur asked me to take on the job I made clear my concerns about the lack of support for such a visit. DI Arthur explained that both the Home and Foreign office believed that Zhao's change of title meant that he now stood outside those roles mandated to receive personal protection by signatories to the Vienna and UN conventions. These conventions required signatory countries to provide protection to foreign heads of state, heads of government or Foreign Secretaries on official or working visits to their country. There was no requirement to protect heads of foreign political parties such as the Chinese Communist Party's General Secretary and so no protection was offered, even though the Communist party was synonymous with the State and as such the highest official in the land was the Communist party's General Secretary. I warned DI Arthur, who agreed but whose hands were tied, that my single officer liaison role would be seen by the Chinese as a slight against General Secretary Zhao and the Chinese people. Sensing trouble ahead, I nonetheless felt as though I had no choice but to accept the role.

In a meeting with the *declared* head of Chinese Intelligence at their embassy in London, I explained that the British government wasn't going to provide Zhao with a full protection package. Let's just say that this news was not well received. Therefore, when I arrived at Gatwick to the meet the flight, I was not surprised when the stone-faced Chinese Ambassador made a show of ignoring me. In travelling to Gatwick I was actually doing more than I should have. Normally a liaison protection officer would simply notify the Ambassador or his primary security/intelligence official of his or her contact details and explain that he/she is the primary point of assistance should any security matters arise.

When Zhao landed I made myself known to his Personal Private Secretary (PPS) and accompanying protection team. As my Chinese protection officer colleagues couldn't speak much English and I don't speak Mandarin, I relied on the PPS who had a good command of English to translate my greeting. I made it clear to her that I was not there to perform a protection role *per se*, but to offer the General Secretary's protection team my number and to assure them that if they had any security concerns then they should not hesitate to call me. She took my card, looked at it sceptically and then translated for the protection team who complained bitterly as they loaded the General Secretary into the waiting Chinese vehicles.

I followed the Chinese convoy back to their embassy. En route, I contacted DI Arthur on the radio, via SB Reserve (these were the days before mobile phones). I told him that in my opinion the F&CO definitely needed to reconsider as the signs from the Chinese were ominous. "Okay, Carlton," he answered, "I'll call the F&CO duty officer and pass on your assessment."

As we arrived at the embassy I received a radio message asking me for a number where the Duty Foreign Office Minister could contact me. Conscious that the phones would be intercepted and recorded, not least by the Chinese, in their embassy, when I spoke to the duty Minister I stressed that I was speaking from that location. I hammered out an agreement with the minister. A fuller protection package commanded by me would be provided for the more official aspects of the General Secretary's programme. It was a compromise.

The lack of protection was taken as an absolute slight to the Chinese people and as a result it is highly probable that this was the reason why negotiations concerning the building of the new Hong Kong airport stalled. The Chinese wanted the facility completed before they were due to take back sovereignty of Hong Kong in 1997. They were not prepared to hand over a single yuan towards the airport's construction despite the desperate need for a larger, modern airport. This cost the UK treasury millions of pounds (the Chinese delays meant the airport was not completed until July 1998) and embarrassed British Prime Minister John Major who, when he travelled to Hong Kong on the airport's planned opening date, shortly before the handover in May 1997, could only open a connecting bridge, not the airport. Once again prot had played its part in a political outcome although on this occasion the Branch could say that it was in no way at fault.

In 1987 I was assigned to Secretary of State for Northern Ireland Tom King's protection team. For many in the radical Republican movement, Tom was a hate figure and one of the primary targets for assassination. All of us on the team knew that this was no Hollywood protection; this was a role with a very real and present risk to one's own life. After several months on the team, a member of the public riding her horse in the fields close to the Secretary of State's farm in Ford, Wiltshire, noticed a man and a woman "acting suspiciously". She called the police. The local police force's firearms unit, who provided 24hrs static protection for the minister's house and grounds, deployed to search the area, arresting the man and woman. Wiltshire Special Branch, contacted 'B' Squad at the Yard and after further investigation by 'B' Squad officers, another male was arrested at a nearby campsite. The suspects, all part of an IRA ASU, had intended to assassinate Tom by using a long-range sniper weapon. The ASU members were charged and prosecuted for conspiracy to murder.

Tom's character was such that he constantly attempted to circumvent our procedures, making our job very difficult. Several weeks after the ASU had been captured we were travelling as usual to his Wiltshire home from London. As usual I was traveling in the front passenger seat of the armoured Jaguar with Tom in the passenger seat behind me. On this occasion the regular GCS driver, Tony, was off for the weekend so Bill, a fill-in driver, was driving the vehicle. Our back-up vehicle was on our bumper, which contained the three other members of my half of the team. In travelling to and from the Secretary of State's country home we varied the route, but tended to take a shortcut along a lonely stretch of road which brought us out on the main road not far from his home. As we drove along the route, not far from the main road, a temporary traffic light on red prevented our forward travel. I was edgy. The road was a single lane in each direction with one lane totally blocked and controlled by the traffic light, signalling red. Strangely, we'd had not been informed about these road works by Wiltshire Constabulary when we'd contacted them earlier in the journey. The prot part of my brain took over and I called the back-up vehicle, the boys were already on top of it, trying to contact Wiltshire to check the bona fides of the road works whilst simultaneously readying weapons including smoke grenades should it come on top. We all watched and checked our angles. Tom was hard at work examining the contents of his Ministerial box, oblivious to our anxiety.

Two things stopped me from having Bill drive through the light. Firstly the road works were on a bend - if this was legitimate and we drove through we could possibly drive into an oncoming vehicle. Secondly, there were two or three workmen right where we were. Republicans as a rule were not the sort to self-sacrifice and saw no advantage in killing innocents which always backfired on their political goals. Of course these workmen could be an IRA hit squad. If they were, I felt we were capable of performing our role and nullifying the threat.

Worryingly for me, our GCS driver was just as ignorant as Tom, he seemingly only saw a red traffic light. If I wasn't convinced before that GCS drivers were a security weak link I was now getting there. Just then the lights changed and we passed through cleanly, although I noticed that two of the workers had looked in the vehicle and seen Tom. I decided there and then that on Monday, we wouldn't travel back to London using this route and told Tom of my decision once we arrived at his home. It hadn't been a set-up this time but next time... We wouldn't tempt fate. This meant that on Monday we'd have to allow extra time to make it to RAF Lyneham on time for his flight to Northern Ireland. Tom had been informed.

Come Monday morning the cars were lined up early waiting for Tom to appear. He was late. As we started driving Tom turned to Bill, the GCS driver and a true Cockney.

"You know the shortcut we take don't you Bill?"

"Yes, Sir." Bill replied.

"Secretary of State," I said, interrupting, "I explained that we would not be taking the shortcut because of the road works and the potential for attack. You know this."

"Yes, but we're late."

"Yes we're late, because you didn't come out on time. But we're still going to take the long route." I turned to Bill. "Bill, carry on towards Chippenham as I briefed you this morning."

"Carlton, you're being dramatic," Tom said. "Even if we were seen, there's nothing to suggest any malice."

"There's nothing to suggest there isn't any either."

"Bill turn left, it's coming up soon," Tom reiterated.

"Yes, Sir," said Bill

"Bill, carry on straight." I said, becoming increasingly incensed.

"Er, Okay, Carlton," replied Bill, sounding somewhat torn.

This time Tom practically shouted as he said: "Bill I think you're forgetting who pays your salary. Turn left please."

This was no request it was an order and Bill knew it.

"Yes, Sir."

I turned to Bill.

"Bill, I'm in charge of keeping us all alive, so carry on straight please."

"Bill...." The tone of the Secretary of State was now earnest. Bill knew what he had to do. He was a GCS driver and as such he had to keep Ministers happy. This was something Bill had learnt all his working life. He turned left and we took the shortcut again.

The Secretary of State sat smug and content in the back. The rest of the team and I remained on high alert. An IED dug in at the side of the road would be invisible. Thankfully, we drove through the suspected area without incident. The rest of the journey was silent and uneventful, although I was seething. I didn't blame Bill. As a GCS driver, he'd been placed in an impossible position. I swore then that if I ever had the power and opportunity I'd change this situation and only have SB's specialist protection drivers drive protected principals.

When we arrived at RAF Lyneham, Bill pulled the vehicle over at the waiting RAF aircraft. I opened the door for Tom but prevented him from rushing to the aircraft. Closing the car door to make sure that Bill couldn't hear and also making sure that we were out of earshot of the waiting RAF police and servicemen, I looked Tom in the eye and told him in no uncertain terms that he had overstepped the mark. He'd put all our lives on the line. An ASU had recently been on his land tasked with executing him in the name of the struggle. I wasn't going to die as collateral damage, due to somebody else's stupidity. I made it clear that what he'd done was irresponsible and I wouldn't let it lie. I informed him that I would report the matter up the chain to 'A' Squad's chief, DCS Greenham for further action. He needed to understand once and for all that I, or whichever SB officer was in the lead seat, decided on tactical matters, not him. There were ASU's on the loose and I had a wife and two small children under two who I didn't see every other weekend for at least four days in order to protect him. I wasn't going to needlessly die for him as well. I was a professional and I needed to do my work unencumbered. He would hear more about this.

I gestured for him to pass and silently accompanied him to the aircraft.

As Secretary of State for Northern Ireland, Tom King was effectively the province's Prime Minister, so under the new policy of *Ulsterisation (returning the province to Stormont rule)* 'A' Squad did not protect Tom in Northern Ireland anymore, that job now went to RUC SB. However, the moment he left the province to travel anywhere in the world, even Eire *(The Republic of Ireland)*, our team took the reins again.

Greenham told me to leave the matter with him. Unlike today's incumbents, Greenham didn't ignore requests like this, nor did he have any fear of any politician. He contacted 'Head Girl', which was the nickname Tom and other cabinet ministers gave Margaret Thatcher. The Iron Lady knew that if Tom had been assassinated then she would have had no choice but to intensify the war on Republican extremism. In a time when the government was attempting to achieve a breakthrough in the peace process, this would have been utterly devastating.

As normal we picked Tom up 48 hours later back at RAF Lyneham. He entered the back of the Jag as I closed his door and took up the front nearside seat commanding the travelling protection operation. My DS and Tom didn't get on at all, so on my half of the team I tended to be 'closest' to Tom, always occupying the front seat of the lead vehicle. Upon entering the vehicle Tom had greeted Tony, the regular GCS driver and I, in the normal friendly manner whilst adding that we needed to travel directly to No10. I knew what at least one of the discussion points of this urgent No10 meeting would be. I don't think Tom did. After that Wednesday afternoon meeting with Head Girl, I wouldn't say Prot was ever easy with Tom, but he'd never second guess me again.

Chapter Eleven - Deutschland: Cold War, Luke Warm Politics

The late 1980s saw the fall of the Berlin Wall, putting East Germany on the ropes. I was now a Scotland Yard Special Branch detective on 'E' Squad's Sub-Saharan African section when I received a call from 'A' Squad. The new Minister President of East Germany, Lothar de Maizière, was about to visit the UK and, because I spoke fluent German and Herr de Maizière lacked English, 'A' Squad asked if I would consider being the primary protection officer on the job. The UK Government of the day knew that Germany would in all likelihood reunite and hence Minister President de Maizière's opinion concerning this matter was of the utmost importance to the UK national interests.

Herr De Maizière arrived early in the morning from the United States where he had been the guest of President George Bush *(senior)*. On meeting and talking to Minister President de Maizière, he told me that he wished to do some sightseeing before his meetings with Mrs Thatcher and the Foreign Secretary.

Minister President De Maizière was not at all Presidential. He had been a dissident musician who had risen to represent the anti-Honecker coalition as its main spokesperson prior to being voted Minister President in their first truly democratic elections. Herr de Maizière was keen to talk and learn all he could about the West. During our discussions he told me of his great interest in musical theatre. He also mentioned that whilst he was in the US he had wanted to visit Broadway but the US Secret Service, fearing for his safety hadn't allowed him. I explained that if he wished to visit Shaftesbury Avenue, to see the home of the British Musical, he could, as I foresaw few security concerns. We had no intelligence to suggest any particular threat and although an absence of knowledge is not an absence of malice, we had a number of factors in our favour. De Maizière's face was not known to the wider public, so he would not stand out and attract attention, making it easier to secure any area he was in, and any would-be miscreant would have to be especially fleet-of-foot as this would be an unannounced, spontaneous trip know only to us.

De Maizière was excited and was keen to attend the location but had to comply with one condition: he would first need to get permission from the head security officer at the East German embassy. This was apparently the case even though his East German protection team, with whom we were working well together, agreed to the visit. We therefore travelled to the East German embassy in Central London in order that the Minister President could run the proposal past the head of Security and Intelligence at the Embassy.

On arrival Minister President de Maizière asked if I would speak to the security officer to explain what I was proposing and that it was safe. As we walked into the reception area of the Embassy of the DDR, the man who Herr De Maizière wanted me to convince walked towards me. He was the chief STASI officer in London. As we neared each other and I prepared to shake his hand the STASI man stopped and shouted at me in triumph: "You! I knew it! I always knew you were a spy!"

*

As a kid I had avidly watched the hit 1970s TV show *'The Man in a Suitcase'*. In the show, the star, an American ex-CIA officer called Mac, travelled around the UK and Europe investigating various matters on behalf of wealthy clients. Each week Mac would inevitably end up getting beaten up by a mafia member or some other individual connected with his investigation. However, what I liked about the series was that no matter where Mac was in the world, he would bump into an old CIA or other intelligence agency colleague who would help get him out of a tight spot and subsequently help him solve the case. What I didn't know all those years ago was that there existed more than a grain of truth in this interpretation, in that the 'state' intelligence and protective security world is relatively small and therefore one often meets colleagues - and foes - time and again.

About three years before I joined the Met, whilst I was still an AAFES Exchange Detective in West Germany, I was travelling to West Berlin with Angela in my three-litre, petrol-guzzling BMW along the South-North Transitstrasse. At the time, three roads were designated by international treaty as routes from West Germany through East Germany to West Berlin. Westerners were authorised to utilise these routes but they were prohibited from deviating from them. The transit-roads came from three different locations in West Germany - South, Central and North. All of the roads were at some distance from each other and of varying lengths, but all were in excess of a hundred kilometres.

When Angela and I were some way into our journey along the southern Transitstrasse I noticed that the red ignition light on our vehicle was permanently illuminated, this meant that my battery was not charging and would be drained by the time we reached West Berlin. There was also another problem. It was a bank holiday in West Germany, so no garages would be open in West Berlin. As we continued to drive along the Transitstrasse, I wondered what I was going to do. I was sure that if I turned my engine off I wouldn't be able to re-start it again. After a further half an hour of driving I noticed an information sign denoting an up-coming exit. The sign said *'Nur Für LKW' (only for HGVs)*. Hoping that this exit would lead to a truck rest area - and no doubt a garage - I seized my chance. Sure enough, about a hundred metres up the slip road, I spied a junction to the left of which was a garage with several trucks parked outside. My relief turned to horror when I spotted a large Soviet convoy, and they saw me! As I drove into the rest area and stepped out of my vehicle, leaving it running, I noted several bemused lorry drivers looking at me. I walked towards the garage office and opened the door as a man came to the counter. I was now off the Transitstrasse and hence technically in the heart of Communist East Germany.

"Good day," I said in German, "Can you help me? I think my alternator is playing up and I don't think I'll make it to Berlin without fixing it."

I explained that it was a Bank holiday in West Berlin and therefore I would be unlikely to get my car fixed when I arrived there. The mechanic looked as though he was in shock as he warily looked at my vehicle in the distance. After a bit of a pause, he spoke abruptly, yet apologetically.

"Sorry, I don't think we could repair anything like that here."

I should have known better, East German's were used to the 2 stroke 'Trabant' or at a push the big Soviet 'Zill', but nothing as technically advanced as a top of the range BMW three-litre. The man seemed to want to talk, but at the same time he was also strangely reticent. Then all of a sudden, I noticed a change in his eyes, one of growing fear, and I turned to look at my vehicle. Two Volkspolizei officers were standing right next to it! I quickly exited the garage and walked over to my vehicle, but before I could even speak the smaller of the two officers, who like his colleague was dressed in the green Para-military type uniform of the 'peoples police' with shiny knee-high riding boots and Jodhpurs, addressed me imperiously.

"Why are you off the Transitstrasse?"

"My car is not working properly and ..."

I was abruptly cut off with a wave of the hand.

"Why are you off the Transitstrasse?"

Without waiting for an answer, the taller officer spoke.

"This rest place is only for HGVs. You are committing an offence against the laws of the Democratic Republic of Germany. Why are you off the Transitstrasse?"

I tried to explain and pointed to the illuminated ignition light on my vehicle's dashboard as proof. The officers looked, saw the red light on my dash and for a split second they seemed to consider what to do next.

I just caught a glimpse of Angela's petrified face as the officer barked an order.

"Get in your car, return to the Transitstrasse and don't stop driving till you get to West Berlin. We will be watching. If you stop, we will arrest you. Go now."

I didn't need to be told twice. Respectfully making my way past the taller officer, who was partially blocking my entry, I slid into the driver's seat of my vehicle and thanking the officers through the wound down window, I made a 180° turn and headed for the Transitstrasse.

Later on as we speedily made our way along the Transitstrasse, I noticed that the ignition light had gone out. The problem had seemingly fixed itself. Maybe a loose connection had rattled back into place. One thing was for sure, any further examination would definitely have to wait until we reached West Berlin.

Once in West Berlin Angela and I found a hotel and began to make the most of this über exciting city. Whilst West Berlin was a paradise of excess, it was impossible to forget the sights we'd seen of East Germany that surrounded it, during our drive along the Transitstrasse - the automatic free-fire machine gun nests, attack dogs controlled by machinegun toting, great-coated East German border guards, four-metre high electrified fences, ultra-powerful search lights, unending reams of barbed wire along the whole length of the road not to mention a mass of concrete boulders, chicanes and blockers reinforced by anti-tank traps and the ubiquitous clear space running parallel to these contraptions which formed the killing ground of no man's land. So, we planned to cross this border into East Berlin the following day, to see for ourselves the heart of communist DDR.

As an avid amateur WWII aficionado, the sight of the infamous Checkpoint Charlie really got my heart pounding, as did the sign that proclaimed "You are leaving the American Sector". This was followed by *"Stop. You are leaving the American Sector and about to enter the Soviet Sector of East Berlin."* We drove on *(The car was purring. A Turkish garage, which was open despite the bank holiday, had looked at it the previous evening).* Slowly we edged along Checkpoint Charlie's concrete chicane until at the border crossing we were stopped by a US Military policeman. I wound down the window: "Good morning, Sir, you're heading into the Soviet sector of East Berlin."

This was a caution, a reminder of what we were about to do, to make sure that we were not inadvertently crossing this highly-militarised border into what a great many people believed was hell on earth.

"Yes, thank you." I said.

"You're not US military personnel are you sir?"

"No, I'm a civilian, but I'm an AAFES Exchange Detective." I said.

"As long as you're not military personnel, Sir."

The soldier looked at Angela and I in the vehicle as a colleague seemed to record our car's registration number. We were then allowed to proceed to East Berlin, with the words: "Have a nice day."

We followed the narrow twisting single track concrete-shouldered corridor into East Germany, where all the customary repressive border control measures were once again set out before us. We were stopped short of the actual immigration control booth by one of the many East German border guards and asked for our passports. I imagined that the East German guards were probably wondering whether I was an American serviceman too. This was important as, at the time, all military personnel could only officially enter the Soviet Sector of Berlin if they were readily identifiable as such and travelled through certain military crossing points controlled by Soviet Military police and not East German border police officers. This was all a matter of the four victorious powers, post WWII international agreement which the Soviets took very seriously *(after all their three-week battle to take Berlin had cost them an estimated 360,000 lives).*

"Engländerin," *(English woman)* said one of the guards looking at Angela's passport as he turned and walked towards a nearby building. The guard with my passport silently followed suit.

One of the guards returned several minutes later.

"You're English," he said in German.

"Yes."

"When did you arrive in Germany?"

"Three years ago," I replied.

He looked quizzically. "When did you arrive in the DDR?"

"Ah, ok, if you count travelling on the Transitstrasse, then yesterday."

He went away again still holding my passport in his hand. When he returned after a much longer period, he was with several other officers. In the interim, although we hadn't said much to one another, I could feel Angela's anxiety. Other cars in the layby had come and gone. We were clearly being singled out for special treatment. I was also concerned but tried not to show it, least of all because it had been my bright idea, thanks to my love of politics and history, to travel to East Berlin.

"Out of the vehicle."

We got out. The officers then went through the car. Side pockets, glove compartment, seat flaps, the boot, the engine compartment and in the visors. Thoroughly but not forensically. Two of the officers even took away my music and language CD tapes. As I saw this, I asked if I would get them back. One of them muttered something like "We'll see." We were then told to wait back in the car. It was clear that all was not well and I looked longingly towards Checkpoint Charlie. As I did I spotted a US Military Police officer observing us through binoculars.

Three officers, machine pistols at the low ready, guarded the vehicle whilst Angela and I sat quietly inside. Two new officers, obviously senior - I didn't know East German border guard ranks - now walked towards the car and approached my side of the vehicle.

"Please get out of the car," one of them said, speaking Russian. I understood his meaning but not all of the words and I complied. He then spoke in German again.

"Why do you speak Russian?"

"I don't," I said.

"Then why do you understand?" He said.

"I don't," I reiterated.

The officer's question suggested that I had fallen foul of the fact that people often involuntarily react in a given manner when they understand what's being said. The problem is that the person's reaction doesn't always discern their level of understanding.

"So, if you don't speak Russian why do you have Russian tapes?" He asked.

Although the answer was that I was trying to teach myself Russian, it now took on sinister overtones. I explained but the officer wasn't convinced.

"Okay, so you do understand Russian then," he said, smiling knowingly.

I was myself an investigator, so I knew this smile only too well. It meant "I've got you!"

So, getting desperate, I tried to press my point. "No, I don't actually understand. I recognise some of the words, but I don't understand. This is what I've been trying to explain."

As I spoke the officer raised his hand, impatiently, as though I was wasting his time.

"Okay, Mr King."

He stressed my name as though he was disbelieving of even this detail.

"Come with me, you are detained for being in possession of contraband."

"Contraband?" I repeated in astonishment. Angela looked terrified.

"Yes, Mr King, you have a radio communications system in your car, which I'm sure you know is illegal in the DDR."

Suddenly it dawned on me; he was talking about the CB radio that was built into my cassette system. In the late 70's, early 80's before mobile phones, this was all the rage in West Germany. I had never thought of it as a "radio communications system."

"Come with me, Mr King," he said, as two of the armed guards turned their attention from my car and Angela to me. "We have several things to discuss."

The guards walked behind me as the officer led the way in to a single-story control-booth-type building.

"But what about my girlfriend?" I protested, not wanting to leave Angela alone.

"Don't worry, we will look after her."

I was not reassured. I was taken into a dark room, in clear contrast to the natural light of the mid-morning summer sun, where I was told to sit down. The main investigating officer left the room. His two Kalashnikov-wielding subordinates stayed for a few more minutes before leaving.

In front of me was a two way mirror. I knew it was two-way because we used a similar system in AAFES. I was being left to sweat under covert observation before the forthcoming interrogation.

After what seemed an age, probably no longer than thirty minutes but enough time for my predicament to take full effect, one of the Kalashnikov-wielding guards re-entered the room, accompanied by a new officer - in a different uniform: The STASI.

"Ah, Herr King," he said as he entered the room.

The guard straightened and quietly acknowledged the officer. "Herr Hauptmann."

As he said this, the guard's demeanour betrayed the belief that he had just given something away. The officer's rank - Hauptmann (captain). I instinctively reacted to the officer by standing and offering him my hand. Having lived in Germany for several years I had assumed many local habits.

"You are Herr...?" I asked, hoping he would fill in the blanks, which of course he didn't.

However, the Hauptmann did shake my hand, surprising himself, I think, before gesturing for me to take a seat.

"Herr King, or whatever you are called, what is your mission?"

"My mission? What mission?"

"Let's stop playing games," he said, in perfect English, "Shall we look at the facts?"

Reverting to German he began to lay out a long list of facts as he saw them. I had travelled along the Transitstrasse the previous day but unlike 99.99% of all other travellers I had deviated from the sanctioned corridor, I was obviously trying to make contact with somebody off the Transitstrasse. Unfortunately for me however, I was seen by the commander of a Soviet convoy who alerted the people's police (Volkspolizei). He explained that investigations were already underway at rest stop and the surrounding area to find my prospective contact.

He went on, saying that I had made up some story about my vehicle being in a state of disrepair but, unsurprisingly, it was clearly okay now. Furthermore, I spoke perfect German, something that was not the norm with either British or American servicemen, unless of course they were in Intelligence. The Hauptmann also highlighted the radio communications system, which he considered as a camouflaged means of communicating with East German traitors or Western spies in the DDR.

In short, in the officer's opinion, I was a spy and they had caught me red-handed.

"Mr King, I'll use your alias," he said. "We know you are a spy and due to the fact that you have made some mistakes you have been caught, but, all is not lost."

The Hauptmann looked me full in the eyes, allowing his accusation to sink in.

This was the Cold War, and such accusations weren't made every day. The consequences were unthinkable. I considered my defence. If the officer was correct, I must be the world's most incompetent spy *(although to be fair to the Hauptmann, during my career I'd encounter less professional spies than I would have appeared to him in that moment).*

The Hauptmann's statement of *'all was not lost'* had gone over my head. This was his initial attempt to turn me into a double agent, which in itself was a measure of how seriously the Hauptman actually took the charges laid against me. The Hauptmann sincerely believed that I was a spy and he was providing me with a way out. All I had to do was to betray my country.

I instead tried to explain myself to the Hauptmann, with absolute, yet quiet conviction.

"My name is Carlton King. I'm British."

The officer stopped me with a wave of the hand.

"Please, please Herr King, don't waste my time with your cover story. I said you had made some mistakes and this is another. You are an American, in the American military. We have your military identification."

The Hauptmann placed my AAFES credentials on the table as though this was his coup de grâce with a victorious smile. He wasn't much older than me, about thirty. Obviously fit, the Hauptmann's face had the chiselled look of an athlete, whilst his gaze - stark and gripping - was perfect for his role.

"No, Herr Hauptmann, this is what I mean. I am not in the American Military, I work for them, but I'm a British citizen. If I had been in the US Military the Americans would not have let me cross at Checkpoint Charlie."

"Come, come, Herr King, don't insult me. All that would have been arranged ahead of your deployment. But be that as it may, this does not change the matter of your spying and the fact that we have found your American military identification."

The Hauptmann pointed to the words on my credentials *'Army and Air Force Exchange Service.'* He then moved his finger to the small print lower down, having taken the credentials out of their holder. *If found place into any United States Postal Service box.* This was for him proof perfect that I was firstly an American and secondly in the military.

"Your officers didn't 'find' my credentials," I said. "They weren't being hidden. My credentials were in the glove compartment of my vehicle. Why would I have my ID with me if I was trying to spy and why if you are right, are my credentials in my name? As for the Russian language, it is one of the languages that I am trying to learn, unsuccessfully I may add. I am also trying to learn Dutch, Danish, French and Italian; this does not make me a spy. I just enjoy languages. And finally the situation with my car is true, the alternator was not charging but luckily I found a Turkish garage open in West Berlin last night. The guy looked at my car and explained it was a faulty connection, it's now fixed."

Was that a flash of doubt across the Hauptmann's face?

He continued. "I don't believe in such coincidences, Herr King…"

We stayed in that dingy room for another couple of hours or so, batting accusations and defences back and forth. A couple of times the Hauptmann left the room for about twenty minutes, no doubt checking my answers against Angela's, and against any intelligence updates from his team.

After the last such break, the Hauptmann re-entered the room and fired another question at me.

"What about the communications system in your vehicle?"

"This is a CB radio. It is built into the cassette player, this is normal in the West. You must know this"

"This is contraband. It's illegal in the DDR."

"I didn't know that it was illegal to have such a radio in the DDR and if I did I would have respected your laws."

"But you as a Detective should know that ignorance of the law is no excuse."

I could only accept this.

"Why have you come to Berlin, what is your role here and why are you wishing to visit our capital?"

I made it clear that I had no mission. I was on holiday and as a person interested in history and politics I wanted to see East and West Berlin. I was just an interested tourist.

The Hauptmann left the room again, no longer smiling. The door closed behind him.

A few minutes later the original border guard officer came back into the room.

"You can go."

I didn't hesitate. When I arrived back at the car, Angela was still in the passenger seat. She had not been taken for questioning. They were apparently only interested in me. Understandably, Angela simply wanted to turn around and go straight back to the safety of the West. I refused. I didn't want to let the Communists win. I was by no means an anti-communist and was in fact, compared to many of my US military friends, a fluffy 'pinko', but this was a matter of pride. I wanted to see East Germany. I would take a quick look at the tourist sites and venture up the Funkturm, the tallest radio tower in Berlin to have a look at the city from that vantage point. I would however, make sure that we were back in the bosom of the West by nightfall. It was a lovely warm summer's day so we had some several hours of sightseeing light left.

When we re-entered West Berlin later that evening, through Checkpoint Charlie, one generally needed to return to the West using the route one exited, the US MPs were waiting. The Watch-Officer, a lieutenant, said that they'd noted my situation and had been worried when we did not return earlier. So due to this a report had been raised. I spoke to the duty Intel officer and gave him a provisional brief of what had happened. It was agreed that on my return to work I would travel up the two flights of steps from my office to the Military Intelligence office and provide them with a full debrief.

The intelligence world is schizophrenic, a fact that I now fully appreciate, but at the time I had no idea that I was being debriefed with the aim of making sure I had not been turned by the East Germans, among other things. The MI officers were trying to establish if I was targeted by the East Germans and if so, why? If it was just a chance situation why had they only concentrated on me? Was in fact Angela the target? Could she be trusted? If Angela and I were indeed loyal, could we have inadvertently given anything of significance away? In intelligence one has to cover all the angles.

Fast forward eight years and there to my utter amazement was the unmistakeable face of Herr Hauptmann! The face was older but the stare and the blue green eyes were the same. He was convinced he'd been correct in his assessment and we shook hand, before he concluded: "Well my friend, the game is now over for me, you have won the war."

The Cold War was ending and although he'd done well, rising to the rank of Colonel, he was finished. A STASI Colonel would not exactly be the most popular candidate for any role in the unified Federal Republic of Germany. Time and again throughout my career, I would be reminded of how small the world of intelligence and protective security is. I would bump into friends and foes in the most unexpected places - and I would see so many familiar faces in different lands in different roles that it was often impossible to remember where and when I'd first met them. However, at least one person on de Maizière operation I wouldn't forget. This was his economic advisor. In the late 1980's, this little known academic, outside of East Germany, with whom I had some interaction would go on to become the most powerful politician in Europe – German Chancellor Dr. Angela Merkel.

Chapter Twelve - Rumble from the Jungle

In the mid 80's US President Ronald Reagan enlisted the Thatcher government to help fight the War on Drugs. Amongst other actions, our assistance would include covert operations carried out against Narco-traffickers and left wing revolutionaries in Colombia. As MPSB's Colombian desk officer, I would also have a small role to play in this transatlantic effort.

Although London's Colombian expatriate community was small, we had some cause for concern. The Libyan State had trained Colombian terrorists in the same camps as Irish republicans and supplied both groups with weapons via their People's Bureaus. As a result, the Irish and Colombians developed a 'friendship'. I'd have to take such intelligence into account when early in 1990 an 'A' Squad DI asked for my assessment of the potential threat to the new Colombian President Elect, César Gaviria - should he visit the United Kingdom?

President elect Gaviria had embarked on his bid for the presidency of Colombia when the original Colombian Liberal party candidate, Luis Carlos Galán, was assassinated in a hail of automatic gunfire delivered by Pablo Escobar's drugs cartels' *sicarios (dagger-men/assassins)* during a large open air rally outside Bogota on the 18th of August 1989. As Galán's campaign manager, Gaviria was seen by the Liberal party leadership as the person best placed to take over as leader and run for the presidency. With some understandable reluctance, Gaviria accepted this poisoned chalice and won. The US government was delighted, not least because Gaviria had promised to continue the Reagan-era extradition policy of trying, sentencing and incarcerating major Colombian drugs traffickers in the USA. This was the very policy that had led narco-king pin, Pablo Escobar, to declare war on the

Colombian Government. Needless to say, Gaviria jumped to the top of Escobar's hit list.

Officially, the President Elect's visit to the UK was billed as a pre-accession to office consultation with British politicians. In reality the visit's aims were much simpler - to keep the President Elect alive until his inauguration. Not easy. At least three presidential candidates had been assassinated during the Colombian presidential elections, not to mention scores of regional and local politicians and perhaps hundreds of officials, police and judges. Colombia was in a near-state of war.

The 'A' Squad DI tasked with the Gaviria protection was Dan Smith. Dan was a measured man from the Welsh valleys who had excelled at school and university and made his way into the Branch as a DC after five years in uniform and two failed attempts at the Branch exam. Dan now 20 years into his Branch career was a safe pair of hands. Dan explained that he intended to provide only a limited protection package to the President Elect; his rationale being that as neither Head of State, head of government nor Foreign Secretary of Colombia, Gaviria was not entitled to prot under the auspices of the UN convention on protected individuals which the Branch utilised to inform its provision of armed personal protection to foreign dignitaries. However, Dan was no fool, he understood that protection was being granted at the behest of the *Head Girl*, so with this in mind and an eye on the available resources, he intended to provide the safe minimal package to the principal. His package consisted of one SB protection officer and an SB specialist protection driver, although he intended to harden some venues visited by the President Elect with uniform colleagues and specialist uniform units, such as the Diplomatic Protection Group *(DPG)*. Finally, Dan had come to me to provide him with the most up-to-date intelligence assessment around which he could base this proposed protection package.

I wasn't able to provide much reassurance. Although the secret intelligence I had access to and my own 'investigations'/monitoring of UK Colombians seemed to rule out any real threat from extremist left-wing Colombians inside the UK, it was worth first of all bearing in mind the Libyan and IRA connections to the Colombian left. Although it was improbable that activists from the Colombian left in Britain would attempt an assassination, there was always the danger of a 'lone wolf' *(a single dedicated individual assassin working completely in isolation)* or just as problematic, an opportunist *(devil-may-care)* assassin from performing such a feat on the spur of the moment. Such attacks are nigh-on impossible to prevent *(as long as the attacker keeps his intentions to himself)*. Of course, such assassins would generally be caught as they were glory seekers looking for their fifteen minutes of fame. However, the President elect would not generally lend himself to being such a target, at least not for UK glory seekers. I assessed that the most likely threat to Gaviria was from individuals who would be rewarded by Pablo Escobar and would therefore wish to escape to spend it - but of course, one couldn't discount Escobar holding a man's family hostage until he killed the President Elect. I wanted to make the point to Dan that there were some things that simply couldn't be analysed and assessed. As US Secretary of State for Defence Donald Rumsfeld would put it some years later - 'You know what you know, but you don't know what you don't know!'

The most likely threat to the President elect however, was from a planned attack by either of the main drugs cartels – in particular Escobar's Medellin cartel. Our problem was that the cartels had unlimited funds. They had previously hired highly-skilled ex-special forces soldiers as their assassins abroad. So Dan might be facing SAS-types who could operate anywhere in the world. To highlight this point, I told Dan the story of a highly-respected senior Colombian Narcotics Police officer who, in the mid-80's led a raid on a jungle drugs factory near the Orinoco River. The Island boasted an airstrip, a cinema, workers dwellings and a bar. The drugs factory workers, mainly innocent cámpesinos, were treated well and paid about ten times the average basic Colombian salary. When the commander and his team raided the facility they found cocaine processed and nearly ready for transportation with a street value of up to a billion US dollars. Unable to hold the area for the central government, the commander burnt the drugs and razed the camp to the ground. Once back in Bogotá the commander was feted and hailed as a hero of the nation.

 Prior to the raid, all those who should have known of the camp's existence did or could have if they so wished. However, few if any in power wished to openly acknowledge the camp's presence, as ignorance of the narcotics trade is often healthier. Generally, most Colombian politicians or officials preferred to accept the drugs cartel's 'gold' or at least not to openly challenge the trade. So, fearing for the life of the narco-police commander, the Colombian government sent him to serve behind the Iron Curtain as the Colombian Defence Attaché to Hungary.

 In the Cold War countries behind the Iron Curtain were regarded as impenetrable for foreign criminals. And the commander thought he was safe until the day he was gunned down in broad daylight on the streets of Budapest by assassins unknown. The message sent to all Colombians that day couldn't have been clearer, the cartel's reach was limitless.

 I recommended that Dan beef up the President Elect's security package and to his credit, he did. Dan added additional protection officers, a back-up vehicle and other police resources, as well as sniffer dog searches who hunted for explosives at every venue, DPG to guard and secure all visited premises and SEG motorcyclists to escort the President elect's convoy to and from all venues.

Dan also asked me to join the team as his 2ic *(second-in-command)*, taking up the role of an extra protection officer and the operation's intelligence co-ordinator. I cleared my desk of my other 'Americas Desk' secret intelligence work and immediately commenced the pre-operational assessment work by meeting my contacts on Colombia in HM Customs & Excise's National Investigative Service *(NIS)*, the police Regional Crime Squads *(RCS)*, the Yard's Central Drugs Squad, Colombian IOs at their London Embassy and my other key 'Colombia' players in the United States Drug Enforcement Agency *(DEA),* based at the US embassy in London as well as Colombia centric contacts in the Security Service.

Throughout the years of the Colombian 'narco wars' it had always been very easy for others to label the Colombian police as corrupt but when drugs gang members are so emboldened that they can enter a police headquarters and offer the police chief the choice of the 'lead or gold', with the *'lead'* signifying not only the officer's death, but the death of his entire family. When one considers such consequences the concept of corruption becomes less a notion of absolute choice and greed and more one of survival. In those days I often wondered how many of us would chose the lead.

Just before the President Elect left for the UK I spoke with his 'PA' via telephone. The PA, obviously a member of ACI *(the Colombian Central Intelligence Agency)* or DNI *(The Colombian Security Service)*, said that some months previously during the campaign he had received an anonymous tip-off that President Elect Gaviria should not travel on the flight they had covertly booked to travel to Cali from Bogota. Heeding this anonymous warning the PA tried to persuade the then Presidential candidate not to board the aircraft. Initially Gaviria resisted but was eventually persuaded to relent. The aircraft exploded five minutes into its flight from Bogota Airport killing all 107 passengers and crew as well as three people on the ground.

The PA confided in me that he suspected that the President Elect's secret travel arrangements had already been compromised from a mole within his camp and that the leak had actually come from within Gaviria's 'security detail' *(protection team)*. Despite these concerns, the President Elect's plane arrived safely in the UK. Gaviria's immediate family travelled with him. As the President elect stepped off the plane our security package kicked in. Official meetings took place at No.10 and the Foreign and Commonwealth Office. We travelled out of town to the Prime Minister's country seat at Chequers and visited other parts of the Home Counties including 'Shakespeare country', Stratford-on-Avon. On our return to London we went to the theatre to watch the musical 'Buddy' and visited top restaurants and tourist sites. A few days into the trip, the Colombian PA asked to see me alone.

"We want to create a fully trustworthy presidential protection unit. I want you to tell me how we can do this."

I suggested that there were two main options. If he wished to keep the team Colombian he would need to create an atmosphere where officers in the unit did not feel vulnerable to threats from the cartels, terrorists or revolutionary organisations. If this was successfully achieved for the officers, and most importantly their families, then the unit would be much more secure. To achieve this, the protection team would have to be provided with excellent pay and conditions, good secure accommodation for close family as well as appropriate schooling for the officers' children. The unit would also need to closely vet applicants seeking recruitment, thereby identifying vulnerable officers or those attempting to infiltrate the organisation on behalf of third parties such as the cartels. Most importantly, the unit would need to be staffed by elite officers, small in number, with an excellent *esprit de corps* and an intelligence-based ethos at the core of its operational planning. This was my preferred model.

The other method of attempting to create an 'untouchable' body of protection officers would be to create a team of foreign volunteers whose extended families, living outside Colombia, would not be so vulnerable to threats. The downside of this 'mercenary' unit would be a question of motivation and loyalty. Furthermore, the Colombian media would no doubt attack the president for not trusting his own security forces and the mercenary protection unit for being solely interested in earning large sums of money, which one would have to pay to get the best people. Moreover, if the main driver for participation in the unit was money, as opposed to other factors such as national pride or a will to uphold the laws of the state of Colombia, then this in itself would be a vulnerability for the team, as one thing the drugs cartels had in abundance was cash.

Some years later I would undertake various operations in Colombia. On one of these ops I observed first-hand how helicopter borne narco-police and officers on the ground destroyed some of the coca fields in the jungle regions not far from Bogota. The narcotics 'war' is unending and in my opinion, futile. Prohibition alone will not solve the problem. As with alcohol, harm reduction, purity controls and legalised fiscal architecture would take most of the criminality out of the drugs trade, including stopping most of the deaths, as these are mainly due to poor product control or the battle for market share. Criminalising vast numbers of people in various ethnic groups and classes involved in the drugs trade, as we presently do, is not the answer.

The President Elect's visit passed off without incident. As is often the case with protection, one never knows if the actions one took prevented an attack or whether an attack was never considered.

After the Branch's successful UK protection operation, the PA actioned some of my ideas which, along with others from US agencies, helped bolster President Gaviria's protection package. Although ex-President Gaviria outlived Pablo Escobar *(who was killed in a rooftop shootout in 1993, while Gaviria was still in office)* and survives to this day, there is only so much one can do against enemies with almost unlimited financial resources. In April 2006 Gaviria's sister, Liliana Gaviria, 52, a real estate agent, was the subject of an attempted kidnap in the province of Risaralda, 110 miles west of Bogotá. Approximately six men intercepted Liliana who was traveling with the single National Police protection officer assigned to protect her. A desperate close-range firefight ensued but the officer and Liliana were killed. Mortally wounded, the brave NP officer was able to return fire injuring two of the kidnappers before he succumbed to his wounds.

Unfortunately, when it goes wrong, 'Protmen' nearly always pay with their lives.

Chapter Thirteen – SDS (The Special Demonstration Squad)

On 17 March 1968, an anti-Vietnam-War protest that began in Trafalgar Square moved on to the American Embassy in Grosvenor Square, led amongst others by the writer Tariq Ali and actor and human rights campaigner Vanessa Redgrave. The events were given a Rock 'n Roll edge by the presence of Mick Jagger, who stood on the steps of a house in the Square, looking towards the American Embassy, where fighting soon broke out. The crowds started to overwhelm the police who, even with the help of mounted officers, could not bring the rioters under control.

Inside the embassy US personnel watched as the fighting threatened to breach their gates. The commander of the embassy's United States Marine Corps guard force reportedly opened the armoury and issued the guards with M16 automatic rifles so that they could defend their sovereign territory. For many Americans the Marine Corps was the 1960's military embodiment of all-American values, values which viewed the demonstration's 'long haired Brit Communist hippies' with loathing. Their sworn duty was to protect the embassy's personnel as well as the highly classified CIA, diplomatic and military secrets therein. However, before the Americans were required to consider actually using deadly force, the Met police were finally able to regain control - but only after 86 people were injured and two hundred demonstrators were arrested.

MPSB had warned senior uniform colleagues of the potential for violent disorder but had been unable to provide grade-A, top-table intelligence on the intentions of the more radical factions of the demonstration, the elements who would go on to inflict the most criminal damage and led the charge to storm the US embassy.

So, as a result of these riots, the escalating troubles in Northern Ireland, the French student demonstrations and allied riots and national strikes in France that threatened the very existence of French Republic; the Home Office requested greater 'proactivity' from MPSB. Government knew the British state was at potential threat and demanded that the revolutionary extremist and subversive organisations that utilised legitimate struggles and demonstrations to create violence and undermine The Queen's Peace be combatted. The Under Secretary of State for the Home Office, with the then Home Secretary James Callaghan's blessing, sanctioned the formation in MPSB's 'C' Squad of a permanent Top-Secret covert ultra-deep cover monitoring and intelligence gathering unit – The Special Operation Squad *(SOS)* - eventually renamed the Special Demonstration Squad (SDS). From this point on, an extremely small number experienced MPSB officers recruited into SDS, would infiltrate extremist radical organisations intent on overthrowing the UK by non-parliamentary means or damaging the peaceful well-being of the UK's public order, in doing so these officers would live under ultra-deep cover within these subversive organisations, hour after hour, day after day, year after year for years on end severing all contact to police and official organisations!

SDS' aim was to prevent violent disorder before it could occur, so that the government of the day did not get caught on the hop again. The Branch was happy to oblige. It knew that radical revolutionary movements around the world were increasing their memberships: the Red Army Faction in West Germany, the Red Army in Japan, the Weather Underground in the USA, the various paramilitary organisations in Northern Ireland and the mainland's own short-lived urban radical extremist/terrorist organisation – the Angry Brigade – which even attempted to bomb London's Post Office Tower in 1971 but was successfully combatted by the Branch probably utilising SDS intelligence. These organisations all had one thing in common, their activists had all graduated from street protester activity into urban terrorists. Moreover, many, if not all of these groups enjoyed some level of support from the Soviet Union, the Warsaw Pact or other states 'antagonistic' to the West. Consequently, the Branch was keen to play its part in defeating this Cold War game of high stakes poker.

At its inception the Home Office was the body that defined SOS's (SDS's) role, rationale and intent. Although most of MPSB's work was already classified as Secret, the knowledge and activities of the SOS would be classified even higher at Top Secret. To maintain this Top Secret nature, the Home Office directly funded and assisted SDS for nigh-on two decades. In 1970 Deputy Under-Secretary of State for the Home Office Sir James Waddell wrote to the Commissioner of the Metropolitan Police, Sir John Waldron, explaining the need for the utmost secrecy vis-à-vis 'SDS': "Plainly the arrangements could if made known in the wrong quarters be a source of acute embarrassment to the Home Secretary." Waddell wrote. Politically therefore, from its inception, the SDS was seen by those in government as a potentially problematic yet necessary evil, that for reasons of political expediency had to be kept Top Secret.

Unlike provincial police forces, which were steered by a mixture of police committees, the Home Office and local councils, the Metropolitan Police was directly answerable to the Home Secretary who had direct political control and oversight over its functions. This anomaly had resulted from the Met's size, its unique position as Britain's first police force, its location as the capital's police service and the quasi-national investigative role performed by Scotland Yard's detective departments such as Special Branch. So until the turn of the Millennium, when this oversight role was turned over to the Mayor of London, it was part and parcel of every Home Secretary's brief to be conversant with what the Met was doing in their name and under their DIRECT control. This was especially the case as regards MPSB's covert activities, which had national and international significance. Thus, it was impossible for any Home Secretary up until the year 2000 to deny a broad strokes knowledge of the MPSB's activities including SDS. Consequently, from its inception the SDS was designated and would remain Top Secret, so as not to embarrass the Home Secretary.

I was introduced to the world of SDS once I was rotated into 'C' Squad as a desk officer. The intelligence secretly gained from SDS officers *(even though most of us in C-Squad were not told of its provenance)* was a major factor in helping us achieve our goal of maintaining the peace and tranquillity of the British way of life.

From the safety of my desk, I witnessed the high price paid over many years by spouses, children and extended families of Branch colleagues selected for SDS. The apparent lack of close support and the almost total submersion into their undercover lives seemed to leave many SDS operatives reeling. In fact, at least one military physiatrist informed the Met that the requirement on SDS operatives to maintain a separate 'real' life, which posed a major danger to their long term ultra-deep cover life, along with the need to continually deceive extremist comrades who would invariably become best friends, coupled with the fear of physical harm and even death if unmasked as an SB officer, was a perfect recipe for mental illness.

On top of this, the fact that every SDS officer knew that there was no support or back-up for them as they lived 24 hours a day every day amongst these often violent activists, was another huge and constant stress factor. Unlike the future National Public Order Intelligence Unit's *(NPOIU)* undercover section and other undercover Police, Customs or Military units – who generally had back-up officers often only minutes away - SDS operatives were well and truly on their own. Day in day out SDS officers worked totally in isolation, save for the *'I'm alive'* bi-daily telephone calls to SDS's covert office and the bi-weekly safe house meets. SDS operatives had no back-up and no contact with any other official body they were totally alone. It was Jekyll and Hyde territory and in time it would break many, if not most officers.

The main influence on an SDS officer's psychological well-being was the inordinate amount of time he/she spent totally immersed in the target organisation in their undercover alter ego. It was only logical, and part of human nature, that they ended up forming true friendships with activists in the organisations they were monitoring. The effect of this day-in day-out, year-in year-out submersion was debilitating.

In the UK, this type of officer-based long term deep penetration undercover *(UC)* role was unique to SDS. In fact there weren't many units in the world that practiced this model. Most British UC units, regardless of the organisation *(Police or Customs etc.)*, deployed their UC officers as and when they were required, normally on relatively short evidential investigations. When not engaged on UC investigations such UC trained officers generally performed normal police, customs or military duties, until required for a further UC deployment. As you've seen this was not the case for SDS officers.

The closest UC operative to the SDS was the classic Warsaw Pact *sleeper* agent. They took on an identity and lived it forever, though this is also not a favourable comparison. Such sleeper operatives *(we arrested one in my early years in the Branch)*, were generally only caught by their mistakes – treachery – or through sigint *(Signals Intelligence)*. When caught however, there was no way for us to find out who they really were because they only lived one life and identity. An SDS officer however, couldn't leave his real identity behind. He was a Met Special Branch officer and generally had a partner and family not far from where he/she was deployed. The operative knew that on those occasions that they were able to return to his/her suburban life to see their loved ones and become their 'real' selves that they could be spotted by their activist comrades at any time. That's why it was generally considered safer for SDS officers not to inhabit their real lives, but to remain in their deep-cover alter egos for longer and longer periods giving their fake 'self' primacy over their real 'self'. This process led to unacceptable pressures that often surfaced in illnesses - stomach ulcers, bile, mental illness and emotional paucity not to mention the breakdown of families. This was the toll SDS officers paid for years of lying and deceiving extremist 'friends' and comrades, not to mention 'real' family and friends, all in the cause of Queen and Country.

One friend informed me that once their tours were either completed or prematurely abandoned, that as many as thirty five per cent of her ex-SDS colleagues never returned to mainstream Special Branch duties. Instead, such officers would often leave the Met, the country or sadly, suffering from obvious extreme stress and mental illness, were required to retire from the service prematurely. For those who did return to mainstream Branch work some four, five or even six years after commencing their SDS deployment it was possible to see that their personalities had changed and they tended to seek and at the same time suffer from isolation. Because SDS officers never really got closure on their deep-cover lives, having to remain 'covert' for the rest of their days, for fear of being spotted by their erstwhile friends and comrades, this isolation multiplied.

Other UC unit's officers didn't suffer from these problems. Normally, once UCs from such units finished their generally short-term evidential operations their status as an officer was made known to the courts and defence council to gain criminal convictions. SDS as a Top Secret intelligence gathering and not evidential unit, tasked solely with obtaining covert secret intelligence, didn't have this luxury. Its operatives' covert status would never be declared. Consequently, the pressure on ex-SDS operatives remained, even when their lives returned to 'normal'.

Like war veterans, many ex SDS operatives would not speak of their deployment, especially not to anyone who was not indoctrinated into the unit's existence. Hence, with no opportunity to vent fears, anger, frustrations or problems, the cycle of pressure and the slide towards the spectre of mental illness was never ending.

One of the first cracks in SDS appeared in 2013 when the media reported the claims of former undercover SDS officer Peter Francis that SDS 'investigated' the family of Stephen Lawrence in order to seek possible evidence to smear them. Peter also stated that some SDS officers had relationships with activists involved in the organisations they infiltrated.

Hundreds of ill-informed column inches have been written about Peter Francis and SDS, some of which I must dispel. Neither Mark Kennedy, another UC officer who came forward to speak about the negative effects of his undercover work, nor any other NPOIU undercover officer, was ever in SDS. SDS was solely an MPSB unit working to a completely different brief from that of the NPOIU UC officers. SDS' brief was solely intelligence driven, any arrests were to some extent a by-product, not the goal of SDS operations. SDS targeted subversive/extremist organisations not individuals, whereas like practically all other Police and Customs UC work the NPOIU's aim was that of arresting offenders. This placed a completely different onus on NPOIU ops as opposed to SDS deployments. Clearly as a *national* Special Branch body under the auspices of Commander MPSB and the Met's ACSO, the NPOIU was connected to the Metropolitan Police Special Branch, as MPSB officers like me ran some of its units *(I ran the NPOIU's Strategic Analysis Unit)*, but it was in no way associated with

SDS. These units were two totally separate entities, with totally separate goals.

As for Peter Francis, in the best tradition of Special Branch and especially SDS, he was an extremely dedicated and professional officer who committed his life to the service of his country. Unfortunately, like many SDS operatives, Peter paid a heavy price for this dedication by succumbing to the relentless pressure of years of gut wrenching fear, self-loathing and deceit executed in the name of a higher purpose - the well-being of the British State. Unfortunately, the psychological, emotional, familial and cognitive damage experienced by Peter during his deployment would leave him broken and alone. He was not the first SDS officer to suffer this fate, nor would he be the last.

The need for unending secrecy during and post deployment was such that SDS operatives developed the most robust aliases and 'legends' possible, prior to deploying into the field. The hope was that these aliases would stand up to lifelong scrutiny. Consequently, up until the late 1990's, in common with others in the covert undercover world *(the Intelligence Agencies, general police UC units, the Military and Customs)*, SDS utilised the best known method of creating a resilient alias - the so-called *Day of the Jackal* technique.

The best thriller writers turn to the real world to give their books the authenticity that readers crave. Arguably, the master of the genre is Frederick Forsyth, author of *The Day of the Jackal*, published in 1971. In his book about an English hit man *(the Jackal)* is employed to assassinate French president Charles de Gaulle. The nameless anti-hero acquires a genuine UK passport, in name of an actual individual who had dead young. The Jackal then travels through Europe, where he commits several murders and evades the police – thanks to the passport, which in the book and film MPSB are left trying to trace. The amazing thing was that Forsyth had exposed a genuine loophole. It was shockingly simple. The Jackal is pictured searching through three village graveyards to find the headstone of a baby boy who would have been about the same age as he is. Taking the details to the Central Registry of Births, Marriages and Deaths *(based in London's Somerset House from 1836)*, the Jackal buys a copy of the deceased's birth certificate – all the proof he needs to apply for a passport, which is issued four days later. It has been estimated that 1,500 passports were acquired in this way in the UK each year - and not by UK undercover officers and agencies - but by a range of international ne'er-do-wells, from Soviet spies to IRA terrorists to fraudsters of all types, have all strolled into Somerset House to collect their fraudulent birth certificates. It wasn't until 2007 that the Identity and Passport Service finally set up a system to close the loophole. They quickly uncovered 1,200 cases, leading to 290 arrests, 100 convictions and 38 deportations, showing just how popular the scam had become. In its time the Jackal technique was invaluable to SDS - operatives' their lives even depended on it. SDS also required the highest level of 'other' documentary identification *(drivers' licences, passports and birth certificates in their false name etc.)* as it was not uncommon for activists in a target organisation, their family members or their friends to have access to official public sector records, these documents had to be real.

In the final analysis absolute success in SDS was measured by its ability to help keep peace and public tranquillity in the United Kingdom - as well as maintaining SDS' secrecy so that an operative's 'comrades' would never suspect that their organisation had been infiltrated by a government spy even after the SDS operative had long since left the target organisation. Of course this was blown out of the water post Peter Francis' revelations. While SDS officers took no pleasure in being continually deceitful to their subversive friends and comrades, they were proud of the fact that they provided intelligence that saved lives and prevented hundreds of millions of pounds' worth of property damage in my time alone.

I've too often read uninformed commentary about SDS operatives spying on 'pink' and 'fluffy' well-meaning citizens going about their lawful business, when actually, SDS operatives only ever infiltrated groups that were intent on making the UK less-governable by destabilising our industrial, social, racial, economic or political fabric; to undermine the nations communal peace and security. Promoting conflict was the prime intention of the subversive organisations Special Branch targeted for SDS infiltration. Additionally, a favoured tactic employed by many subversive organisations was that of entryism into legitimate protest groups, such as the Stephen Lawrence campaign, in order to cynically utilise the pain and anguish of such causes to create the conditions for anger driven strife and public disorder. *(The Stephen Lawrence Campaign, was a legitimate grass roots social justice campaign dedicated to unearthing the truth about the racially motivated murder of black teenager, Stephen Lawrence, in 1993.)*

SDS officers did not infiltrate legitimate protest groups. However, if activists from a subversive group infiltrated by SDS entered a legitimate campaign, the SDS operative UC in that group would obviously have to do likewise, primarily to maintain his or her cover, but also to assess what the subversive group's intentions were vis-à-vis the legitimate organisation. This is what happened with the Lawrence campaign as subversive groups attempted to hijack and steer the campaign for their own nefarious and hostile ends.

A spy doesn't simply infiltrate an organisation one day to be shown all its secrets the next, that only happens in the movies. Organisations bent on undermining public tranquillity are understandably cautious; they guard their secrets. In the real world trust has to be earned and it often took many weeks, even months, before an SDS operative could get anywhere near a target organisation, never mind being in a position to gain high grade intelligence from it. More often than not, the operative wouldn't even make the first move. Ideally it would be an activist who would suggest the link-up, which cleverly, on occasions, the SDS officer would initially rebut.

A good case study of the difficulties of infiltrating an extremist organisation and gaining activists' trust would be the extreme right wing. Infiltrating Britain's subversive extreme right wing organisations was for any operative a daunting proposition. Firstly, most local extreme right wing activists tended to know each other, they'd generally been to the same schools, played on the same football teams and been in the same gangs. Secondly, the sections of the 'right' of most interest to the Branch worshipped violence and, of course, were extremely racist. So, to start to crack this nut the SDS operative would have to first affect the same physical and mental prejudices of the target group *(not easy when you have to learn to speak and act like the people you revile)* whilst seeking a point of access to the group. An SDS operative might initially attend several overt 'fluffy' right-wing public meetings. This initial entry phase could last for many weeks or months. During this period the operative would spend countless hours living his/her bogus life, in their bogus flat, working at their bogus job, making friends and laying down strong roots in the local area. Whilst attending these public meetings the operative would be aware that he is being furtively evaluated by key party members. Primarily this evaluation is aimed at recruiting right-wing talent, but also in common with all extremist organisations, right wing activists are paranoid of police or Security Service infiltration.

In line with Nazi ideology, most extreme right-wing parties run a twin-track policy – the ballot box and street action. This policy allows such parties to have a degree of democratic legitimacy whilst also attracting street activists with a penchant for extreme violence. SDS operatives had to be careful not to undermine legitimate right-wing politicking especially if electioneering was involved but deal with the violent and extremist aspects of the organisation. Conscious of this, SDS officers were circumspect in how they dealt with any genuine constitutional actions of these parties, so as not to undermine their legitimate democratic rights.

Mindful of the media's interest in race, and keen not to 'publicly' act contrary to any anti-racial legislation, at first glance some extremist right wing parties might appear 'fluffy', non-violent and legitimate. However, as the weeks and months go by, and the SDS operative is progressively accepted into the 'extras' of the party's life, this begins to change. As trust grows and members begin to let their guards down the operative will aim to be invited to the party's covert conspiratorial meetings by tactfully making himself useful to the organisation and befriending the more extremist activists. Depending on the group and the SDS operative's gender, physical appearance, demeanour and legend, he may be given a subordinate security role by the right wing party at public meetings. Obviously during this stage the SDS operative will be under constant covert assessment by the extremist group. They will most probably drop by his/her bogus home unexpectedly, check his/her bogus workplace and note his/her answers to questions for later retesting. Everything will be checked, sometimes officially by the extremist group's covert fellow travellers in the Civil Service or public sector *(Many extremist groups have contacts/members who work for the British state)*

SDS officers have to make tough decisions on a daily basis. A male SDS operative would want to infiltrate the most extreme members of the right wing and therefore would have to prove his mettle in battle, that way gaining access to the skinhead, blood-and-honour and football 'hooligan' orientated elements of the extreme right, those elements that the Branch and uniform colleagues in general had immediate and acute interest in. These were/are the groups that on occasions inflicted unwarranted physical harm on their enemies - the Visible Ethnic Minorities *(VEMs)*, Jews and left wing activists - in what were named 'street actions'. These more violent sections of the right generally had good international contacts with likeminded bodies and groups overseas, which were generally even more violent than their British comrades. Many overseas groups where in fact terroristic in nature. German, Polish, Russian, Scandinavian, South African and American white supremacist grouping often did not shy away from multiple murders of 'immigrants' or members of VEM groups. Today its members of these groups that are most likely to travel to the Kurdish areas of Iraq, the Ukraine or various African conflict areas to learn how to kill or to increase their knowledge of killing *(having previously been in the army)* VEMs or Muslims in the name of fighting ISIS, Al Qaeda or various African guerrilla organisations members. These are the individuals who when they return home – to the UK or elsewhere – are the most likely to involve themselves in future anti-Muslim 'actions' in an attempt to cause 'race wars' in their respective countries including the UK. Indeed, as regards this goal, both the extreme right wing and extreme Jihadis have the same agenda.

Whilst serving in 'E' Squad's European Liaison Section *(ELS)* at the turn of the decade 1980 -1990's, I regularly read German BKA reports which described how VEM citizens or immigrants had been thrown off high buildings or burnt to death by right wing suspects. The Dutch CRI reports also noted such street actions. Thus SDS intelligence on right wing circles was highly prized by these countries having the potential to save lives both here in the UK and abroad.

As political activism is national, if not international in nature, MPSB SDS officers were never confined to London. That said, every SDS operative knew that whilst on his/her travels with extremist comrades that the dangers of the deployment would increase exponentially. Without back up and often functioning in complete isolation, even if abroad, the dangers were obvious. Another exacting area for SDS operatives was the ever encroaching legislative environment. 'Legals' were always a concern for SDS officers. To gain access to the best intelligence on their target groups, SDS operatives needed to make it into leadership level positions. However, this in itself was a balancing act. If an officer reached the upper echelons of an organisation and was able to direct its tactics and actions, it would defeat the purpose of an officer's deployment, as one could quite rightly be seen as sustaining the extremist organisation's activities by acting as an *agent provocateur*. This was not the goal of SDS, operatives knew full well that they should never become organisers without whom the extremist group could not function or be as effective. The ideal position for an operative would be upper-middle-management within an organisation's operations, logistics or strategic command; such roles would provide one with an excellent overview of the extremist organisation and its capacity to do harm but not unduly influence its actions. More importantly, such roles would provide the operative with the potential to prevent harm to the public.

In addition to other problems, SDS officers in right-wing organisations also risked being targeted by agents of foreign powers, left wing infiltrators into the right and violent anti-racist groups. Unsurprisingly, Jewish organisations in particular, supported at length by Mossad, kept tabs on the right-wing activity throughout Europe, including the UK. Moreover, the streets of the inner cities were not free from political violence in the early to mid-1990s. Vicious tit-for-tat beatings of right and left wing activists were not uncommon.

The role of an SDS operative was not to target individuals on the right or the left or in other potential subversive arenas, but to monitor organisations that wished to undermine the Queen's Peace or parliamentary democracy and to reduce harm to the community. In achieving these goals SDS operatives involved themselves in seemingly trivial events because the target organisations' did. As Peter Francis explained, being an SDS operative was not a part time role. SDS officers lived the 'job' 24 hours a day 365 days a year. For all intents and purposes they were who their legends said they were. Simply put, SDS operatives took part in all the activities of the target organisation in order to fit in and prevent greater harm overall. Consequently SDS operatives were engaged in 'fluffy' as well as the hard core actions, something that was particularly the case for SDS operatives deployed into the subversive left.

Many extreme left-wing organisations tended to perceive any activity against an organ of the state as a building block towards revolution. For them, any activity that was likely to cause a stir was encouraged. Accordingly, acting as general members of the public, the activists would often attempt to highjack local single issue campaigns such as keeping a local hospital open or preventing the closure of a local school in order to steer the campaign towards conflict. To achieve this, activists purporting to be general members of the public would swamp a local campaign's public meeting or primary steering group and attempt to usurp a campaign's key roles of Chair, Treasurer and Secretary by standing and seconding each other for these posts, backed up by a show of hands. This was often easy to achieve as 'Joe Public' tends not to promote himself publicly. Their goal attained, from this point on a campaign would be steered by the extremist organisation. This technique was known as *'entryism'* and the extremist left wing were its undisputed masters. The radical group Militant Tendency performed this manoeuvre on a massive scale to takeover Liverpool City Council and various Trotskyist and other ultra-left wing socialist factions utilised the process to exert major influence over trade unions.

The Stephen Lawrence campaign was targeted in this manner by various extreme left wing organisations who saw the campaign as a vehicle to attempt to mobilise and radicalise the masses from various poverty-riven London estates. From these extreme left wing groups perspective their organisation would provide a focus to combat the mindless violent racism of the right-wing with their own 'legitimate' defensive-violence against the repressive organs of the British state. Fortunately, the Lawrence family's legal representatives were able to keep most of these extremist groups at bay. That said, both Mark Ellison QC's report - *the Stephen Lawrence Independent Review* - and the Operation Herne Report by Chief Constable Mick Creedon accept that the Welling Stephen Lawrence march in October 1993 was to a degree highjacked by various left wing extremist groups who attempted to turn the demonstration into a violent juggernaut. Some activists even planned to use the demo as an opportunity to attempt to burn down the BNP HQ with its right wing activists inside.

In the weeks prior to this march and in an attempt to increase the march's potency, extreme left-wing groups of various persuasions attempted to gain the maximum participation of as many angry young people as possible. These groups deliberately canvassed the attendance on the march of youth from Britain's volatile inner-city estates, such as Broadwater Farm, and provided them with subsidised transport from their areas to Welling, South London. All of this was to ensure the highest possible turn out on the march of these 'disenfranchised' masses. SDS field operatives ensconced in many influential positions in extreme organisations were able to provide the Branch with the rationale articulated by the leaders of these organisations regarding their group's attendance on the march. As suspected, although dressed up in anti-racist clothes, the reason for their organisation's effort was simple. It was to create as much havoc on the streets of South London as possible.

However, for many tens of thousands of sympathetic, law-abiding and well-intentioned, unsuspecting anti-racists members of the public such intent was an anathema. For many extreme activists, these genuinely concerned demonstrators were perceived as ballast from which those wishing to cause havoc could emerge and do damage before melting back into the masses. Critical SDS reporting leading up to the demonstration fully exposed such tactics, allowing the Branch to provide uniform police with the ability to substantially lessen the disorder caused by the demonstration, although major rioting would nevertheless occur. Once again, in this instance, SDS operatives were instrumental in saving millions of pounds in property damage and perhaps many lives.

The importance of SDS' intelligence on the run up to the Welling demonstration would be difficult to overstate. It allowed uniform colleagues to plan containment strategies to prevent a substantial number of demonstrators, perhaps in the many thousands, from breaking away from the main demonstration to burn down the BNP HQ and generally cause riotous havoc. The powers that be knew what could have happened had this intelligence not been available and so both the then Met Commissioner, Sir Paul Condon and the Conservative government's Home Secretary, Michael Howard, set aside time in their busy diaries to travel to an SDS safe house to thank the team for their efforts. Unfortunately, on the day, Mr Howard was unable to attend but Sir Paul personally delivered the Home Secretary's *"heartfelt and sincere thanks for the team's excellent efforts"*. It's a shame that Lord Condon's memory presently appears to have lapsed on this issue.

The murder of Stephen Lawrence and the police's subsequent failure to bring the perpetrators to justice mobilised many extremist groups to try and attract tens of thousands of potential activists who were brought into these extremist groups orbits via sham 'anti-racist' satellite organisations. For a while this resurrection and recruitment strategy was successful, allowing the extreme left to stage various high profile street demonstrations in London and beyond. Several of these anti-racist rallies degenerated into riots, as desired by these extremist groups. Fortunately, as with the Welling demonstration, SDS' infiltration of the subversive parent organisations of these 'anti-racist, groups, meant that many of these riots were short-lived and were quickly brought back under control thanks to large contingents of police reserves at strategic locations. These reserves were on hand due to the provision of sanitised SDS intelligence funnelled by 'C' Squad to senior uniformed police area commanders. These 'C' Squad area liaison reports, provided area commanders with an understanding of the organising group's militancy, the likely level of participation on the march/demonstration and the mood and intent of the key violent activists attending the demonstrations. An unintended and positive affect of these demonstrations and rallies not foreseen by the extremist leaders, was that tens of thousands of *real* well-meaning anti-racist citizens, schooled solely within the norms of parliamentary democracy, worked tirelessly for an end to racism within their communities. These citizens wished to build up society, not tear it down. It was a positive, yet for the extremists, an unintended outcome.

Most significantly, what I can categorically say, is that at no time did SDS operatives infiltrate the Lawrence family or its campaign. Nor did any section of the Branch, including the SDS or any other part of 'C'

Squad, seek to smear or indeed undermine the Lawrence Family in any other manner. This was simply not the Branch's MO and more importantly, SB officers would not have countenanced it. As regards the Lawrence Campaign, it should be noted that with the exception of Peter Francis, SDS operatives had already infiltrated the extreme left-wing organisations that would attempt to enter the Lawrence campaign years before Stephen's murder. Operatives were not tasked to spy on the Lawrence family campaign; but as mentioned about, they simply reacted to the murder within their undercover character and role within the extreme subversive organisations they inhabited. Therefore, in line with many campaigns that their radical organisations were 'entrying' they reported the efforts being made by 'their' extremist organisations to hijack and subvert the Lawrence campaign for their own political ends back to the Branch.

From its Home Office inspired inception onward the ultra-secret SDS was of great value to 'C', 'E' and 'B' Squad Desk officers, the Security Service, the Home Office, the Home Secretary and government in general; not to mention the Great British public at large. However, due to the immense mental, physical and all-consuming effort required by SDS operatives over an unending number of years, the major losers in this whole escapade were the SDS operatives themselves. Therefore, it is absolutely unacceptable that as Home Secretary, Prime Minister, Theresa May, implied that the SDS was a rogue and underhand organisation whose officers were somehow corrupt. This is a distasteful slur on an organisation that was formed at the behest of one of her predecessors and for over three decades was funded and assisted by her former organisation - The Home Office. Moreover, there is no evidence whatsoever to substantiate any charge of corruption against SDS operatives.

For those who happily saw SDS destroyed *(it was terminated shortly after MPSB was disbanded)*, I would ask them to consider this question: From whence do terrorists hail? Terrorists are generally forged through 'struggle'. Terrorists, and definitely the progenitors of terrorist groupings, start out as committed activists in some cause or another long before they migrate towards deadly political violence. Indeed, terrorism often raises its head when activists make the rather rational judgement that the quickest way to bring their cause to prominence, and potentially to fruition, is to use violent means.

The task of the police and the state's security apparatus is to assess when and if, there will be a transition from peaceful activism or aspirational extremism, into actual violent extremism and terrorism. Unfortunately, this is not an exact science and so MPSB *(particularly through the SDS)* monitored the evolutionary paths of extremist groups. Unfortunately, with the Branch now defunct and the SDS tactic now vilified and terminated, the state at some stage in the future may well pay the intolerable price of protracted communal violence for its short term political expediency.

One of the main elements of Britain's, and particularly London's, present day success is the MPS's ability to maintain the security and tranquillity that has made London a relative nirvana when measured against some of the world's other major cities. This stability has helped fuel the desire of the globe's super wealthy to live, invest and build prosperous service and creative industries in the capital and throughout the UK.

The degree of communal harmony that allowed Mayor Boris Johnson and present incumbent, Sadiq Khan, to continually laud London as the safest major city in the world has not been achieved by chance. It's something that the Branch, and in particular SDS, has played a major part in sustaining. The SDS-derived grade 'A' intelligence that Scotland Yard's Special Branch, along with other SB intelligence, used to assist territorial police colleagues to prevent mass public disorder, major racial violence, major criminal damage, subversion and terrorism in London and the UK for over 130 years is now no longer available to police. The major riots of 2011, where the police clearly lacked intelligence on the mood, intensity and levels of anger and frustration which community and extremist activists taped into; clearly left the MPS and other police forces hamstrung. Therefore, I contend, that we the citizens of the UK have already paid for the lack of MPSB and one of its key units, the SDS. Let's hope the price we pay for this lack of infiltrating and monitoring intelligence isn't even higher, in terms of a Paris style killing spree.

The Cold War was not so cold in many third world countries. It cost tens of millions of lives in Africa, Asia and Central & South America *(Afghanistan, Vietnam, Korea, Congo, Angola, El Salvador, Chile and Indonesia are but a few locations.)*. The first and Second world casualties of this undeclared conflict were far fewer, as the super powers tended to fight hot wars on the territories of poor countries. In *major* first world countries, the Cold War's *'damage'* generally took the form of extremism and terrorism, yet the greatest effect on citizens was to their freedoms rather than their lives. Britain was no exception to this, with the relatively benign MPSB being the most transparent aspect of political policing in the UK and its SDS being its secret cutting edge. The few who paid the price for the freedoms of the many, were often anti-state activists who intended, often with malice, to undermine, overthrow or destabilise the state. Clearly the state has a right, if not a duty, to defend itself against those who would wish to over throw it. That said, the Branch was only one cog in the British state's domestic national security apparatus, the Security Service *(MI5)* was an even more central component, as was the Home Office, the judiciary, the Press and of course the politicians, in particular cabinet level government ministers who sat at the centre of this machine and could therefore tweak it to their advantage.

It is the job of the Security Service to vet and assess senior politicians; the Branch assisted with this duty where and when required. When the Branch came across intelligence relating to politicians *(through its agents, desk officers or SDS operatives etc.)*, especially if it believed that the information could be utilised by Soviet bloc IOs or other states to blackmail or gain leverage against politicians to the advantage of these foreign powers, it would pass this intelligence to the Security Service. It was then up to the Security Service and others to decide what should then happen, unless it was 'purely' criminal, which would then be a matter for the police and criminal justice process. Of course, the needs of the nation's national security could obviously even mitigate how such offences were dealt with.

The Cold War was not an abstract concept, it was a conflict that cost the UK hundreds of billions of pounds to wage. The tools used were many and varied of which, on the home front, MPSB's SDS was just one. The present stuttering investigations into the *high-level* historical child sex abuse inquiry can be seen as a consequence of Cold War era national security norms, which unless reformed, could well hinder the enquiries progress. Finding a non-tainted establishment figure to chair the inquiry has already proved to be very difficult, not least because of the British establishment's extremely interwoven ruling *elite*. Just as importantly, the simplistic media analysis which eagerly grasps on to the theme of police corruption and wrongdoing belies the complexity of this issue. An example in case is the situation surrounding Cyril Smith MP (Member of Parliament). If thoroughly scrutinised, the tentacles of the Smith investigation will stretch to the office of the DPP *(Director of*

Public Prosecutions) of the day, as well as the AG's *(Attorney General)* office and potentially beyond. Over the years files and correspondence on this matter and its fallout will no doubt have been raised in the Cabinet Office, Home Office *(when it included the Department of Justice)* and the Security Service, as well as the MPS and other police forces. So to limit the investigation to the *police* will no doubt have the desired political effect of driving the culpability down to the least establishment body – thereby insulating the primary power brokers. However, the media has the capacity to prevent this, albeit their track record is not good when it comes to matters potentially appertaining to *national security*. The BBC and many historical Fleet Street outlets will no doubt have their own files relating to Smith et al. But perhaps as a result of that Cold War relic the 'D' notice programme, the open secret that was Cyril Smith et al, escaped national press exposure for more than five decades. The fact is that the Cold War's national security umbrella and the OSA were very potent tools, and still are!

As for me, by early 1998 having been posted or undertaken operational missions in practically every MPSB squad my knowledge and experience of this highly specialised work was vast. Throughout my time in the Branch I'd regularly worked in conjunction with the Security Service, many specialist police squads, specialist UK military forces, Her Majesty's Customs & Excise, Her Majesty's Immigration Service and a plethora of foreign security, intelligence, police and military services. However, I was now poised to step into an arena that was even unique for a highly experienced Special Branch officer – I was to become a senior member of Her Majesty's Secret Intelligence Service (MI6).

Chapter Fourteen - Becoming the Black Bond

The role of MI6, more formally known as: The Secret Intelligence Service (SIS), is to mount covert operations overseas in support of British Government objectives by obtaining and providing information and performing other tasks relating to the acts and intentions of persons overseas: in the interest of the UK's national security (in particular the government's defence and foreign policies); for the purposes of upholding the economic well-being of the UK and in support of the prevention or detection of serious crime.

When SIS officers are performing their authorised duties on behalf of Queen and Country, outside the British Isles, they have a license to commit acts that would be contrary to UK civil or criminal law not to mention the laws of the land in which they are operating. Thus SIS officers acting in such circumstances are exempt from prosecution by the British courts.

In 1997 MPSB was offered a unique secondment opportunity, a single Detective Inspector was to be selected to undertake the highly coveted and influential role of an SIS Case Officer in the Service's Counter Terrorism (CT) Section. After a series of tough interviews the head of SIS's CT section selected me. I would be the only police officer in the UK to be seconded to MI6 as a Case Officer. Case Officers are the top third of SIS' personnel and for a want of a better description it's sufficient to say that Case Officers perform the real-life James Bond role.

The day I entered that iconic office on the banks of the river Thames was truly unforgettable, a career highlight. When, years earlier, my FBI boss had steered me towards the Branch I thought I would struggle to make it into the police, let alone the Branch. And now I'd been given an opportunity that only one other UK police officer had ever had. I was both excited and terrified.

From its inception, life in the Branch had opened my gaze to the role of the Security Service with whom practically every MPSB officer worked very closely. As an MI6 Case Officer I'd have a different relationship with the Security Service, which allowed me to see a different side of MI5. In my SIS role, I came to admire the Security Service's analytical capacity and the guile and verve with which it maintained its relevance in the corridors of power. One of MI5's strengths was that its members mirrored the ruling elite, while the Branch was part of the police a body whose hierarchy was generally perceived subservient to its political masters. In spite of this, or perhaps, because of it, MPSB personnel were often far more dynamic than their Security Service colleagues who frequently appeared timid.

As a result, MI5's world-wide reputation was that of a 'competent' organisation but not necessarily a vibrant one. Moreover, the blot of the 1960s Soviet infiltration had never really faded.

SIS was very different. SIS' personnel were clearly as resourceful as those of the Branch and no less daring. Educationally, Case Officers to a man and woman had attended the very cream of Britain's educational establishments and had generally distinguished themselves throughout their curricula. Additionally, many SIS officers possessed great linguistic abilities and prodigious literary agility. In short, I was stepping over the threshold of an extremely capable organisation.

*

It was five to ten on a warm Monday morning when the unarmed SIS security guard in the hallway just inside the great entrance checked my warrant card and phoned upstairs to the CT section. Five minutes after receiving a return call from the section, the guard escorted me into the far left body pod some 25 metres from his desk. He used his pass to swipe the card entry system and beckoned me to enter the body pod.

Later that day, I'd have to be indoctrinated into the buildings' procedures and the Service in general. The indoctrination I required had nothing to do with my security clearance. As an MPSB officer I already had the highest clearance possible for over ten years. The indoctrination I required related to me gaining total access to all SIS' secrets as a matter of course, as and when I required. In the Secret World all agencies, including MPSB, have their own secrets. These are the secrets that one only gets access to when one is a member of the agency. Normally, as an MPSB officer, I'd only have gained access to SIS's secret intelligence on a need to know basis and after a specific request or as a result of SIS supplying the information to the Branch as one of its intelligence customers. It would now be different.

From the moment I entered Vauxhall Cross on that splendid Monday morning, what to my delight became clear, was that the Secret Intelligence Service didn't intend to differentiate between me and any other SIS Case Officer in any way whatsoever. Other than the fact that the MPS paid my salary, I was a fully-fledged member of the Service from day one. So much so, that most SIS officers were unaware of my non-SIS provenance.

The pod door closed behind me. There in front of me, through the all-glass pod I could see my new boss. My heart began to beat just that bit faster as the pod's mechanism opened the inner door and allowed me inside British intelligence's inner sanctum.

After my indoctrination I was sent on numerous bespoke espionage related courses including *(photography, communications, dead letter drops, anti and counter surveillance etc.)* at a number of intriguing establishments, before taking up the role of a fully-fledged

CT Case Officer based at the iconic Vauxhall Cross HQ on the river Thames. Because of my extensive Branch experience I didn't require the full training that a newly-selected Case Officer would receive, which generally lasted about six months. I was up and running within the month, although of course one never stops learning and I was sent on other courses throughout my deployment, as and when they came along.

Over the years of my service as an SIS Case Officer I'd undertake many agent recruitment and exploitation missions and lead and direct many highly sensitive counter terrorist operations against the UK's enemies in various parts of the world. In addition to case officers, the pinnacle of the service, other SIS roles included 'R' officers *('Requirements officers'- individuals who analysed secret intelligence, information and reports to provide customers, generally government bodies, with the sensitive information they require)*, administrative officers, analysts, linguists, technicians, locksmiths, computer experts, printers, forgers etc. etc., but more importantly the service could also access resources from many other agencies and organisations as well as the military at home and abroad. The access to resources was seemingly limitless. In SIS one could formulate a plan and, as long as it was deemed practical and sensible by the operational and legal assessors, then one generally had the power to acquire all the resources necessary from whichever quarter to make it happen. Although Case Officers were encouraged to express themselves and the Service was bold, brazen and accomplished, it was not foolhardy and operations always took safety into account. The role of the Case Officer is inherently dangerous, especially in the area of counter-terrorism. To mitigate this, Special Forces teams were on occasions built into operational plans to effectively protect Case Officers. I tended not to use them as when entering a country illegally *(using a false name and documents)* in order to execute an illegal purpose *(recruiting a national of that nation or from a third country)* I found it easier to slide under the radar as an individual rather than as a member of a group. Additionally, the military tends to build traits into its personnel that they involuntarily exhibit, a certain bearing, a sense of confidence, characteristics that are just as evident in Special Forces staff which can be picked up by foreign Special Branches and Security Services, as indeed they were by us.

Another important aspect of being an SIS officer is that your opinion is generally respected throughout Whitehall and in the corridors of power. In Britain the secret world is part and parcel of the establishment. The fact that MPSB was part of the police diminished the Branch's standing throughout the 90's and into the noughties. This was a result of the police having never discarded its blue-collar image, a death knell, in a time of style over substance.

I was a good fit in SIS but for one important exception. Everybody in SIS seemed to be a master scribe. From the day I joined the Branch it was made very clear that any report we composed could find its way to a Minister's desk. In SIS this was almost a given. Ministers were hungry for secret intelligence. As a dyslexic individual who graduated late in life, I spent an inordinate amount of time in drafting reports, writing late into the night to achieve this, whilst my Case Officer colleagues generally whizzed through them. So, once again the 'job' was detrimental to my family life. Of course Angela had been supportive of my move to SIS, and was obviously indoctrinated into the fold, but having previously been often away on Prot and then engaged in ultra-sensitive MPSB work which for numerous years required my almost constant absence from home, working in SIS was once again highly-demanding of my limited private life.

Intelligence agencies live or die by their capacity to recruit sources that can provide high grade secret intelligence. Thus recruiting *'agents'* - the secret sources of this intelligence which nations and organisations jealously guard - is a task given to a relatively few highly experienced officers. In SIS these officers were almost exclusively Case Officers. Agent recruitment is a deadly serious business. It can cost the officer his or her life as well as that of the agent. Moreover, failure will almost always have major political ramifications, causing diplomatic incidents, even the fall of governments.

I was not new to agent recruitment, a significant aspect of a Special Branch desk officer's role was just that. However, recruiting individuals in a foreign land far from home, directly contravening the laws of that land, is a different matter and not for the faint hearted. Recruiting agents is always dangerous. So much depends on trust. Yet trust can be highly perilous. When recruiting agents the stakes are very high.

Khost is just across the border from North Waziristan, the lawless Pakistani tribal area from where al-Qaeda and the Taliban routinely launch attacks on NATO positions in Afghanistan. It is home to Forward Operating Base Chapman, one of the most secretive and highly guarded locations in Afghanistan. In recent years it had evolved into a major counter-terrorism hub of the CIA's paramilitary Special Activities Division, used for joint operation with Special Forces and Afghan allies, and was a housing compound for American intelligence officers. It was where the CIA received intel about the location of al-Qaeda leaders and passed the coordinates on to the drone pilots.

On the late afternoon of 30 December 2009, one of the CIA's double agents, a Jordanian man, arrived at the base by car, having been driven from the Pakistani border. He was admitted through the multiple layers of security to meet with the CIA's station chief for the base, along with several other CIA officers and the agent's handler, Al Shareef Ali bin Zeid, from Jordan's General Intelligence Department *(GID)*, who also happened to be first cousin to King Abdullah II of Jordan.

The CIA had come to trust the agent, who had been vouched for by the Jordanian spy agency *(It's not abnormal for rich, first world, worldwide operating, primary intelligence agencies such as CIA and SIS to jointly handle agents belonging smaller countries intelligence and security agencies)*. The agent had already provided very useful intelligence over several weeks of *undercover* work in the region and he was seen as a key agency asset in the battle against high value al-Qaeda leadership targets.

On this occasion the agent was about to deliver intelligence relating to the location of al-Qaeda leader Ayman al-Zawahiri. The CIA considered that this would be one of the most important meetings with an agent since they'd been in Afghanistan. They'd even flown in a special debriefer from Kabul and were planning to call President Obama as soon as the meeting was over.

As the men and women gathered to meet the agent, he detonated a suicide body bomb, which had been hidden under his clothing, killing nine and seriously wounding six others. The station chief and the agent's Jordanian handler were amongst those lost.

The attack was the worst committed against the CIA for twenty-five years and it effectively shut the base.

On 9 January 2010, a Pakistani television network showed a video that had been released by the Tehrik-i-Taliban. It showed the agent – Humam Khalil Abu-Mulal al-Balawi – *(now lauded in Jihadi circles as the 'Khost shahid (martyr)'* vowing to avenge the death of a fellow terrorist and leader of the Pakistani Taliban, Baitullah Mehsud, prior to undertaking his self-sacrifice mission.

These CIA and GID officers had unfortunately died by their recruitment decision.

When recruiting agents, at some stage it is generally best practice to let them know who he/she is working for, especially if the agent is to be used for long term penetration. In such circumstances the recruiting officer needs to know if one can conceivably trust the person he/she is recruiting. In making such assessments officers must always attempt to establish why the person they are attempting to recruit is willing to betray their organisation, family, friends or country. It is important to know what the potential agent's motivation is. Is the motivation money, avarice, hatred, fear or do they just hope for a new life in UK? Sometimes, even though the actual grounds for his/her recruitment appears to be obvious, such as if the individual is being blackmailed, the true reason must nevertheless be unearthed. Knowing a person's motivation in the field of secret intelligence is more than academic as those who choose or agree to work as agents in the terrorist or drugs fields etc., are generally putting their lives on the line. Informing on such organisations is no joke, as if unearthed, death, and a painful one at that, is the most likely outcome. Moreover, death may not be confined to the agent alone, but be first extended to his or her loved ones. Afghanistan and Iraq are littered with the bodies of those who were only suspected of being agents for one Western intelligence service or another.

Therefore, knowing why somebody is willing to take on this risk is imperative, not least because the officer recruiting and running the agent will often have to meet the agent in some pretty inhospitable countries or areas around the world, where the officer will also be at risk.

Having this knowledge of the individual's motivation is also important as it aids the effective running and managing of an agent and allows for better assessment of an agent's needs and provides the ability to control his/her demeanour. An 'Agent Handler' *(in SIS the officer running the agent, generally the Case Officer who recruited him or her)* needs to be able to spot an agent's character changes, emotional spurs and any mood swings in the agent before they become life threatening; as such changes can create dangers for both agent and handler. If the officer catches these character changes early enough he/she can take action to steady the agent before he comes under suspicion from his extremist comrades, as a result of these nervous *ticks*. Registering these changes can also save a handler's life, as such changes in character could result from the agent having been compromised, and turned, in order to entrap the handler. This is why in the initial agent recruitment phase the recruiting officer needs to develop the very *essence* of his potential agent. To do this the recruiting officer must ask him or herself some discerning questions about their potential agent: is he/she a double agent, a dangle, a dangerous chancer, an 'undercover' security/intelligence officer or has he/she already been recruited by a friendly agency, such as the CIA, etc.? All of these circumstances could have far-reaching repercussions down the line, so it's imperative that the recruiting officer can fully answer such questions.

To combat the dangers of dangles, double agents, thrill-seeking Walter Mittys and those seeking money without access or knowledge; the CIA has always been extremely fastidious in vetting its agents. In an attempt to make sure that agent recruitment disasters do not befall the agency, the CIA generally polygraphs the sources its officers wish to recruit as agents. As for SIS, it too goes to great lengths to make sure that agents are who they say they are *(or who the SIS officer thinks they are)*. Thus, even though the gaining and exploitation of intelligence assets is the primary focus of every intelligence agency, in most intelligence organisations, SIS included, only relatively few officers are authorised to run agent recruitment operations as the damage that a malicious agent can wreak on an intelligence organisation is immense. Consequently, for a secret intelligence officer, agent recruitment can be the most dangerous and tricky task that one can undertake. I was one of those few officers in SIS authorised to perform this agent recruitment role.

Some months into my posting I was given the task of targeting and destroying an extremely vicious terrorist organisation that had cost the lives of many innocent people. To progress a particular aspect of this operation, I was on the verge of recruiting an agent with connections to another radical extremist group. This group had good links to the murderous organisation I was actually targeting. Therefore, I intended to use the potential agent to gain intelligence and later to access my target organisation via this radical group. In the secret intelligence profession this is known as the classic, *'back door/entry'* manoeuvre. This op was even further complicated as I had not yet informed my potential agent that I was from British Intelligence.

It was now decision time, should I impart my provenance to the potential agent or cast him back into the sea? I had manoeuvred my prey into an excellent position, background checks had confirmed his antecedence and his potential access. It all seemed to add up. Nevertheless, something - perhaps my copper's instinct - screamed caution. Up to this stage, in the months I'd been dealing with this character, I'd been working under natural cover *(an assumed identity and role)*. Consequently, 'Anton' had no idea of my true identity.

Throughout the months I had manoeuvred Anton into believing that I was some type of dodgy entrepreneur that he could milk for a few thousand dollars. Indeed, he already had. However, the more I talked to this guy the more I began to realise that he was no doubt already working for some other country's intelligence agency. This was not abnormal as the secret intelligence world is not particularly expansive and often we're all seeking the same goals and people to help us to achieve them, especially where terrorism's concerned.

During one of my many conversations with Anton he explained that he had a friend who had contacts in an American intelligence agency *(he didn't say which)* and that as a result he often got information that put him ahead of the other venture entrepreneurs. Anton mentioned that this friend had recently provided him with information that could put him ahead in Iraq *(this was two years before the Allied Invasion of Iraq and some six months before 9/11)*. Apparently, this friend *(Anton said he could get me access to him if we forged a close working relationship)* stated that the Americans had drawn up plans to cut Iraq into three, with the Kurds having their own state in the North. I had of course heard this well-trodden aspiration before and thus, still in knowledgeable entrepreneur role, I pooh-poohed the information adding that neither Iran, Turkey nor Syria, not to mention the Iraqi ruling elite, would countenance such a Kurdish state. Such a state could lead to Kurdish minorities in Iran, Turkey and Syria agitating to be part of this entity, or spur them on to greater endeavours to create their own such independent states. This would cause insurgency *(or in Turkey's case, greater insurgency)* within the borders of these neighbouring countries. Hence, it would be resisted at all costs by these states.

The persona I had adopted for this part of the operation was that of a shark who swam in murky waters and in lands that were on the cusp of law or disorder, failure or success. Such countries often offer the greatest potential profits coupled with the fewest restrictions. However, entrepreneurs in this game need to keep up to date with world geo-politics as, if not, there's the potential to lose more than one's shirt. As a rather unscrupulous fellow himself, Anton inhabited the same world and found nothing abnormal in such discussions.

As we continued discussing these geopolitical manoeuvres Anton, a larger than life fellow was in his element. Holding court was where he belonged and he loved it. So he continued. Conspiratorially:

"No, you're missing the point Louis. This will be after the war!"

"What war?" I said.

"The war in Iraq."

The hot sun in the country we were in beat down, as we sipped cocktails on the veranda of the five star hotel's bar packed with wealthy international and local movers and shakers. Anton ever the salesman studied my reaction, as he looked at me over his sunglasses pulled momentarily from his eyes, no doubt for effect. Surely this information must be worth paying for he must have computed. So now in full flow, Anton continued, pushing home his analysis.

"After this war Louis, Iraq will be occupied by the Americans and split into three. This partition will allow them to manage the country's resources more easily. Ideally, these three parts will be separate states, but if the countries you mention, Iran, Turkey and Syria, complain aggressively, Iraq will be maintained as a loose federation with the same goal having been achieved."

"What goal?" I enquired.

"Oil, Louis! Oil! Oil, run by US oil companies. Three separate countries will mean that each will have a weaker bargaining position and will need its oil revenues to support their independence. Even if this ideal of three independent states is not achieved a federated Iraq will suffice, as the federated parts will be so mistrusting of each other that they will still effectively seek independent oil deals. That's win-win for Uncle Sam. It's just a matter of time my friend, it's just a matter of time."

Agents are the lifeblood of any intelligence agency and as a security/intelligence/law enforcement body the Branch was no exception, consequently, as an SB desk officer, I'd amassed a great deal of agent recruitment and handling experience in the past. It would be this experience, and that gained in SIS, that I'd call on to finally make my decision regarding Anton.

In the end I didn't recruit Anton, he just didn't feel right. Nevertheless, I never doubted the veracity of his Iraq analysis nor his absolute conviction in it. My personal analysis for what it's worth was that Anton was probably half right. The war would not only be about oil, other world and regional geo-political forces would also be at play in the coming war and de facto partition of Iraq; a land I would come to know very well indeed.

Chapter Fifteen - From MI6 to Room 1834 via the NPOIU

Being a Case Officer in CT is one of the toughest roles in SIS. I was the longest serving CT Case Officer by far, most officers being rotated out after two years. The job took its toll. The hours were long, I was away a hell of a lot and I owed it to the family to have a regular hours job, at least for a short period of time. I could have resigned from the MPS and joined the SIS direct, but I'd have to take an overseas posting meaning I'd have to move the family with me or put the kids in boarding school, which frankly was not my scene. Moreover, I only needed to work another 14 or so years in the *job* to receive my pension, in SIS I'd have to work longer. No, the best option was to return to the MPS, after all I'd be going back to the Yard and anyway, I was a Branch man through and through.

A sign of this came after the 9/11 attacks. Once I – like everyone else – had recovered from the shock that such an operation had got through, I considered what this would mean for the Branch. As a case officer in Secret Intelligence Service I was now in an excellent position to observe, first-hand, what MI6 and the Security Service were immediately considering in terms of restructuring their organisations to meet the new challenges of the 9/11 attacks on the USA. I immediately put my mind to considering the Branch's future in this new world order. Here, I thought, was a chance for the Branch to grow and to help bolster the nation's security. In the days after 9/11 I drafted a paper recommending the formation of a national Special Branch *(NSB)* run from Scotland Yard. In my restructuring plan I decided to headquarter my proposed NSB at the Yard, primarily because the structures were already in place and the Yard is close to the UK political and economic power centres. Moreover, if initially NSB remained part of the Met it would ease the unit's implementation. My proposals for restructuring were as simple as they were extensive. The modifications foresaw NSB absorbing all personnel currently assigned to provincial Special Branches as well as their premises and their intelligence files. Provincial Chief Constables would therefore relinquish all control over these officers their premises and their intelligence collection processes. In return Chief Constables would be provided with fiscal compensation for their premises and timely and relevant SB assessments for their police areas, from an overarching national perspective, as required or requested. And finally my proposal recommended the absorption into NSB of the Met's Anti-Terrorist Branch *(SO13)*. In effect I was turning the clock back. NSB would reflect its 1883 SIB roots, fully able to deal with all aspects of political crime under its own auspices throughout the UK and close by British dependent territories. I was working on this paper in the margins of performing my SIS counter-terrorism duties at this hectic time. I worked on this paper night and day in any spare moment. Why? Quite simply, I knew the Branch had only one chance of survival, as the Security Service was using 9/11 to make a final push for total supremacy and leadership over all matters concerning the UK's domestic security.

On the eve of the 17th of September 2001 I provided my paper to the man in direct charge of the Branch - Commander MPSB - Roger Davidson. I knew the Commander well, he was a very capable man, but he made a fatal mistake that day! Roger tasked a Superintendent, who I also knew, with the role of assessing my recommendations and bringing them to fruition. As I left Roger's office that day, in my heart of hearts I knew the Branch was doomed. The Superintendent tasked was not a combative individual. He didn't have it in him to push my concept. The effort required to implement my paper would have been substantial.

MPSB remained the same, in terms of national control and structure. Yes the Branch grew in numbers in the coming years, but its national influence stagnated and waned as the Security Service worked to fill the gap. Senior MI5 officers wined and dined heads of provincial Special Branches who, as general duty officers, were already in awe of the Security Service's allure. The final coup de grace would come later from within the Met when effectively, in 2006, the SO13 'policing' ethos would take over the secret intelligence gathering philosophy of the Branch.

In 2001 though, MPSB still had an impressive structure, it was just not future proofed against a more nimble, politically Machiavellian and media savvy beast, the Security Service.

I had several options as to where to lay my hat upon my return to the Branch which came in early 2002, the main three being the Jihadi section of 'C' Squad, ELS on 'E' Squad, which had expanded to take in many more countries beyond the original Western European Union States, or the Prosecutions Section of 'C' Squad which dealt with Official secrets Acts offences and the arrest and prosecution of cases such as espionage. I was most probably set to head to 'C' Squad's Jihadi section when out of the blue I was asked by Roger, Commander MPSB, to join the National Public Order Intelligence Unit *(NPOIU)*. Strictly speaking the NPOIU was not MPSB, in some ways it was what I'd suggested to Roger on September the 17th a truly national Special Branch body – although the NPOIU's remit only pertained to Domestic Extremism. Hopefully though, I thought, it could be the beginning of my NSB idea. That's also how it was sold to me by Roger. So I bit the bullet.

I'd now been a DI for more than six years so my role in the NPOIU was to be the head of the Strategic Analysis Unit *(SAU)*, which meant I'd be a departmental head and one of the leaders of the whole organisation. This was an ideal position from which to drive the NPOIU forward towards my original NSB goal. Unfortunately, it wouldn't turn out like that.

In 2002 the NPOIU was a relatively new body. It was made up of officers from Special Branches from throughout the UK and dealt nationally with domestic extremism perpetrated by the far left, the far right, animal liberationist, anti-capitalist and extreme environmentalist. The strategic head of the unit was Roger as Commander MPSB but the tactical day-to-day lead was a DCI from Wiltshire Constabulary, the aim being that it would show the organisation's inclusive nature. However, to prevent it going astray due to lack of expertise, all of the departmental heads were MPSB Detective Inspectors. This would now include me. I'd soon learn that this set-up was flawed.

Firstly, although the DCI was a capable officer, being from Wiltshire Constabulary, a small force with a minuscule Special Branch, which was by no means a full time or career specialism in that force, meant that the DCI had never dealt with national police *politics,* senior security and intelligence agency officials or senior politicians at a national level. All of which in the NPOIU she'd have to do on a daily basis. Wiltshire Constabulary was just not a good training ground to gain such experience. But, secondly, and most importantly, the DCI saw herself as being sandwiched between MPSB officers. The result was that she tended to try to miss out the MPSB department heads to deal directly with the DS's under their command. Like the DCI most of the DS' were from provincial police forces so seemingly she thought they had a natural affinity with her. It was all very parochial and not at all what most MPSB officers were used to. Consequently, I'd begin to feel that it limited the organisation. Of course, when the role was put to me I didn't know this. When I was sold my role I was told that I'd have a great degree of independence from the main body of the NPOIU, dealing as I would with strategic level analysis and management.

My role in the NPOIU was to head up a new section known as the Strategic Analysis Unit. My first task in the SAU was to take over the NPOIU's weekly newsletter, which was constrained by its geopolitical outlook and style of production *(I would bring SIS methodology to it, in order to capture its readership.)* as my literary perseverance in SIS had to some degree paid off. However the main role of the SAU was to produce *'informative research papers'* for chief police officers. This limited role was too nebulous for me, so I went back to Roger with some new parameters for the proposed unit, agreeing them with him and the NPOIU DCI. Under this agreement the SAU would seek to expand its original goals and produce extremely in depth strategic papers outlining and analysing future threats and trends that might affect the UK's internal security, public order or domestic extremism within the following two to five years. To achieve this I proposed that, my DS, an extremely capable MPSB guy and I, would utilise both secret and open source material. I'd decide on the themes and the timeframe of the documents we wrote, although, on occasions when required by senior management, we'd produce less in-depth but urgently required analysis on fast moving critical issues. Additionally, it was my intention to broaden our readership to inform not only chief police officers but central and local government leading officials, the Intelligence and Security services, the Military and, on occasion, academia. I decided to include academia as the SAU would need to team up with leading academics in order to expand our analysis. I'd also use my SIS contacts to work with the cabinet office's focus groups and strategic analytical staff as well as the military's strategic school at Sandhurst. Consequently my team and I would produce documents at different security classification levels from Unclassified through to Top Secret depending on the recipient and of course the content.

The SAU became extremely successful with my team and I producing papers that touched on issues as diverse as:

The extreme right wing's future political, tactical and street level policies.

The Animal liberation movement's strategic and tactical targeting.

The potential for urban terrorism and the splintering of left wing factions into single issue protest groupings.

Religious extremism and self-sacrifice activity in the UK.

The potential for protest should the UK up-scale nuclear power production.

The consequences for social cohesion as a result of an increase in faith schooling.

Integration of the British South Asian community in the UK.

Many of the SAU's papers elicited interesting feedback from our readership, including No.10, which was interested in faith schooling and the Secretary of State for overseas Development and the Home Secretary regarding *'the consequences for the UK of the allies bombing of Afghanistan during Ramadan in 2002'*, among many other topics.

The SAU provided me with the opportunity to delve into the minds of some of our state's natural extremist enemies. I tried to get permission from the French penal authorities to speak with Carlos the Jackal, to gain his perspective on post-Communist urban terrorism. The Jackal was languishing in a French prison. I also tried to secure the authority to question and analyse the thoughts of various *'failed'* suicide bombers incarcerated in Israel, and finally I sought permission to speak with David Copeland *(the London nail bomber, sentenced to serve six life sentences in 2000)* regarding his descent into extreme right wing racist 'lone wolf' terrorist activity. Unfortunately all of these attempts failed – the French didn't want the Jackal questioned, the Israelis fluttered one way and then the other and although originally Copeland agreed, he changed his mind. As I thought Copeland's reticence might be due to my racial heritage *(Copeland was a self-professed white supremacist)*, I reassigned the paper to my DS, but he was also blown out.

After less than a year, due to the continued in-fighting within the NPOIU, my DS and would leave the SAU. Jealousy, wanton obstruction and the 'them-and-us' campaign would make it difficult for us to stay. Throughout it all, despite the problems, the SAU had been going great guns. We'd received many accolades from our senior and influential 'readers', yet both my DS and I wanted out. The atmosphere had become too toxic. So, after agreeing a post with the head of 'A' Squad, Sam Bait, and with the blessing of Commander SB, I readied myself for a return to protection. Although this time in a leadership role – I was sure I'd be able to make things happen!

Although a capable MPSB DI had replaced me in the SAU, she would soon claim that she couldn't work with the Wiltshire DCI and her coterie of provincial DS's. Therefore, within less than a year of my departure, the SAU would fall into terminal decline. In the end, the whole unfortunate episode would end in a *'discrimination at work'* grievance brought by the MPSB DI, who would allegedly garner some fifty corroborating statements to support her case. As for the Wiltshire DCI, she would be promoted back to her force as a Superintendent.

This sort of petty infighting baffled me. We were supposed to be protecting the public yet too often naked self-interest and style over substance continually blurred this duty.

*

I returned to MPSB proper to find the Special Branch I left vastly changed. The Met's personnel policies that had been put in place some seven years earlier had begun to kick in, and not for the better. Unfortunately, the Branch's history of secrecy and high intrigue had long left it vulnerable to jealousy and claims of elitism from senior Metropolitan Police colleagues as well as UK senior police officers in general. So, when in the 1990's the then MPS Commissioner, Sir Paul Condon changed how specialist officers were recruited, retained and promoted in the Metropolitan Police, the Branch's pleas to retain its tried and tested system of recruitment and promotion fell on deaf ears.

Traditionally, MPSB's selection process had always been academically rigorous with a tendency to favour grammar and public-school educated officers with university degrees and a bent for politics and foreign languages over alternatively skilled officers. This, in tandem with the high degree of secrecy gave the Branch the unwelcome reputation of being discriminatory and snobbish. The reality was different however, although the Branch's selection process was demanding, extremely competitive and focused on politics, applicants from any background with the right interests, ability and skillset could pass the selection process. I was a prime example of this. In my opinion, the Branch's rigorous selection process was an excellent mechanism for unearthing those officers with the right talent and temperament to deal with the myriad of sensitive and complex roles MPSB undertook on behalf of government and the police service.

Training a rounded MPSB officer was a very expensive and time consuming procedure, so the highly selective recruitment process with its attrition rate as high as nine out of ten candidates, was designed to weed out those who might not easily take to this challenging post selection instruction and development model. Unfortunately some non-SB officers would see this high attrition rate as proof positive of the

Branch's elitist tendencies. In the opinion of these Branch detractors Sir Paul's new personnel policy would finally address the Branch's talent grab, by making such high-calibre officers available to all parts of the MPS, in particular uniform community based policing.

It's not too theatrical to say that Sir Paul's personnel policy, known as the 'Tenure Policy', destroyed the Metropolitan Police Special Branch and many other specialist policing arms of the Met. The Tenure Policy universally prescribed a maximum number of years an officer could serve in a particular specialism regardless of his or her continued competence, thus Tenure was no respecter of excellence or experience. Conversely, MPSB valued experience and longevity, actively seeking to retain its hard won recruits in the Branch, throughout their careers, once they'd achieved initial selection. Additionally, because initial recruitment to MPSB was solely possible at the base rank of Constable, all Branch supervisors had a deep and expansive understanding of the Branch's role, jurisdiction and ethos from the ground up. However, upon the introduction of Sir Paul's Tenure policy, the Branch ethos of longevity and experience was obliterated overnight. Suddenly, every SB officer with more than nine years in the Branch, but less than 22 years police service, was shortlisted to move from the highly specialised Branch duties to uniform general duty policing. Moreover, any exceptions to this policy were based on extremely strict criteria that took little account of extenuating circumstances. It was an extremely rigidly enforced policy.

Due to my unique Case Officer role in SIS and the fact that I had previously undertaken extremely sensitive work in the Branch, I was exempted from Tenure. That said I took little comfort from this, as the Tenure Policy affected the organisation I'd given most of my adult life to in a plethora of negative ways. Primarily, Tenure ensured that numerous SB officers of various ranks left the Branch in quick succession generating an irreplaceable exodus of experience and talent. Secondly, to fill the void left by Tenured supervisory officers, supervisors with no previous SB experience were recruited directly into the Branch creating a critical supervisory knowledge gap. Thirdly, because historically the attrition rates of the MPSB examination and selection process were as high as nine out of ten applicants, the Branch was forced to simplify the selection process in order to recruit the large number of officers now required to fill the vacancies created by Tenure. Worse still, senior MPS management directed the Branch to make its recruitment examination and selection processes more 'police friendly' by severely limiting the political, historical and geographical content of the Branch exam and expanding the general police elements. Some few years later, 'in the interest of fairness', the Branch was directed to abandon its examination process altogether.

The effects on the Branch's professional capacity of all these changes were incalculable. Previously, in addition to the general Special Branch induction course, SB recruits were guided through their initial period in the Branch by seasoned officers and supervisors who provided them with detailed and sensitive intelligence transfers of practises, procedures and covert techniques often on a one-to-one basis. This mentoring process was a relatively simple procedure due to the small number of recruits joining the Branch each year. After Tenure however, this detailed and collegial method of training was no longer available to recruits as to fill the gap left by the Tenure Policy some fifty-plus recruits were required yearly. Worse still, because the Tenure Policy had decimated supervisory level Branch officers, too few experienced officers were available to train these new recruits. Tenure had created an unholy mess.

What in time would become most damaging of all though, was that an unsophisticated and universal uniform-centric corporate community policing model was foisted onto the Branch, and the Met as a whole. This 'community policing model' took no account of the complexities and breadth of modern day law enforcement in all its facets. In time this naive corporate approach, as it pertained to the Branch, would directly impact on the nation's security and in my belief, it would manifest itself directly in the 7/7 bombings and the riots of 2011.

The uncertainty caused by Tenure and other changes in the police service allowed the Branch's competitors to manipulate the situation for their own ends. Accordingly, the Director General of the Security Service *(MI5)* between 1992 and 1996, Dame Stella Rimington, launched a campaign in Whitehall to wrest primacy for exploiting Irish Republican terrorist intelligence in Great Britain from MPSB to MI5 in an effort to secure her service's continued existence in the wake of the fall of Communism. In the ensuing one-sided battle, Mrs Rimington remorselessly utilised the Service's high-level contacts in Whitehall, the media and friendly police services to good effect. The Branch was totally out-manoeuvred, having put its faith in the belief that those that mattered in Whitehall would be aware of its effectiveness. When the government of the day agreed that the Security Service should take over primacy for combatting Irish republican terrorism *(primarily the IRA)*, the Branch was devastated. Sometime later, due to a problem with the Security Service's relatively poor handling of this lead role, MPSB regained a measure of 'joint' responsibility for the issue. However, this would only ever be a *joint* responsibility in name only, with the *real* power still vested in Security Service. To the Branch the loss of primacy was palpable and with its historical raison d'être wrested from it; its cultural assets ebbed slowly and irrevocably away.

When Sir Paul's term as Commissioner ended and Sir John Stevens took over the reins at the Met, a ray of hope emerged as conscious of the damage reaped by Tenure on specialist operations, Sir John attempted to re-establish the Yard's crippled specialist policing and intelligence capacity by immediately banishing the Tenure policy. Unfortunately for the Branch, Sir John's reign as Commissioner proved to be no more than a cruel stay of execution as, upon the accession of his successor, Sir Ian Blair to the post of Commissioner of the Metropolis, the whole of the MPS once again reverted to a uniform-centric, community-policing model. Thus, on 3 October 2006, at the stroke of Commissioner Ian Blair's pen, the Metropolitan Police Special Branch was disbanded and confined to annals of history! Through the years leading to its final demise in the 2006 the Branch - despite its problems - still had a well-structured organisational core of squads and units in which all Branch officers could serve dependent on the exigencies of the counter-extremist landscape and an officer's individual skill set. So, as I took control of 'A' Squad's Room 1834 in late 2002, I was determined to put my skills and those of the squad's officers to maximum use.

*

My many duties in Room 1834 included the line management of 'A' Squad's administration, resources and deployments. This often entailed leading operations and juggling personnel to staff protection teams for visiting foreign dignitaries by utilising officers normally assigned to the permanent teams protecting senior UK politicians, or those protecting UK based foreign Ambassadors. I also used this robbing-Peter-to-pay-Paul technique when attempting to staff overseas deployments for British Ministers who did not receive protection in the UK but were travelling to countries that the RMV considered so dangerous that 'A' Squad personal protection was authorised. In moving these officers around, fatigue management was always my greatest concern as we were woefully understaffed. Although I continually asked, I could never get enough officers to do the job. It was ever thus. Consequently, like my predecessors I often attempted to negotiate the use of protection trained officers assigned to other SB squads, especially 'E' Squad, when staffing teams for visiting foreign dignitaries. Unfortunately, the other squads often had their own staffing problems.

As supremo of 1834 I also managed 'A' Squad's fleet of prestige vehicles. This included a range of armoured vehicles from a Bentley to Jaguars, Range Rovers and BMWs as well as a variety of soft-skinned *(non-armoured)* executive vehicles. I also had control over the allocation of the specialist protection drivers to chauffeur these vehicles. As soon as I entered Room 1834, I did everything I could to remove Government Car Service *(GCS)* drivers and to replace them with the Branch's own specialist protection drivers. This stemmed from my problems with Tom King and ambiguity as to who had ultimate authority over the driver. Fighting vested interest is never easy. Add job security, tradition and money to the mix and it becomes almost impossible, but after many protracted battles my concept would finally win out, and we'd replace GCS chauffeurs with specialist protection drivers.

I was also responsible for the Branch's armoury. In 2002/3 the Branch housed various firearms mainly for 'A' and 'S' Squad use. 'A' Squad were by far the primary utilizers of firearms in the Branch deploying Glock 17 semi-automatic pistols, Heckler & Koch MP5A3 submachine guns and MP5K *(Kurz = short)* submachine pistols. These weapons were more than sufficient for the role 'A' Squad had traditionally performed in the UK and abroad with its full-time principals such as the Prime Minister and the Foreign Secretary. These principals generally travelled to well-heeled locations in the first world or equally upmarket hotels and other locations in second and third world capitals. In these environments the ability to carry concealed weapons was paramount, hence the Glock pistol was perfect. If more firepower was needed officers could consider deploying either variant of the MP5, with the Kurz being the easiest to conceal and therefore tailor made for protection operations. If semi-overt carriage was acceptable, then the MP5A3 carbine provided an accurate support weapon at slightly longer distances. With its larger ammunition reservoir, this weapon was suited to urban conditions especially with the 9mm soft-tipped round generally utilised by MPS.

In addition to administration, firearms, vehicles and human resources, I founded and commanded an armed covert counter-reconnaissance unit (CCRU). Everything I'd learned in the Branch and SIS made it clear to me that such a unit was necessary and so I designed, implemented and deployed the CCRU - a unique unit. The CCRU was a clandestine outer protective security shield that could, with a moment's notice, be bolted on to and complement any traditional overt protection team. Experience had taught me that the best way to proactively catch a Lone-Wolf assassin and hence any assassination team, was during the assassin's reconnaissance stage or when he/she was lying in wait to spring the trap on the day. The CCRU took the fight to the enemy and sought out assassins in their preparatory or entrapment phases. My concept transformed personal protection in the UK but few senior officers in MPS embraced the change. In fact, the resistance to the creation of the CCRU was so ferocious that it made the opposition posed by the Security Service to my SIS ports agent recruitment concept, look utterly genteel in comparison. By early 2003 I was still in the throes of bedding my CCRU concept in against this fierce resistance of the die-hard traditionalists and some jealous senior officers who hindered my unit's every step. These were powerful enemies. One of the MPS's senior uniformed public order gurus, a Superintendent in CO11, even threatened my career. "I'll do your fucking legs," he promised. Other senior officers, who believed I was stretching the personal protection remit beyond the immediate overt protection bubble into the domain of uniform policing, also swore they would cut me down to size. I knew that I'd never be promoted again. Sometimes I wonder what it is about the status quo that so shackles individuals that they can't conceive change. Yes, I was opposed to ill-considered change such as that wrought on the Branch by the Tenure Policy. But I was all for measured thought out change, the kind of change designed to improve capacity and meet new challenges – such as pre-empting self-sacrifice assassination operations by creating a CCRU. However, the most damning aspect of the resistance to my CCRU concept was that many of its detractors seemingly acted out of a sense of jealousy and anger. The main reason for this anger was in part due to the British policing's *bête noire* - guns. I had designed my CCRU as an armed protection orientated unit. In my opinion if the CCRU wasn't armed, it wouldn't be capable of doing the job I'd designed it to. Assassins carry weapons and the only way to defend against a weapon is with a weapon, albeit that in the first instance CCRU operatives were to remain covert and call other officers in to deal with any assassin. But professionals are always equipped to deal with the obvious *(which is why every dentist has access to pliers although they rarely pull teeth)*, a principal that was just as true for the CCRU and firearms, in case they were required to act instantaneously. Had I created the CCRU in 1992 instead of 2002 I would not have been challenged for arming the unit with handguns. At that time the Branch still enjoyed a level of autonomy that allowed it to control its own destiny. But, the intervening years had not been kind, so although the Branch had grown in number, it had lost a great deal of influence. The senior corporate men and women placed within the Branch's structure had busied themselves by scuppering its independence. I explained my concept to all who'd listen and had a need-to-know, that I was not trying to gain status or personal advancement; but simply attempting to save lives. Since re-joining 'A' Squad in late 2002 I had analysed assassinations and attempted assassinations worldwide. All my research had taught me that if protection officers waited until the enemy chose to attack them, prior to adopting any counter-measures, then the Principal and often his protection officers would almost certainly die. During my Branch career I had often monitored and analysed Middle Eastern and religiously inspired extremism, so combined with my international counter-terrorism experience in SIS, I became convinced that it was just a matter of time before a *self-sacrifice* attack would hit the UK. Moreover, I considered it likely that such an attack might be tied to an attack on a protected principal, thereby generating the high degree of publicity that many Jihadi attackers seek. By virtue of their role, protection officers are highly visible and hence vulnerable to attack. Furthermore, as close protection officers generally have a limited arc of observation, attacks are seen at a very late stage and any reaction is generally designed to limit the attacks effects. So if the assassin has managed to shoot, as John Hinckley did when US President Ronald Reagan left a Washington Hotel in 1981, the prot team's actions were focused on stopping the attack and immediately rushing the President to a place of safety and medical aid. At the time, Reagan and the ruler of the Soviet Union, Leonid Brezhnev, were poised to decide the fate of the world - having agreed to 'discussions about negotiations' with regard to Russia's ever-expanding nuclear weapons programme. Hinckley had fired all six shots from his revolver in 1.8 seconds with neither Secret Service nor

Washington Capital police returning fire. President Reagan suffered life-threatening injuries. Had President Reagan died, the course of history could have changed, as the talks with the Soviet Union could have been put on hold, and Vice President George H W Bush did not support negotiations with the Soviets. My CCRU who would loosely encase the overt team, yet not be readily identifiable as protection assets, were a great tool for dealing with these and other Prot-orientated limitations. Firstly, would-be assassins, self-sacrifice bombers or extreme protesters would not know where the covert operatives where, so it would be much more difficult for them to judge the best moment to attack a principal. Secondly, the CCRU would generally pick up on would-be assassins or extreme protesters attempting 'dry runs' prior to any attack and thirdly, CCRU's operatives would be in a position to seek out multiple and ever changing sight lines upon deployment much expanding on the traditional overt protection team's field of vision. This is something that Protmen, tied to their principal, cannot easily do. Moreover, CCRU operatives are free to monitor suspects and, if they deem it necessary, they can tactfully and quietly vector overt police units to the suspected target(s) whilst continually updating the overt protection team with intelligence and options for evasive action. And finally, because the CCRU could be bolted on to any existing overt protection team, I structured it in such a manner that the tactical option of neutralising a threat by themselves would only be undertake as a last resort. In short, covert and unseen, the men and women of the CCRU were everywhere and nowhere. Because the CCRU's tactics were revolutionary, in creating the team I had already drawn up new training, tactics and equipment requirements. Hence, CCRU training would be extensive, including exercises on how to infiltrate crowds and enclosed premises, the use of subterfuge, the delivery of advanced first-aid techniques, protection related firearms, Chemical, Biological, Radioactive and Nuclear countermeasures *(CBRN)* and non-lethal defensive weapons training. Further, I'd also provide team members with secret personal encrypted communications equipment, technical back-up systems, covert reconnaissance and surveillance technical training, technical training for covert reporting, covert containment of suspects, covert handover to overt police units and procedures for split second transference from covert to overt protection methods. I had been able to sell my concept to 'A' Squad's top man DCS Sam Bait, who, as a forward thinking guy was open to radical change. What Sam didn't have though, was a willingness to fight for a difficult cause. Even more importantly, I'd been able to convince an extremely senior officer of my concept's merits - David Veness - the Met's Assistant Commissioner for Specialist Operations *(ACSO)*, known to the media as Britain's top counter-terrorists cop. For many entrenched officers my concept was too much to countenance but David Veness was different, he gave it his whole-hearted support, going as far as to ask me to present my concept to a high-level US counter-terrorism fact finding body. Unlike Veness, many other top-tier officers were promoted via flawed managerial *'competency'* framework processes valuing style over substance, as opposed to leadership, ability and professional knowhow. Hence, many senior officers seemed to lack gusto, an understanding of what motivated their more junior colleagues and a lack of actual vocational competence. These senior men and women tended towards 'managing' their officers as opposed to leading them, this meant that the safe option - the one that offered the least potential for career-damaging blowback - was often promoted as the optimum course. Luckily, with ACSO Veness this was not the case and I was given the authority to implement my concept nationally through the committee he chaired as the head of the Association of Chief Police Officers' Terrorist and Allied Matters Committee *(ACPO - TAM)*.

Although I received TAM's blessing, meaning I could deploy my unit anywhere in the UK, the attacks on my concept by these career-minded enemies did not end. Throughout the months and years that followed my CCRU concept's potency was continually diluted with obstacles being placed in its way wherever, and whenever, the detractors could. However, in spring 2003 I had won a major battle; the team was up and running and quickly proved itself with at least two major successes. In mid-2003 I deployed my CCRU on its first operation, the State Visit of President Vladimir Putin of Russia. During the visit my team gained information that a person purporting to be an FSB officer *(The Russian Federal Security Service - successor to the KGB)* was asking questions about the President's agenda at various locations. I spoke to the FSB chief in the Russian embassy and established that the individual was bogus. My CCRU was then able to find, surveil and disrupt the bogus individual before he could trouble or harm the President during his visit. Later in 2003 at the second major outing on the world stage for my CCRU during the State Visit of US President George W Bush Jr. to the UK. The CCRU was able to covertly surveil suspicious individuals and infiltrate activist demonstrators both in London and in Sedgefield *(the then Prime Minister Tony Blair's constituency)*. The intelligence gained was covertly communicated to 'A' Squad protection teams, US Secret Service colleagues and to uniformed public order commanders. Thus the CCRU was able to prevent several public-order related plots that would have embarrassed HMG had they been put into action against the President. These successes, which came so quickly after CCRU's implementation validated the new unit but my powerful new enemies would not let me be and although I'd won the battle, I knew I might still lose the war.

Chapter Sixteen - Royal Flush

'A' Squad's remit extended to individuals who were not politicians or diplomats but, á la Salman Rushdie, were at extreme risk of being murdered on political grounds. Hence, all 'government' sponsored personal protection operations in the UK, excluding those relating to the British Royal family, came through my office.

The actual reason why the Branch did not protect the Royal family may never be established beyond doubt. However, as with many irregularities in UK public life, competing folklore concerning the establishment of this anomaly have developed over time. For example, in the late 1880's, Queen Victoria, who had been the subject of several assassination attempts, overheard one of her protection officers speaking in a broad Irish brogue. The Queen asked from whence this officer hailed and was informed that he was an Irishman from Scotland Yard's Special Branch. Upon hearing this, the Queen is said to have stated that she would not be protected by secessionists. Hence, from that moment on, the Branch is said to have lost the role of protecting the Royal family. An equally plausible motive for the formation of Royalty Protection *(RP)* was said to be the Queen's dislike of the Branch's political remit. According to this version of events, upon finding out that the officers protecting her were from the recently formed Special Branch, the Queen, perhaps conscious of the antics of her son, is said to have remarked that she would not be protected by the 'secret police'. I imagine that the actual reason for the formation of Royalty Protection is lost in the throes of time.

In the summer of 1988 I was undertaking the single-officer protection of the Governor General of Canada (GGC) Jeanne Mathilde Sauvé. Scheduled to visit the theatre one evening I contacted the Yard to de-conflict with any other potential protection teams who might also be visiting the theatre that evening. I was informed that HRH the Queen Mother and The Princess of Wales would also be attending the performance. A great royalist, once the GGC heard this, she asked me if she could be introduced to HRHQM. So during the interlude I spoke with Royalty Protection colleagues and walking to their box, I presented the GG to HRH the Queen Mother and Princess of Wales. The GGC curtsied to HRHQM and turning slightly to Princess Diana, who was standing slightly behind and to one side of HRHQM, she bobbed politely. As she rose, HRHQM passed a genteel hand to the GG and smiled, Princess Diana smiled likewise. Knowing my role, HRHQM did not acknowledge me. Polite conversation ensued for a few minutes until HRHQM graciously thanked the GG for her time. With a slight bow of my head, I respectfully acknowledged the HRHQM then smiled at the Princess of Wales. It was then, seemingly breaking with royal protocol that the Princess reached over to shake my hand. I happily complied. From the look on the face of one of the RP guys I'd clearly broken some royal code of conduct. Courtly protocol and deference not being my strong point, I'd in no way reproach myself.

Some months later I was in the back of a protection vehicle on Park Lane. We'd just placed a foreign dignitary on a flight back to his homeland from Heathrow and were returning to the Yard. Although protection vehicles are totally unmarked, the black dot matrix police signs of that era, which sat in our armoured Jag's rear windscreen, could be illuminated by the sun's rays reflecting on it. When switched on the sign offered various options *'police security slow', 'keep back police security keep back'* etc....

I happened to be leaning forward talking to the team leader *(TL)*, a DS in the front passenger seat, when I noticed a car horn beeping. As usual the traffic on this section of the road by the

Dorchester Hotel was extremely slow moving so I was able to orientate the location of the beeping quite easily.

"You need to look, someone's trying to get your attention." The DS pointed out,

"Look there, the vehicle in the near lane."

We were in the outside lane so I looked to my left again.

"What have you been doing?" he exclaimed.

I spotted an attractive woman leaning over her driver, pressing the vehicle's horn. I turned to get a better look, first recognising the driver as a Royalty protection officer sporting a very pained expression. He was driving an up-market open-topped sports vehicle. The woman was the Princess of Wales and she was trying to attract my attention. Now having achieved this, she smiled and waved to me. I smiled and waved back. Then, close to the fork, the traffic freed up a touch, providing the Royalty officer with his opportunity to whizz Princess Diana off down Park Lane toward the roundabout onto the Mall. Charles, my DS, was keen to know what on earth I'd done to merit the most photographed woman in the world seeking to gain my attention?

Special Branch were responsible for protecting foreign royalty if they were politically active, consequently in the late 80's I was the DC tasked with single-officer protection of HRH Queen Aishwarya of Nepal, during her visit to the UK. The Queen was an attractive, sensitive and dutiful woman who appeared to be missing her children. Shortly after her arrival and settling in at the Ritz hotel, her PPS asked me if the Queen could go shopping for children's toys at Hamley's in Piccadilly. It was late but I was able to get in touch with a manager who said he had just closed the store. I asked him if he'd reopen the store for a VVIP. He happily agreed. So when we arrived the manager and two or three of his staff were waiting for us. As Queen Aishwarya, the manager, a member of his staff and I walked up and down the aisles, the Queen's PPS and two of her Nepalese protection officers followed behind, shopping trolleys at the ready as she pointed out the toys she wished to buy. We returned a satisfied Queen safely to the Ritz, where I'd stay in the room next to her throughout her visit. After breakfast the next morning, the Queen informed me that she wished to travel to the country estate of a member of the British aristocracy to meet her eldest son HRH Crown Prince Dipendra Bir Bikram Shah Dev, who was at Eton with the aristocrat's son. When we arrived the boys were out on the estate, so I borrowed a jeep-type vehicle with two seats from the estate and began to drive the Queen across the grounds. She loved it. I asked her if she'd like to drive, she looked sheepish at first as though it was against royal protocol but relented and said she would. As we changed seats, her Nepalese head of protection, holding on the back of the vehicle for dear life, seemed more than a bit ruffled. Bumping up and down on the uneven terrain, the Queen's eyes shone with glee. She was delighted with herself. At the silent, yet deafening behest of the Nepalese Prot team leader, I told the Queen that I'd take the wheel again and drove back over the rolling fields back to the large stately home. Upon arrival at the main entrance I could see the Crown Prince, his school chum, the PPS, the rest of the Nepalese Prot team and my Nepalese embassy driver waiting for us. The Queen visibly stiffened her countenance as the Crown Prince, not best pleased, glared in our direction. Her fun was well and truly over.

Thirteen years later, on June 1 2001, the very same Crown Prince used an automatic weapon to massacre nine members of the Royal family, including the King and HRH Queen Aishwarya of Nepal, during a regular family gathering at the Royal Palace in Katmandu. The Crown Prince then turned the weapon on himself.

One afternoon in late January of 2004 I was called to David Veness' office. As Assistant Commissioner for Specialist Operations David Veness was the head of all Scotland Yard's specialist operations units including Special Branch, Royalty Protection, SO13 and the Yard's flying squad to name but a few.

Having received the call I immediately made my way from 1834 to the Yard's Victoria block and down onto the fifth floor. ACSO's formidable secretary allowed me entry to the outer office before directing me to enter the Assistant Commissioner's inner sanctum. I'd had quite a lot of contact with ACSO Veness due to my time in SIS, NPOIU, my forming and leadership of high threat operations team in Afghanistan and Iraq, plus I'd also been commended by him for my long term top secret highly sensitive work within Special Branch and as a result of my creation and implementation of the CCRU, so I knew what to expect when I entered his large office. Gingerly making my way through the mass of files stored on the floor, his desk and every other available surface, I shook the assistant Commissioner's hand. As I did, I recalled the time when returning from ACSO's office, my senior boss at SIS, a Controller *(one of the top four officers in SIS and equivalent to an Assistant Commissioner)* asked if I would apologise to 'David' on his behalf for bungling into his office whilst he was obviously preparing to move accommodation. Smiling, I explained to the Controller that ACSO wasn't moving, it was just how he functioned. ACSO's office reflected a man with a massive portfolio who was on top his game and knew his brief in depth.

Gesturing for me to take one of the few seats free from files and various correspondence, he got straight to it. Prince Charles intended to visit Saudi Arabia at the request of Crown Prince Mutaib bin Abdulaziz Al Saud. As it was HRH's intention to be in Saudi for quite some time, painting in the dessert, the Assistant Commissioner was quite worried.

At the time JTAC's *(the Joint Terrorism Analysis Centre)* terrorist threat assessment for Saudi Arabia was such, that the F&CO recommended only essential travel to the country. If he went, HRH would be highly vulnerable to attack from Jihadi forces. Unlike 'A' Squad, Royalty Protection officers did not have an intelligence background. Therefore, because ACSO felt there was a need for an intelligence officer to interface with SIS and the Saudi intelligence and security services to make sure that RP were kept up to date with the latest security intelligence picture, he asked me to travel to Saudi to act as the intelligence coordinator for what would be a large multi-layered operation.

I left for Saudi the following day and was soon at the centre of a large protection operation covering practically all aspects of the visit. The joint activity between the Saudi police, military, security and intelligence agencies, as well as the visiting UK protective security apparatus, worked well. The Prince was kept safe and UK interests were advanced.

At the conclusion of the visit, Crown Prince Mutaib offered HRH the Prince of Wales the use of his luxury 747 airliner to travel back to the UK. This was an offer that Prince Charles was keen to accept. When this request was passed to me, I told the RP commander to try and stall the HRH whilst I checked a few things out. I quickly checked with various sources and established that the Saudi Royal's aircraft was not as well equipped in terms of defensive aids as the state-of-the-art Royal Air Force's Queen's flight aircraft was, that was scheduled to fly HRH back to the UK. I soon confirmed that I could not recommend that HRH travel out of Saudi Arabia on the Crown Prince's aircraft. I told the RP prot commander that I was willing to inform HRH in person of my decision. The prot commander declined and imparted my decision to

HRH himself. My decision was accepted and HRH declined the Saudi Royal's invitation.

At the conclusion of the operation, instead of taking a business-class flight back to the UK, I decided to save the job some money by trying to bump a lift on the Queen's Flight that HRH would be taking back home. I asked the RP Commander if there was room on the aircraft for me. I knew numbers were always tight on the Queen's Flight as the biggest was only the size of a large private jet. I'd travelled on these aircraft several times before on missions with various Secretaries of State and knew space was always an issue. There was enough space, I was told, so I gratefully climbed aboard and we took off from Riyadh without incident en route to the British sovereign base in Cyprus where we'd refuel *(this aircraft couldn't travel back to the UK in one leap)*. Prior to landing in Cyprus HRH's equerry ventured from the royal accommodation back to the general cabin, which is still quite plush, and informed me that HRH would like to meet me upon landing.

When we landed I exited the aircraft to see the HRH waiting on the tarmac. Seeing me, the equerry hurried over.

"His Royal Highness is waiting for you." He stressed.

Following the equerry as he scurried towards HRH I wondered how I should address him. Moments later I'd take my lead from the equerry.

"Your Royal Highness this is Detective Inspector Carlton King."

I wanted to shake hands as is my bent, a trait honed by my time in Germany all those years ago. But I noticed HRH kept the fingers of both hands in the pockets of his overcoat, a much mimicked trait, which I now knew from personal experience, was clearly his own peculiar mannerism.

"Detective Inspector King!"

"Your Highness."

"So, you are the intelligence man who forbade me to travel back on my good friend Crown Prince Mutaib's aircraft."

"Yes, I am Your Highness"

"I see. On what grounds?"

I explained that I was a Scotland Yard Special Branch officer, that I'd first read the JTAC collective report on Saudi Arabia and indeed the specific report concerning this proposed visit in our 'E' Squad office before travelling out here. I mentioned that I'd travelled out some several days prior to his arrival in Riyadh. I also told him that I'd made contact with colleagues in our embassy, Saudi officials, police, military and UKSF and that I'd passed, where necessary, sanitised intelligence to his protection commander in order to make sure that his visit occurred without incident.

"Yes, and I thank you for that. But about the aircraft?"

That was quite simple, I explained. I'd used my risk, threat and vulnerability matrix to consider this option. I then spent some time sharing the negative intelligence picture with HRH and outlining my concerns. It was not an exact science, intelligence never is, I told him, but I would have hated to lose him on the way back from a successful operation because I'd let my guard down at the conclusion of the mission. It was simply a matter that I knew our enemies' capabilities and the RAF's capacity to counter those capabilities, which the Crown Prince's aircraft did not possess. I smiled and then added: "Although, I now have a feeling, that in the not too distant future, it will also possess these counter-measures."

HRH listened intently throughout. For a second I detected a slight smile as I passed my final comment. He then mentioned that he considered my decision to be "seemingly thorough and sensible."

Changing the subject, HRH asked me if I knew that he'd been to the area of Bam in Iran, prior to his arrival in Saudi to observe the assistance mission resulting from the major earthquake there. I said I was, as it had cut short his Saudi visit. This comment led HRH to engage me in discussion for a further few minutes, whilst on the side lines his equerry, hopping ever so slightly from toe to toe, seemed to be having trouble clearing his throat. I took this, as I believe did the Prince, as a not too subtle method of indicating that our conversation had run its course. Working to his equerry's not to subtle timings HRH bade me farewell, and followed by the scurrying equerry, he re-entered the 146 for take-off. I resumed my place in the commoners section via the rear door.

Chapter Seventeen - When It Goes Wrong...

... It can really go wrong.

My aim in close protection, regardless of where I was in the world, was to prevent it coming on top. If I needed to fire my weapons, I'd failed.

When undertaking protection operations, in addition to considering almost everything that could possibly go wrong, I'd also put strategies in place to deal with any perceived or proven deficits, take account of any previously logged learning - positive or negative - and rectify or evaluate my operation in line with these findings.

The know-how I gained from my initial high-threat-low-infrastructure *(HTLI)* ops during and shortly after the war fighting stage of the US led invasion of Iraq, would lead me to instigate, design and implement the model for all such future 'A' Squad operations. I would conclude that lightweight body armour was not fit for use in such warzones, that better weapons systems were required, first aid needed improving on, intelligence feeds with the agencies including the Defence Intelligence Agency *(DIS)* and GCHQ needed to be habitually tapped into and of course that MPSB and military interoperability must, always remain under MPSB control. Unfortunately, no matter what one puts in place such ops remain inherently deadly and do not always go to plan.

*

For over two years I was the head of the Secretary of State for Defence's *(SoSD)* protection team. The SoSD, at this time Labour Minister Des Brown, received MPSB armed personal protection *(prot)* 24/7, 365 days of the year wherever he was in the world. As the commander of this team I also ran scratch protection teams for the Ministers of Defence *(the SoSD's subordinates)* when they travelled to HTLI countries and protection was deemed necessary by the Royalty and Ministerial Visits Committee *(RMV)*. Consequently, Afghanistan and Iraq became second homes to me, as either the SoSD or any of his three junior subordinate ministers were in these deadly countries at any one time, buoying up the troops, assessing the needs of our war fighting capacity and negotiating and planning the war tactics with our coalition allies. These deployments, as well as the countless other HTLI ops I undertook as the subsequent head of the Foreign Secretary's team as well as such ops for countless other senior ministers, including the Prime Minister, continually put me at serious risk.

Des was at one of the main British command facilities in Baghdad inspecting and commending the troops and I had decided to cover the ceremony by stationing myself and another officer relatively close in on the parade ground, whilst placing my other officers, along with regular soldiers on a loose outer cordon covering the main strategic points. The Secretary of State had started awarding citations when I heard the cracking whoosh of an incoming mortar. Initially I ducked as the mortar exploded somewhere behind. Everyone had hit the deck except the Minister who was half crouching, possibly trying to remain composed. Within that split second I pulled myself together and ran towards Des as did my close-in DC, Tom.

In running towards the Minister both Tom and I were knowingly putting ourselves at massive risk. Mortars are fired in salvos. We both knew that getting under hard cover was the thing to do, which is what every soldier around us did automatically. To run into the open parade ground was - in any other circumstance - dumb! But, we were Protmen and saving the principal is what we do.

"Down, Minister, down! I yelled as another mortar whooshed into the parade ground.

Tom reached the Minister before me and pulled him down, covering him with his body in time to beat the second explosion. I was there a split second later and together we wrapped ourselves around the Principal, hoping that our body armour would stop any shrapnel bound for our backs as more mortars cascaded into the parade ground. The first salvo over, Tom and I picked up the Minister and propelled him to the hard cover of the nearest building's wall before bundling him into a solid building that we'd identified during our earlier recce of the facility. After fifteen or so minutes, and the military's air defence system declaring all clear, we escorted the SoSD back onto the parade ground to finish the ceremony.

No one was injured. What Tom and I did to make sure that the Minister was safe is not taught on any course or contained in any manual. It was a reaction of sorts, a considered and deliberate act, an understanding of duty. Tom and I both knew that had those mortars been any closer, our raised position on top of the Minister could have put us on offer. For my part, I did not consider the Minister to be better than me, or as a man worth more to society, but I did calculate his worth as a political entity to be in some way greater to the symbolic well-being of my nation. So I guess in those spilt seconds between the whoosh and the bang I'd calculated that my potential sacrifice would be worth it. I can only imagine that Tom had reached the same conclusion. Perhaps there was also an element of the fact that we'd both taken the Queen's shilling and therefore had a job to do. In my case though, perhaps the greater burden was that of command - I led by example and I was not prepared to ask my men to do what I wouldn't, even if it cost me my life.

As with many of my actions on Prot or indeed on intelligence missions, there was no official acknowledgement of our deeds in terms of tea and medals, in the police Queen's honours tended to be bestowed on very senior officers who'd never seen an angry man and had steadfastly avoided putting themselves in harms way. We accepted this. Sadly though, I don't remember Des Brown managing to thank us. Maybe it was just an oversight.

*

I often came under indiscriminate mortar or rocket fire whilst advancing the HTLI ops ahead of the arrival of whichever SoS/Minister I was protecting. On many occasions mortars were much too close for comfort. This was especially the case with regard to my operations in Iraq between 2004 – 2007 when British bases at Basra Palace, Basra Airport and the hotel on the Shatt-Al-Arab were constantly under attack by indiscriminate fire *(IDF)*. At times, these Southern Iraqi venues were amongst the most bombed locations on earth.

Iraq wouldn't be the only location where ops weren't as peaceful as I would have liked. In Afghanistan, IEDs were a constant threat, be they VBIEDs *(Vehicle Borne Improvised Explosive Devices)* or suicide bombers. Suicide bombers were perhaps the hardest to handle, in every sense.

In late 2005 I was once again in another of my home from homes: Afghanistan. I was 'advancing' *(planning & organising)* the forthcoming visit of the Minister for the Armed Forces *(MINAF)*, Adam Ingram to Kabul. The Minister was dispatched by the Secretary of State for Defence, at the time, John Reid, to speak with senior coalition military leaders, the Afghan military, police and senior government officials. Whilst advancing and recceing the operation, prior to the minister's arrival, I made connections with various intelligence agencies, including the excellent Intelligence Corps of the British Army *(Int Corps)* who warned me there was at least one vehicle-borne suicide bomber in the area. Although they'd provided me with the vehicle's make and colour, my experience in the Branch and MI6 taught me any of these 'facts' could be wrong.

For many reasons, secret intelligence rarely provides the full picture. Perhaps the agent was only in the room for one part of the conversation, perhaps some of the details changed without him/her knowing, or he could simply have misheard the details. If the Intel came from sigint, many points may not be known. Were those being eavesdropped on using code? Such language could use basic substitution of vehicle makes and colours, e.g., red meaning black or Ford meaning Mercedes, etc. Any mix up could be caused by something as simple as intercepted speech being incorrectly deciphered. Hence, in my Prot commander role, I only used secret intelligence as a valuable 'multiplier'. This meant that Intel heavily informed my actions and decisions but did not define my tactics. I based my operations on a risk, threat and vulnerability matrix, with intelligence helping me deal with a defined issue. Unfortunately, when the Branch was disbanded in 2006 and SO1 was formed in its place, too many people did not have my experience and took intelligence or worse still, an absence of it, as gospel on which to design their whole operation. This could cost lives. Thus on this op, as normal, I'd use the ICorp Intel to allow me to try to harden a potentially identified weak spot – the minister's movement between bases in Kabul. I'd try to achieve this by sending advance vehicles to circle the route ahead, to search for the suicide bomber's car using the known details and anything that appeared out of the ordinary. I had attempted to gain the use of a helicopter to provide these advance vehicles with some 'top cover' but unfortunately, due to combat operations, I was unable to obtain one from any of the coalition forces in theatre *(at this time the Americans did not have a major presence in Afghanistan and the UK military has a perennial deficit of helicopters)*.

Once the minister was on the road, I knew - thanks to updates from ICorps - that we had a potential window of about thirty minutes before the bomber would be able to position himself along the minister's route. So knowing this timeframe, or at least considering I did, I had to decide whether to prohibit the minister from leaving the British embassy in Kabul or not. If I prohibited his travel he would be unable to meet most of the partners he'd travelled to Afghanistan to see. He wouldn't be in a position to formulate a first-hand evaluation of the war's progress and he'd be sending a strong political message about how badly the war was going *(as often the case, we had the press in tow who would willingly publicise this message.)*. The minister also wouldn't have the chance to discuss strategies with his interlocutors face-to-face – unless of course they travelled to us. But the Afghans were generally loathed to do this for the same reasons we were cautious of travelling to them. So, if I decided to permit the minister to travel, then I'd be risking all our lives.

Although, I was not a gambler, especially with my life, I was sure that taking everything into account - the Intel, the environmental conditions and my team's professionalism and knowhow - that I'd be able to get the minister to most of the proposed appointments without incident. Those few appointments that I felt were just too dangerous and too far away, I'd abandon. I informed the minister of my intention to change his schedule, outlining my reasons. He agreed, bowing to my advice and professionalism.

The op was extremely tense from the off. We were travelling between venues when IntCorps routed an urgent call: the suicide bomber was in our vicinity. I immediately reconfigured and elongated the convoy in the hope that those vehicles at our furthest edge would provide us with early detection of the suicide bomber's vehicle. I also plotted the route to a 'safe-haven' military camp.

Unknown to me, the bomber struck at this moment, apparently detonating his device amidst a German patrol a couple of miles ahead of us after organising a fake accident to disorientate those in the convoy. We came across the still-smouldering vehicles some minutes later. The dead and injured had already 'bugged-out' using their remaining vehicles, but it was clear just how devastating this explosion had been. Glimpsing the bloody, burning mess brought home the fact that it could well have been us. The minister, who I had protected on numerous occasions, was as always calm, cool and collected as we sped onto the next venue. It was as if he hadn't even noticed.

*

A few weeks later I was once again in that other UK military hotspot, Basra, Iraq. On this occasion I was protecting the Secretary of State for International Development *(SoSDFID)* Hilary Benn. I'd brought Hilary to Southern Iraq, after we'd attended talks in Baghdad, so that he could meet two other key players in the British occupied south to discuss civil society building in the region. Consequently we'd meet Sir Hilary Synnott, the British regional coordinator for Southern Iraq, at the US led Coalition Provisional Authority *(CPA)*, and the British military commander for southern Iraq, Lieutenant General Graham Lamb. The three men had an initial meeting at General Lamb's military HQ for the southern region, Basra airport. This was a multi-pronged operation and in the recce phase I'd first 'advanced' the Baghdad element of the Minister's mission before travelling down to Barsa to advance this section. So when Hilary actually arrived in Baghdad with two of my men, I had already flown back to Baghdad, leaving two of my guys in Basra to await Hilary's arrival and to lead the initial Bagdad leg of the operation. On the advance phase in Basra we'd recced the British military HQ in the city with the assistance of colleagues from the Royal Military Police *(RMP)* protection wing tasked with protecting General Lamb in the region. The British Military HQ in the city was some twenty or so miles from the airport. Once in Basra, as per the programme, SoS Benn wanted to see the city for himself and speak to General Lamb's subordinates there. Sir Hilary Synnott, making use of this opportunity for face time with the Secretary of State, asked if he could tag along. I agreed. I put Sir Hilary and the Secretary of State in my vehicle so they could talk along the route. General Lamb stayed back at his HQ.

As usual I had control of the convoy and its actions, although several organisations were involved. I had agreed with Sir Hilary's protection team, who were from the United States Naval Criminal Investigative Service *(NCIS)* that they'd slot one of their armoured vehicles behind my vehicle containing the Minister and Sir Hilary, then I'd have my back–up vehicle containing some of my SB officers and RMPs behind that vehicle, followed by the remaining NCIS vehicles. The pilot vehicle leading my convoy and its back-up was staffed by the British Army's security regiment for Basra Airport HQ area, whose six-month tour had just gotten underway. The actual airport security detail was provided by the RAF Regiment, but because Basra Airport was so large and its area extended into the city, a British Army security unit was also stationed there. The route from Basra Airport into the city was part of this regular Army regiment's area of operations, so I was depending on this regiment *(who shall not be named here)* to provide my convoy with the 'local knowledge' and know-how relating to their area of operation. As the regiment had recently arrived in theatre, I checked with their Major concerning the units' local knowledge and readiness for the operation. The Major, who I accommodated in my MPSB back-up vehicle, assured me that his guys had done their drills and knew the roads 'like the back of their hands'. I was therefore confident that this was the case. In addition to the Minister, Sir Hilary and myself, my armoured vehicle was driven by a first-class RMP driver who I knew was on the ball. I'd placed one of my SB officers in the pilot vehicle with one of the security regiment's staff sergeants and driver. In that way I'd keep some element of control over the convoy whilst we were rolling.

Weapons and comms now readied, we began to move off, out of the base into no man's land along the highway. Basra was becoming a more dangerous place by the day. Its proximity to Iran meant that munitions and IED know-how were easily finding their way to the Shia insurgents. Some several minutes had elapsed when my RMP driver asked me where we were going. The RMP driver was four months into a six-month tour and knew his ground well.

"Basra, I hope." I told him.

"The numpty's going the wrong way, Carlton. We're heading to Iran, we're not far from the border."

I immediately contacted my officer in the pilot vehicle. "George, I'm told we're heading for the Iranian border not Basra! Ask the sergeant exactly where we are and come back to me ASAP."

The answer was not long in coming.

"The driver's kept it to himself, Governor, but he's now admitting that he's been winging it, hoping he'd recognise a landmark."

The chances of that weren't great on a straight desert highway. I told them to slow the convoy.

"George. Does the staff sergeant know the way?"

"He's just told me that he's not sure either, Governor."

This was embarrassing for the British Army and of course for me. I'd accepted the Major's word that his men knew what they were doing but I was in charge and would therefore carry the can for anything that went wrong. I checked with my RMP driver who confirmed we needed to turn around. To do this we'd have to cross the central reservation on this deserted road, which in itself could be dangerous - who knew what was planted here? But there was no other way. I contacted my second-in-command *(2ic)* in the SB back-up, quickly explained the situation to him and told him to pass his radio to the NCIS special agent in-charge *(SAC)* in the vehicle. As the SAC answered I asked if he knew the route to the Basra venue.

"You're damned right I do, I wondered where your guy was going."

I wanted to say he's not 'my guy, he's Army' but of course he was my guy, he was a Brit and I had put the convoy together.

"Okay, then," I said reluctantly, "NCIS should take the lead and pilot us in to Basra."

"Okay, Carlton, will do. Sit back first whilst we do the cross over drill of the median strip."

Nick gave the Branch radio back to my 2ic and contacted one of his back-ups to 'take over the pilot role from the Brits' as he put it. As he did, I passed the message over the main military radio so all in the convoy knew to wait for the NCIS to safely traverse the central reservation before we all followed the NCIS pilot vehicle's tracks onto the opposite side of the highway, in the same formation but for the NCIS lead. The NCIS got us safely to the British military HQ in Basra without further incident.

As I got the Minister and Sir Hilary into the safety of the HQ, I pulled the Major aside. His "nothing happened so we're okay" attitude didn't wash with me, nor I knew would it with General Lamb. Only when I mentioned General Lamb to the Major did he get the message and began to show at least some contrition. I let him know that every extra minute that the SoS was out on the road put him at great danger. If something had happened, his regiment would have been at fault. This would be the case not least because it was in his regiment's specialist area of operation that we were travelling. Worse still, an American NCIS unit had had to pull his arse out of the fire. I let him know that I was ashamed for him and his guys, so I couldn't understand how he wasn't.

The truth was of course that the Major had embarrassed me. I'd learn from this. In future in travelling to countries where I didn't know the lay of the land and depended on other professionals for this crucial aspect of my operation, I'd try to verify what individuals told me, even if it was the group's leader who was making the claim. If nothing else, the Major had taught me a memorable lesson.

*

Throughout my career, I've performed many different types of ops in Palestine, Israel and the region. I've been on the end of Palestinian rockets fired from Gaza into Sderot, Israel; attacks from the Israeli IDF into the Palestinian West bank; rocket attacks from Hezbollah on Hebron, Israel and rocket attacks from South Lebanon into Israel, as well as attacks from the IDF on Beirut.

In June 2007 I was once again commanding a protection operation for Secretary of State for International Development, Hilary Benn. The plan was to visit Gaza's central hospital, amongst other locations in the strip, to assess the effectiveness of British aid to that area and to decide what future UK sponsorship should be provided to the region. As usual I had undertaken exhaustive preparatory work and as well as consulting SIS, I sought out US intelligence, touched base with Palestinian security and Intelligence officials and had talks with Israeli friends in Shin Bet *(Israeli Special Branch/Security Service)*. Although the threat to the visit was high, it had to be otherwise the RMV wouldn't have authorised my team's deployment, according to the agencies I consulted it seemed relatively quiet.

So, as I exited the main doors of the rudimentary, dirty and over-stretched Gaza Central Hospital on that late June morning and was met with a long burst of automatic gun fire, I could only conclude that we were subject to an assassination attempt!

Everything happened in an instant. I automatically stepped in front of the Minister. First decision: Should I backtrack fifteen metres and go firm in the hospital building, or should I move forward three metres and enter our vehicle, whose armour at the time, wouldn't defeat sustained 7.62mm or 5.56mm rounds for long. The positives of the vehicle were its proximity, the fact that I had covered its position with my men and loyal FATAH units from the Palestinian Presidential Guard and Palestinian Special Police. But more importantly the vehicles provided me with the opportunity to bug out. If I went back to the hospital building we might leave ourselves open to a subsequent all-out assault from multiple attackers or some form of suicide attack? Armoured vehicle it was. I reckoned we'd have enough ballistic cover to make good our escape.

I briskly manoeuvred the Minister into the vehicle, at the same time radioing my two guys armed with G36 assault rifles stationed on the flanks outside the hospital, to provide me with information on the shooter(s) location, whether they had a bead, and if they could confirm that we were the intended target. Neither the principal nor I had been hit. I ordered my guys to collapse the bag, re-join the convoy and move off rapidly. My independent actions, vis-à-vis the protection of the SoS, were being mimicked by our local escort - the Presidential Guard and Palestinian Special Police. All of us were dumbfounded in the initial confusion as to where the rounds had come from and indeed had ended up. Another burst of fire went up as we began to move away, but I couldn't see or feel incoming.

As we moved, I began to explain to the Minister, whom I knew quite well, that Tim and John, now in the vehicles behind us, had had one of several gunmen in their sights. They had not taken any deadly action, as they seemed to be firing off 'celebratory' rounds into the sky, not at us. The minister was remarkably calm. I did caution him though, that 'what went up must come down' - bullets shot into the air fall at a rate that can easily kill.

Some substantial time later, I received a message from the embassy in Jerusalem: Hamas was attempting a coup d'état against ruling Fatah government in Gaza. The hospital shooting, which I'd informed them of, was linked to a Hamas assassination attempt on the life of the General in charge of Palestinian General Intelligence, FATAH's Central intelligence organisation. The ambush failed, but both of the General's young sons who were also in his vehicle at the time of the attack, *en route* to their school, had been killed. When the children's bodies had arrived at the central general hospital, funerary shooting had erupted.

Realising that a coup was underway, I knew I now had other potential worries. Could I trust my local escort? My initial thought was to get my Principal out of Dodge back to the relative safety of Israel without delay.

In initially arranging the protection package I had fully considered *trust* factors. Consequently, I had tactically placed one of my officers in the Palestinian Special Police's CAT *(Counter Assault Team)* vehicle alongside their CAT team members with the aim of overseeing competence, functionality and loyalty of this heavily-armed team. If this was a coup scenario, then my officer, Jim, was potentially at risk. He could be murdered or kidnapped, to be executed months later, if the loyalty of the CAT officers to FATAH was not guaranteed. Jim was a top man. He had come to SO1 from the Met's Specialist Firearms Unit SO19 once the Branch had been disbanded and SO1 had been formed from the remnants of 'A' Squad. As a former SO19 man Jim had great experience of CATs and of armed ops in general, so I consoled myself with the fact that if anybody could look after themselves in a shooting match, it was Jim.

Jim was armed with an MP5 A3 with folded stock which he'd stored in his quick access rucksack, he also had his Glock 17 pistol in a quick release holster on his hip under his suit jacket. So even though I was fearful, I was conscious that he at least had the means to defend himself if it all came on top.

I next spoke with my opposite number in the Palestinian Presidential Guard. General Ali was a good guy, I'd known him for several years so I had no hesitation in getting straight to the point. Ali confirmed the assassination attempt, but stated that FATAH were in control of the situation. I tried to confirm this with my sources in the embassy but they knew less than Ali. The Minister wanted to continue the visit and as I couldn't swear that he was in immediate danger - none of my contacts had any information to say otherwise and Ali's explanation appeared plausible - we pushed ahead with the visit, but as a consideration I did make some compromises. We'd visit the programmed venue that was the nearest to the inner border with Israel, so if the coup developed we could quickly make our way to the crossing.

With my large SO1 team, I thought that I'd be able to keep an eye on all of the Palestinians with us. In fact I felt that the Presidential Guard were most probably trustworthy and didn't require close observation, but I wasn't so sure about the Special Police's loyalty as they were Gaza-based and so potentially infiltrated by Hamas. The positive was that I had them semi-covered by Jim, so I had the option of playing the wait-and-see game. Prot is not an exact science. It's all about risk management.

The Minister's visit to the partially sealed-off goods border crossing at Karni had been designed by the Department for International Development *(DFID)* staff to show solidarity with the Palestinian people. The UK government wanted the crossing fully opened, allowing Palestinian produce to flow out to Israel and the wider world, making Gaza more economically viable. The Karni stop was therefore an opportunity to visit this practically closed facility from the Palestinian side of the border so the Minister could inform himself of what might be required to get the site up and running again. It was a project close to Hilary's heart.

I had previously agreed protocols with the Palestinians that the CAT would follow the advance lead and back-up vehicle onto the Karni site. After all the job of any CAT is that in an attack scenario its members take the fight to the attackers, whilst the principal bugs out, prior to the CAT retreating itself. No matter what, I had planned to reattach Jim to the inner SO1 component of the convoy once the Karni element of the visit had been completed. Indeed, the role I'd already assigned to Jim and a DC once we arrived at Karni, was to observe the Special Police CAT in addition to covering the rest of my SO1 team from an outward position. I had no choice but to bring Jim back to the inner SO1 circle at Karni, because under treaty obligations Palestinian security services were not permitted function within the several miles no-man's land of the actual border crossing area where we'd travel to directly after leaving Karni. After Karni our next stop was Israel.

Our convoy entered the Palestinian side of the Karni facility. Suddenly, I received a radio message from Jim. The CAT driver had apparently stopped short of the Karni site and appeared to be unwilling to follow the convoy on to the facility. This was absolutely contrary to my operational agreement with the CAT team commander.

My phone rang.

It was Jim.

In a hushed voice Jim explained the situation. The CAT driver was simply refusing to move. He would not enter the site.

Concerned, I told Jim to stay on the line. "Whatever you do don't hang up Jim!"

I immediately sought out General Ali. He assured me he'd immediately order the CAT to close up to the convoy. Ali summonsed a Special Police Major to him appearing to pass my demands on. The Major immediately complied, speaking to the CAT commander over the radio. Although, I'd taken Arabic lessons in the Branch many years previously and in SIS sometime later, my Arabic language skills were frankly next to useless. I just hadn't grasped the language, although now I wished I had.

Within a heartbeat Jim's voice crackled through my mobile's earpiece now permanently plugged in my ear. "Something's coming over the radio Carlton."

"Good. So, what's happening now?"

Jim, who also couldn't speak Arabic, had no way of knowing what was said. He could only report the CAT's team's reactions as he perceived them.

"Nothing Carlton, they're doing nothing, except turning around and looking at me! The atmosphere's turning ugly."

I heard Jim cajoling the five-man Palestinian crew to catch up with the convoy. But in reply, all I heard was silence.

I'd made a massive mistake, I'd put my DS in harm's way. If I'd miscalculated and something happened to him, it would all be down to me.

I addressed Ali.

"General! Your CAT team isn't complying with your orders. I need you to tell them again to meet us here and let my officer out!"

I could hear the strained voice of Jim, controlled yet almost pleading:

"Okay then guys, let me out here, I'll walk the rest of the way."

The alarm in Jim's voice was palpable. He addressed me directly.

"I've asked them to let me out, Carlton, but the team leader's said NO. He's just laughing in my face. They all seem to be discussing something. They're whispering, so you can't hear them?"

Then suddenly, even more alarmingly, the ever steady Jim exclaimed,

"Governor, the driver's now putting the vehicle in reverse. We're beginning to turn around to leave your position!"

My heart missed a beat. This was now serious. I turned to General Ali, still nearby. Now strident, I demanded action from General Ali.

"Ali, your CAT is still not complying. They are now moving away from our position. You have to stop that vehicle."

Ali looked at me, trying to play down the situation, in that laissez-faire Middle Eastern way.

"Don't worry, Carlton, I am sure there's an explanation."

"Like what? CATs always stay with the principal behind the back-up vehicle, otherwise it's useless. Add to this the team's disobeyed your orders twice. We have a big problem do we not? Even worse, my officer now says that the CAT's driving away from us and they have refused to let him out. Ali, I'm taking no chances. I want you personally to immediately call your CAT leader and tell him to allow my officer to leave the vehicle. I also want you to dispatch several of your officers and men to stop that CAT from leaving."

I let this sink in for a second and then I attacked Ali further.

"Ali I want you to make this happen immediately, otherwise two things will occur. I will remove the Minister immediately and not authorise further meetings with your government due to a lack of security. And I will stop your CAT, and free my man, myself - regardless of what it takes."

I knew this was a dangerous tactic. If elements of my team and I chased down the CAT, in an effort to forcibly free Jim, it could escalate out of control. Moreover, I couldn't spare many men to do this job, as I also needed to protect Hilary. I was hoping that Ali would work out that British support for FATAH, especially at the time of an attempted coup, was imperative. So, hopefully, I calculated, he'd act as I required.

Meanwhile, sitting as he was behind the CAT team in the back of the Landcruiser, Jim had unzipped the rucksack containing his MP5A3, which was fully loaded, cocked and ready to go. Leaving it inside the rucksack, Jim slowly positioned the weapon on his knees and covertly placed his finger on the trigger, discretely taking up the pressure. Should the need arise he'd decided to rock and roll. No matter what, he was not going to be taken hostage.

General Ali immediately complied with my demands this time stopping the CAT with his Presidential Guard who collected Jim and delivered him to me. Jim explained that his handover had been like a mini Mexican standoff, the Special Police finally letting him out, before leaving the scene. We were both relieved, Jim obviously more so than me. On Jim's return, I cut short the Minister's visit and immediately headed for the border, leaving the turmoil of Gaza behind.

I'll never know what the CAT team had intended, what we do know is that they insubordinately left the scene. Intelligence would subsequently show that many Gaza based Palestinian Police did not remain loyal to FATAH. Anything could have happened.

Back in Blighty I debriefed Jim and more importantly I spoke to the F&CO and SIS to try to get to the gist of the intelligence failure that left a Government Cabinet Minister's Prot team dangling with no knowledge of what was happening in the surrounding area.

I'll say it again: Intelligence and Security are not exact sciences, so maybe nobody knew anything more than we did. For my part, I knew I had miscalculated. So in future, as a general rule and when at all possible, I'd make sure I never left a lone officer in the company of potentially hostile host forces again.

Chapter Eighteen - Poison Chalice – Head of Iraqi Special Branch

Baghdad International Airport *(BIAP)* was full of its usual mixture of hustle and bustle, oppressive heat and the anticipation of men ready to go to war. As usual, thousands of US personnel from all Branches of the Military, Federal government agencies and US civil administration were all milling around as where a smattering of other nationals militaries and officials waiting for flights, sleeping, receiving and going over orders. Many others were looking for or awaiting transport to central Baghdad, knowing they would soon be leaving the heavily-fortified airport for Baghdad or one of Iraq's other main cities. All would be taking their chances along highways that were effectively deadly fairground shooting galleries for all types of insurgents, Jihadis, militia and Fedayeen types. It had an air of organised chaos.

By the summer of 2003, Iraq had become my second home and on this mission I'd landed at Baghdad International Airport *(BIAP)* with two of my 'Advance Team' on board a US Air Force C17 out of Kuwait. I was back in town to advance, organise and lead the operation to protect Secretary of State for Trade and Industry, Patricia Hewitt during her visit to the Iraqi capital. The visit, to ensure Britain's economy received some of the spoils of war, was due to take place in about a week's time. I had hand-picked both of the guys in my Advance Team; both were extremely able and both had already accompanied me on previous Iraqi ops. They would both become members of my soon to be created HTLI team.

We were met at BIAP by colleagues from the RMP who would transport us via the BIAP road *(aka Route Irish, arguably the most dangerous road in Iraq)* to central Baghdad. So, having loaded our packs into the two lightly armoured Land Rover Discoveries and checked that our Glocks and Machine Pistols were loaded and ready to fire, we took up tactical positions for the journey to the new British embassy/residence in downtown Baghdad.

As soon as we arrived I was informed that General Sir Freddie Viggers would like to see me ASAP. General Viggers was the new ranking British military officer in Iraq and was one of the deputies to the American overall commander of the Coalition Provisional Authority *(CPA)*, retired General Jay Garner. I left my two guys bedding in with the RMP and going over schedules whilst I travelled with an RMP escort the mile or so to Saddam Hussein's main palace, now CPA HQ. It was a monster of a building, which oozed grandeur and obscene wealth, as did Sir Freddie's office. With him was the head of SIS in Iraq, Zachary. I knew Zachary well, having worked on a Special Mission together for SIS's Chief, 'C', shortly before the war in Afghanistan.

"Ah, Carlton," said Sir Freddie, "come on in and take a seat."

He beckoned me to sit down on the chair near Zachary in front of an enormous marble table fit for a king - or a Middle Eastern dictator.

The General, a fit, precise, well-spoken and impeccably turned-out man in his mid-50's, was known to be approachable and polite - in the Sandhurst and British public school manner. Of course this genteel deportment masked a steel core. In the future, after his stellar military career was over, Sir Freddie [KCB](#) [CMG](#) [MBE](#) [DL](#) would gain one of the most venerable establishment positions, that of 'The Gentleman Usher of the Black Rod'; that individual who in high British drama yearly demands entry for the sovereign to the house of commons during the state opening of parliament. Zachary, although much younger, was of a similar mould. Bright, articulate and confident, he oozed capability, an absolute requirement for an MI6 station chief. These men were both the product of an imperial class, nurtured by the British public school system, Oxbridge and Sandhurst.

Zachary got straight to the point.

"Carlton, have you met Kojak? If you have, you'd know, he's not a particularly cerebral fellow."

For a moment I was in the dark, the only Kojak I knew was Telly Savalas from the hit 1970's American TV show. Then I twigged who they meant.

"Aha, yes." I replied, "I've met him on a couple of occasions. I guess he's the type of guy you underestimate at your peril," I said, kicking back at Zachary's assessment that he wasn't very cerebral. "He was the Commissioner of the New York Police, you know."

Seemingly, in keeping with certain class sentiments, not every SIS officer appeared to hold the police in high regard.

"Well, Freddie and I thought you'd be his perfect counterweight," Zachary said. "Of course, he'd be your boss, as would the Iraqi Chief of the National Police, *(under the new democratic model for the Iraqi Mukhabarat)* but in reality you'd have relative autonomy."

Sir Freddie was nodding vigorously in agreement.

Hell, I thought, they're pitching me the job as the head of the Iraqi National Police Special Branch!

"Carlton, you know what the situation is. The Americans have made sure that they've got control of the main organs of state and although this is their show we are heavily committed here, and well, we lack traction with the Iraqis in this area."

It was worse than that I thought, it was as if it was all done and dusted, a *fait accompli*.

"So you'd like me to head up Iraqi SB. Clearly things are worse than I thought!" I replied rather glibly.

Sir Freddie then hit me with the next salvo.

"I've taken the opportunity to speak with David Veness who I know from my days in London area command; he agrees with us that you'd be ideal for the task, especially with your experience in Zachary's field, not to mention your political savvy. David has given the idea his blessing and will expedite the necessary administration."

So they'd roped my boss of bosses into the matter, Assistant Commissioner for Specialist Operations, David Veness. Clearly this could be a great opportunity for me. I could possibly make a deal to be prompted to Detective Superintendent once I returned back to the UK after fulfilling my Iraqi commitments. This would mean I'd jump two ranks and add another unique chapter to my CV. That said, undertaking such a role could just as easy not help with promotion at all. The Met was notoriously ridged in matters of promotion even when one was by far the best candidate, I'd find this out to my cost, in years to come. No, the main lure of the post was that in a strange way this job would be fun, whilst filled with a sense of abject terror. Unfortunately, for mankind, a sense of terror often provides the best fun, as long as one survives of course. I'd be living daily on my wits, whilst controlling history – what better.

That split second of buccaneering spirit flashed from my mind to be replaced by hard-nosed common sense and an intrinsic instinct for survival. I would not accept this post, no matter how exciting it would be, irrespective of the immense power I'd wield throughout Iraq and the rank I *might* be promised if I had the good fortune to survive my two year tour of duty. No, even being at the cross roads of history wouldn't induce me into what I believed would be an impending hell hole. Moreover and frankly more importantly, I wasn't an island, for once I had to put wife and kids before nation. For far too long they'd played fourth fiddle to the job, Queen and country. I'd do my bit, but those who created this mess needed to play the main role in cleaning it up. I would not be their caretaker.

The fact was that Iraq was set to explode, and to save it, I'd have to play dirty. So, if I took the job as head of the Iraq Secret Police the likelihood was that I'd either leave Baghdad in a box or in handcuffs.

I spoke directly to Sir Freddie.

"I'm flattered General, but I think Zachary was already aware of my pre-war assessment of the conflict here in Iraq, which now post war, is if anything firmer."

(In the months after September the 11th discussions concerning the validity and sagacity of a US invasion of Iraq and the UK's undoubted participation in it, were rife in SIS. From the beginning I had expressed my objection to an invasion whilst other colleagues were just as vociferous in their support. Having first heard of the real potential for a US invasion of Iraq two years before 9/11, when 'Anton' provided me with his 'US intelligence agency' derived assessment of the drivers for war in Iraq I had continually assessed the possible impact of such a war on world-wide terrorism. It was clear to me that an invasion was seen by many neo-conservatives in the American Republican Party as a solution to at least some of the problems that plagued US pre-eminence in Middle East whilst potentially also shoring up oil supplies. As Anton put it win, win for Uncle Sam and the Republican moneymen many involved in big oil and allied industries. Yet, for counter-terrorism it would be a disaster. As an SIS counter-terrorism Case Officer my somewhat stark evaluation, revolved around humanities basic conflict drivers, you kill people close to me and I'll do the same to you. Therefore to me, it was always clear that the result of such an invasion would be to unite disparate Islamic,

nationalist and ethnic factions to win supporter for any non-western groups that wanted to wage Holy War against the West.)

Sir Freddie continued: "Yes, but how does this affect your undoubted suitability for the post?"

I explained my reticence.

"As the head of SIS in Iraq, Zachary will have to have very close dealings with his Iraqi colleagues in the Security Service. These dealings will not be scrutinized, as they will, or should be, kept secret. However, if I accept your proposal I would be the head of the Mukhabarat, the Iraqi secret police that in line with our democratic ideology regarding police would have to foster a spirit of openness and place a premium on democratic accountability. Quite correctly, this would mean that most of the unit's modus operandi would be open to the glare of public oversight and scrutiny. Yet, in the situation we are entering into, this will prove to be problematic.

I was against the war for several reasons, but in particular I didn't think that we, and by 'we', I mean the Americans - as they are the only ones with the capacity - would be willing to invest the necessary money and personnel into winning the peace. I've always believed that to stifle resistance in a country the size of Iraq that we'd need to station half a million men here, for several years and nothing I've seen up to now makes me feel that my assessment is wrong.

You're going to ask me, where's the evidence for this appraisal, but would you really be asking for me to act as a counterweight to Kojak if you didn't see the storm clouds gathering. After all, is that not why you believe we need a more conciliatory British style of occupation, before it too late?"

I paused for breath but didn't let either of the men answer my question as I forged forward.

"In life people can generally learn from their past experiences. Many years ago I was a detective for a section of the US Department of Defence in Germany. I had access to the personnel records of all this sections employees. These files stretched back to the immediate post-war occupation of Germany. The older files recorded whether an employee had been de-Nazified. I sought out information about this and learnt that many employees in the past were able to obtain or retain roles within the state apparatus even though they were staunch members of the Nazi Party. This was a conscious decision by the Allies, aimed at preventing the creation of a huge body of unemployable men with nothing to lose - even though the Allies kept over a million men in occupied Germany to counter any potential rebellion *(as well as to ward off the Soviets)*."

"We are now doing the exact opposite here. We are expelling all Baathists from public service, thereby creating the conditions for rebellion by leaving men idle. Worse still, previous senior officials are now devoid of status, ministries are leaderless and there are too many men with nothing to lose. In addition to this, our US colleagues are hell bent on reducing the strength of their forces to the bare minimum to gain a fiscal and political post-war boost. Unfortunately, we are now walking into a situation where a reconciliatory posture by the British would become counterproductive. Why, because I believe that we will soon have a full-blown insurgency on our hands. If I'm right, - I hope I'm not - my style of counter-terrorist and security work, the 21st century British style, will be redundant. Iraq will belong to men like Kojak."

"This type of analysis is exactly why we wish to offer you the post." Said, Zachary. "You understand the politics of conflict." Added, Sir Freddie.

"Yes, General and that's why, regrettably, I will not take the role. Unlike SIS, if I took over the Iraqi Special Branch, I would not be able to hide what would have to be done by my Branch in an effort to prevent even darker deeds by insurgents and terrorists in the conflict to come. Therefore, I would be at great personal risk from all sides."

"Iraq is heading towards a period of low intensity warfare and major sectarian conflict. The only people who will have a chance of preventing this strife will probably be those Iraqi *Mukhabarat* officers who kept a lid on things before the invasion. To achieve this, these officers would no doubt revert to old ways and utilise techniques that no democratic police service could condone. So, if I bring these guys and their techniques back into the fold for the greater good, I would no doubt become the most hated foreigner in Iraq. Additionally, because of Iraq's existing and growing sectarian schisms I'd need to hire what would amount to foreign mercenaries as my protection team, because I simply wouldn't be able to trust all of my Iraqi officers with my life. Finally, even if I was successful and survived my tenure as head of Iraqi Special Branch and I helped prevent or at least limit the coming insurgency, the chances are that in years to come I'd be hauled before International Court of Human Rights in Den Haag for human rights abuses. Sorry, gentlemen, I'm flattered by your offer, but taking this post would be detrimental to my health and against my better judgement."

And that was that. We never discussed the offer again.

The American national who was awarded the post by President G W Bush of Interim Interior Minister of Iraq, who my intended posting as head of Iraqi Special Branch was designed to outflank, was the former New York City Police Commissioner Bernie Kerik. Bernie was liberally known to the British as 'Kojak', due to the fact that he was a large, squat, bald headed man who spoke with a New York accent and was no stranger to the rugged end of policing. Along with his good friend and business partner, the famed former Mayor of New York, Rudy Giuliani, Bernie had received an honour from Her Majesty the Queen for his actions as New York Police Commissioner on 9/11. Although, as Bernie characteristically put it, the honours bestowed on him were not as grandiose as those awarded to Rudi: "Rudi was made a Knight, or some shit like that, I was only made a member of your empire."

I'd met Kojak a few times, most memorably when I was advancing the prospective visit to the Iraqi Police College in Baghdad of Foreign Secretary Jack Straw. The Baghdad police college was a very dangerous location to visit, the police and in particular new police recruits, were one of the main targets of attack in post liberation Iraq. Literally hundreds of Iraqis had died as a result of various IED, VBIED and gun attacks on queues of individuals waiting outside various police establishments, who were simply applying to become officers.

In those early days of the occupation Bernie travelled around Iraq with two bodyguards, a fearsome looking pair of Afrikaner mercenaries, Andre and Pieter. As Bernie put it, these guys knew about killing due to their role as 'specialists' in Apartheid South Africa's 'anti-Communist wars'. Bernie then went on to recount how early on in their relationship he had started to chide one of the Afrikaners because his colleague had not shown up for work on time. Bernie hated unpunctuality.

"So I fucking started in on this guy," he said, "I was telling him I'd dock his partner's wages and he says to me, 'he's not late' Boss. I say, what the fuck, he ain't here, is he? He says 'he knows he'll be right over as he's just mopping up a job'. I say what job? I didn't give him any fucking job. I swear to god, Carlton, he looks at me cool as you like and says that they were coming to work when they saw a bank job going down, grabbing their weapons they jumped out of their vehicle and went to work, halting the robbery. He popped three and a half perps and Pieter, his partner, capped two!"

Deciphering Bernie's words I assumed *'half'* meant that Andre had only wounded the third human being.

Bernie continued. "So because Pieter took down the least he drew the short straw and stayed at the scene to mop up, with some of my Iraqi police patrols who'd arrived a bit later. So Andre came into work alone, like nothin' happened!"

Bernie grinned at me, his incredulity and admiration etched on his face.

"You gotta love these guys, Carlton!"

I asked Bernie how he'd risen to become the Commissioner of the New York police with its more than 40,000 officers, not to mention the tens of thousands of civilians - a body that was even bigger than the Met. He understood I was questioning his less-than-cultured approach, so he fully outlined his professional career path, explaining that he was an educated beat cop who understood the politics of policing and had managed to catch Mayor Giuliani's eye. He and Rudy needed each other. Bernie was the man who could make good on the Mayor's promise to drastically lower the crime rate in New York City, whilst Giuliani had the political clout to keep the liberals off his ass whilst he achieved this.

"You gotta understand, Carlton, power is an ever shifting thing. You can't stand still. Giuli wasn't just talking about being the Mayor of New York; this is about Giuli becoming the President of the United States of America."

Whilst saying this, as if to affirm his analysis, Bernie gripped and practically clapped together the two large pistols that he wore overtly in shoulder holsters on each side of his large frame.

"I can see you're like me, Carlton, you like to get the job done. Some of us are willing to do it, others just talk about it. Let me give you an example. I told you how I got to work for the DEA as part of a task force, didn't I? Well, what I haven't told you is how I made the biggest fucking drugs bust the US government had ever made."

On a previous occasion Bernie had told me how he had moved from the New York City Police Department *(NYPD)* as a street cop *(a patrol sergeant)* to the New York Department of Corrections at Rikers Island, rising to become its chief, before being drafted onto a federal task force with the DEA. He would subsequently return to the NYPD, before becoming its Commissioner under Mayor Giuliani. Bernie knew that I had a criminology degree. He mentioned that this was smart. He explained that he had educated himself to Master's Degree level, as the people at the top only respected paper. Although he mentioned his education, Bernie tended to play his down when speaking to cops or like-minded individuals. Bernie was no fool, he was cunning and one misjudged him at one's peril. He was a smart man who loved to play the rugged cop role. It was his life.

"We knew that this Colombian cartel boss was travelling to Switzerland to get his rocks off, so we went there to give him the good news with a little help from the Swiss. You been to Switzerland Carlton?"

"Yes, many times."

"Working?"

"Yes, often."

"Well, the cops in Switzerland ain't worth shit!"

Bernie noticed my raised eyebrows.

"I see what you're thinking, Carlton. Like I told you, I've worked overseas and got jammed up, so I know cops don't always have the freedom of movement they'd like. So let's say that the cops in Switzerland can't do shit. The whole country's in the hands of the fucking bankers and nothing, and I mean nothing, happens without their say-so. It's the most corrupt place on earth. You see, Carlton, this guy was putting tens of millions of dollars into their banks and the Swiss liked that just fine, they didn't want Uncle Sam fucking around in their shit. So when we submitted a commission rogatoire *(letter of request)* to their judicial authorities to arrest this guy, who was a major known Columbian player, the Swiss Judges rejected it! Can you believe that, Carlton? This guy was wanted by the United States government and those corrupt fucks refused any assistance? So in that circumstance it's about getting the job done Carlton. You know what I mean?"

"You're not wrong, Bernie." I said in answer to his statement.

He looked me in the eyes and reached for his guns again. What's this guy going to tell me now, I thought?

"So, we knew where this Colombian cocksucker was staying and I knew these duplicitous Swiss fucks wouldn't waste any time telling him that the DEA were on his ass, so we had to act quickly before he ran back to Colombia or some other such South American hell hole. I called one of my trusted guys that I'd got on the task force. In this game you've always got to have trusted guys, Carlton, remember that. This guy of mine's a great guy, Italian *(American)*; he was with me on the street so you know he can hold his own. You've got to be tight on the street. So I say to Gino, 'when this Colombian prick comes down those stairs, and he will, 'cos he's walking around Switzerland like a big shot without protection because he thinks he's bought off the whole darn Swiss police, I want you to walk up to him and fuck him up good.' Gino says, "Okay boss."

Bernie was clearly proud that he was able to elicit such unquestioning loyalty.

"Look Carlton, Gino's a really big guy, if he hits you, you stay hit. I said, 'Gino, I don't want you to fuck around with this guy, I want you to beat the crap out him and then get the fuck back to America'. Gino says okay boss. That guy never once asked me why."

"That's impressive," I said and I looked at Bernie as if to ask the question that Gino never did.

"You see Carlton, this guy was a big fish, I knew that if I could get the machinery in Washington to do its thing that it would be able to overturn these Swiss fucks, but I needed time and Gino was going to buy me that time by putting that fuck in hospital for six weeks."

I smiled as though I thought his actions were ingenious, as indeed to some extent they were, there was just one minor problem though. It was contrary to the rule of law!

"When that fucking punk came down those stairs making his grand entrance with a hooker on his arm, my man went to work. Gino hit him, bang, kicked his fucking teeth out and fucked him up good and proper. The rest, Carlton, went to plan."

As he recounted the story to me, Bernie performed Gino's actions as though he was personally delivering each blow. He was in his element.

Bernie was undoubtedly rough and ready but as I had stated to Zachary, he was no fool. During his tenure as Iraqi Interior Minister, Bernie, began to push to overturn the Bush Administration rule banning Baathists from government posts, especially within the security forces. Bernie was experienced enough to know the damage this was doing, not least in the loss of local on the ground community intelligence. Unfortunately, by the time he achieved this goal and re-hired thousands of former Iraqi police, much of the damage, in terms of the vacuum caused by the no-hire decree had already occurred. Less positively, as I prophesied, Bernie also had to re-hire those who knew exactly how the Mukhabarat had to work. I was grateful I'd stood my ground and rejected the Iraqi SB role so I didn't have to make such decisions.

Bernie didn't remain the Interim Iraqi Interior Minister for long, approximately six months in all. It wasn't due to a lack of adequate remuneration that he left. He had told me that he was earning footballers' wages, by which he meant American football, whose salaries are even higher than those who play our beautiful game.

Bernie had greater ambitions and mentioned that somewhere in the mix, Donald Rumsfeld, the then US Secretary for Defence, had something to do with his and Giuliani's security company. Bernie, therefore, already had powerful connections in the Bush Administration and his time in Iraq was nothing, if not a positive CV-filler on which to hang his right-wing credentials. Hence, the next time I heard of Bernie, some few years later was when he was being nominated by President George Bush as his Secretary for Homeland Security *(a senior cabinet post in the US administration)*. Unfortunately for Bernie, he never got past the nomination stage. He had made too many enemies on the left and sailed too close to the wind for too long. So, shortly after his nomination Bernie was quietly withdrawn from consideration by the Bush Administration due to various 'irregularities'.

Some months later, I read that Bernie was under consideration for several criminal charges. Eventually he was placed in front of a grand jury and indicted on various Federal offences. On November 5, 2009 he pled guilty to eight felony tax and false statement charges and was sentenced to four years in a federal penitentiary.

So it was that as Bernie soon found himself back in the USA angling for the position of Secretary for Homeland Security, Iraq continued to be my second home.

Consequently, from 2003 onward, my role as a senior Special Branch Protection Commander, and the demands of the War on Terror, kept me busy, especially after major hostilities were declared at an end by President G W Bush and the insurgencies I predicted in Afghanistan and Iraq began in earnest.

Chapter Nineteen - To Any Length

It was 2007 and I was once again in Basra, Iraq, advancing the visit of Secretary of State for Defence *(SoSD)*, Des Brown. Some weeks earlier the PM and his SO1 team had visited Basra. The PM's team didn't seek the assistance of other more HTLI experienced SO1 staff but instead allowed the British private security firms employed by the F&CO and the Military to direct the protection operation. So, whilst I was recceing Des' visit, the Colonel in charge of Basra Palace asked why I was putting more in place to protect the SoSD than the PM's protection team had done for the Prime Minister, stating that I was "very thorough."

I didn't answer the Colonel's question, but the truth was that I knew full well why the PM's team hadn't utilised all the assets available to them to secure the life of our country's political leader. The deficiencies lay with a lack of knowledge and experience. I knew what was available from our military, Intelligence and eavesdropping services not to mention those of partner nations such as the United States or the Dutch. With the disbanding of the Branch and the coming of SO1, new blood had purposefully been drafted into protection straight from uniform, especially at a supervisory level. Dealing with uniformed policing in London one day to running protection operations in a killing zone the next, was for any officer a massive learning curve. In Special Branch, officers were moulded for years to take on these responsibilities, not to mention that officers had to prove their interest in all things political via the SB exam process, against stiff competition, before one even joined. This lack of political intellect, knowledge of secret intelligence handling and experience, was leading to deadly deficiencies.

During the visit to Basra, Des Brown intended to have meetings in Basra Palace, the British Army's HQ for the region and, at the time, the most bombed place on earth. Recceing the facility, which I knew very well, I spoke to Major Tarquin, who was handling the visit's programme for the army. The Major provided me with the exact detail of the military's proposed programme for the Minister. The Major explained that he intended to transport the Minister in a Warrior armoured troop carrier, but place him in the top cover position so he could see as the convoy swept through the streets of Basra. He then planned for the convoy to stop off at various sites where the Military were assisting Iraqi civilians. Finally the Major planned for the Minister to visit the joint Iraqi-Coalition forces police and security HQ (PJOC) before returning to Basra Palace. This would have been a round trip of some twenty or more miles with the Minister in the 'top cover' position throughout. Top cover is the position whereby a soldier stands outside the hatch of an armoured vehicle with the upper half of his body exposed to the elements, whilst he is protected from the waist down by the vehicle's turret. Once the Major had outlined his plan I asked him if he saw any deficiencies. He appeared nonplussed.

"What about Top Cover?" I asked.

"What about Top Cover?" He retorted. "My men perform Top Cover all the time. How else will the Minister be able to see downtown Basra as we travel through the city?" I pointed out that the Minister was not a soldier and that being injured, let alone dying due to enemy activity was not an option.

"That's unlikely Detective Inspector." Sneered the Major.

I immediately retorted. "I think you're aware that at least ten soldiers from your regiment have been shot performing Top-Cover in the last few months."

As part of my pre-deployment activity I'd read the regiment's casualty reports from DIS *(the Defence Intelligence Section of the UK MOD – now known as the Defence Intelligence Agency (DIA).* This didn't move the Major one iota. He hit back even more sarcastically.

"I think you need to understand the situation on the ground, Detective Inspector." The Major's words were meant to be cutting. It was as though he thought I'd come to Iraq for the first time, whereas of course, I'd been active in Iraq for many years.

So I called his bluff.

"Okay, let's go. Put a patrol together, Major, and I'll stand Top Cover as you want the Minister to do, that way I can precisely identify where any dangers might lie."

A few hours later, ten or so armoured vehicles pulled out of Basra Palace on route to Basra city. I was stood Top Cover, G36 in hand, cocked and ready to roll for some of the journey. We travelled the Major's proposed route visiting the civilian sites: a school for girls – itself a potentially dangerous location, a small medical area and the Police Joint Operational Command Centre where Iraqi police and Security Service officers worked hand in hand with the British and Coalition Military Police and Intelligence, under British control. The PJOC was one of the main venues that the SoSD wished to visit.

The PJOC was located in the middle of an urban area, in ambush country. Getting out of the PJOC would be awfully difficult if we were attacked. I spoke to the PJOC's commanding officer and asked if a helicopter could land on the roof, as I was optioning the possibility of bringing the Minister into the facility by air or at least evacuating him via this method should it come on top.

The commander said helo access was not possible. I could see it was, although, I could also see that any helicopter would be extremely vulnerable to small arms and RPG fire, not to mention shoulder held SAMs. As I said I'd take a closer look to assess this, the commanding officer took me out of the earshot of his Iraqi colleagues and begged me not to consider the air option. The commanding officer apologised for not telling me the truth regarding the helo option. He had wanted to keep this option secret from his Iraqi colleagues, as if the PJOC was ever attacked, the British and coalition contingent would only have this surprise option open to them to affect their escape. The commanding officer was being realistic; he knew he couldn't trust all of his Iraqi colleagues and that every day his life, and those of his men, was on the line. He felt extremely vulnerable working in the PJOC in the middle of a city where many people hated him and all he stood for. I decided to strike the air option from my planning process, the potential compromise to the guys' lives being more important than a ministerial visit on this occasion.

Recce visit over, Major Tarquin led our convoy back to Basra Palace along another extended route, hoping that this would impart to the Minister the dangers his lads faced when patrolling the city.

Upon re-entering the palace grounds we came under immediate IDF. The rockets being fired were accurately targeted and one couldn't help but suspect that enemies within the palace had contacted insurgents outside and informed them of our return. We immediately hit the ground, explosions bursting around us. Amongst other things, I knew I'd have to deal with this potential IDF threat before the Minister's arrival.

I didn't sanction the major's plan for the SoS visit. What I told the Colonel in charge of Basra Palace was that I wouldn't allow the SoS to stand top cover at any time and I'd restrict and harden the programme. I made it clear that the Sos would not stand top cover. In fact, if the operation took place, I'd demand that the SoS transported in a Challenger battle tank, instead of warrior, as warrior was vulnerable to various weapons systems in the insurgents arsenal. As an outer shield I'd have helicopter support over the convoy, Awacs oversight of the route, Explosive Ordnance Disposal officers searching and securing the locations which I believed safe for him to visit and sufficient troops to help my men and I harden each location. None of these elements had been considered by the Major in his plan, as expertise and experience count for much in the protection game. I did not sanction the proposed a visit to the PJOC, scrubbing it totally.

I knew my plan would cause some consternation as I was using up a massive amount of resources. But frankly my aim was to prevent the operation in its proposed form, even with my added precautions. The mission was to take place during the 'Ashura' *(a major Islamic commemoration festival particularly for Shia Muslims)* and as such it was an ultra-dangerous time to visit down town Basra. I believed that if the SoS visited Tarquin's proposed sites during the Ashura it would be like rubbing Shia faces in the dirt. In my opinion it was therefore a politically poor time for such an expansive visit. Whichever member of the SoS' political or special advisor staff planned the SoS' visit at this juncture should be reprimanded, as it was basic assessment and intelligence procedure to consider such issues when making visits proposals. That's why I nevertheless demanded a high level of security should any aspect of the visit take place. I discussed the visit with the Colonel in charge of Basra Palace. He was clearly fearful that we would take in coming fire should the visit occur, but as is often the case with our 'can-do' military; he was unwilling to admit this officially to his senior officers and the military's political leadership. The Colonel's troops had already taken heavy casualties during his tour and he didn't want to lose any more. I called for a meeting with the British Ambassador to Iraq, Rosalind Marsden, who I knew well. Rosalind agreed with my assessment that politically the visit in its present format was not the best move. I put my concerns and those of the Colonel and the Ambassador to General Lamb, the senior British Military officer in charge of Iraq's southern region. General Lamb agreed that the visit parameters should be changed. I passed my decision to the MOD HQ in London and to SO1 at the Yard. I would recommend a curtailed programme to aid diplomacy in Basra and to potentially save British soldiers and Iraqi civilians lives and possibly that of the SoSD and, with his, most probably my own.

In the end, Des Brown was able to see some of the actual situation on the ground and perform his crucial role even though I limited his exposure to danger and possible death. Des was able to evaluate the continuing insurgency, perform his welfare role to the troops and report his conclusions on the conflict back to the Prime Minister, thereby effecting Britain's international policy. What Major Tarquin clearly didn't understand was that frankly, the Minister was not expendable. It's a sad fact of life that not all men's lives are equal.

Nine months later I handed the responsibility for Des Brown's team over to another DI. At the meeting where I discussed the handover and introduced my successor, I asked Des if he wished to comment on any concerns he might have on my stewardship of his and his ministers' protection teams. After initially saying that everything was fine and dandy, I pushed him to be absolutely truthful as I felt he harboured some reservations.

"Okay, then, Carlton" he said finally, "I think it's ludicrous that you and the team travel with me to Afghanistan and Iraq when I have thousands of soldiers including the Royal Military Police *(RMP)* that could protect me there. After all, I am in-charge of the military and this would save money."

I took this opportunity to disabuse the SoS of this position, explaining what his fate could have been:

"If the military had been responsible for your protection you'd most probably be dead by now," I answered.

I recounted the example of Major Tarquin and his Top-Cover proposal before going on to explain why he didn't experience many mortar or rocket attacks while in Iraq.

"Before your arrival on visits to Iraq I arranged with the military - the RAF regiment, Special Forces and on occasions other coalition forces militaries - to try to limit IDF attacks by them identifying and destroying any insurgent mortar base plate firing sites that are targeting any facility where you'll be staying. Additionally, during your actual visit, I'd task RAF, or other coalition air forces AWACs' to seek out any new insurgent firing points for immediate destruction for the duration of your stay. That's why there's usually a lull in that generally constant IDF fire you read about in your daily intelligence reports when you arrive in theatre.

"The interventions I undertake to keep you safe are resource intensive, so when you're not there, Basra Palace is hell on earth for the guys and gals who live and work there. The actions I instigate require such an effort that normally they are not undertaken. My job is to keep you alive, so where I could I intervened to prevent you being exposed to the dangers of the real conditions in Basra or indeed elsewhere in Iraq or Afghanistan. The risks to your life were too great to do otherwise. The RMP don't have the clout to do this and besides they are not as risk averse enough to do so.

"We all know that your assassination would be a major blow to the coalition forces and a propaganda coup for the insurgents. Such an act would prolong the conflict and cost yet more lives. So I've always made sure that everything possible - and when I say everything possible, I mean it - was done to keep you safe."

Des graciously accepted my explanation, admitting he hadn't a clue of the lengths I'd gone to, to keep him alive.

*

One of al-Qa'ida's most audacious pre-9/11 plots took place in October 2000, when a Yemeni-based cell attacked the US naval vessel - the USS Cole. The suicide squad rammed the Cole with their small, explosives-laden boat, causing massive damage to the side of the state-of-the-art US destroyer. The resulting explosion killed 17 US sailors and injured 39, although luckily it didn't sink the US warship as per the operation's intention. In 2008, two suicide bombers set off a series of blasts outside the heavily fortified US embassy in Sana'a, killing 16. In 2009, a Yemeni suicide bomber came close to killing Saudi Arabia's Minister for Internal Security by posing as a reformed militant who wanted to return to the fold. There had been perhaps hundreds, if not thousands of other attacks aimed at Yemeni targets. By 2010 therefore, the Yemen was embroiled in an unending cycle of low intensity warfare, it was a very dangerous place indeed.

On the morning of April 26 2010, Osman Ali Noman Asaloi, a 22-year-old student from Taiz province, South West Yemen, waited by the roadside. Close by, Fairuz Abdullah Buraq, Ali Saleh Alhadji and Noman Ahamati were also going about their business in the impoverished rubbish-strewn neighbourhood of eastern Sana'a. At the same time, the security convoy of Britain's 52-year-old Ambassador to the Yemen, Tim Torlot, converged on the location. Most mornings, after slightly varying their route and arriving at marginally different times, Ambassador Torlot's convoy would pass this choke-point en route from his official residence in downtown Sana'a to the brand new British Embassy on the outskirts of the city. As per normal, on account of the narrow streets, the convoy slowed down.

Osman, who looked young for his age and was wearing a school-uniform as disguise, approached the slow moving convoy as it began to quicken again and detonated his suicide vest concealed under the uniform. The explosion was enormous, Osman's head would later be found on the roof of a house twenty meters away, but the Ambassador and his Yemeni protection team escaped uninjured.

The attack bore all the hallmarks of an al-Qa'ida assassination attempt. The British embassy closed for a short period afterwards, as a precautionary measure. Additionally, all staff were henceforth required to travel in armoured vehicles and under armed Yemeni escort.

So on October 6 2010, when five UK embassy staff members, including the deputy head of mission, were *en route* to work at the new embassy they felt relatively safe until their vehicle suddenly veered off course, as though hit by a truck. It was the result of an RPG projectile fired by Militants at the lead vehicle containing the British diplomats. The armour did its job and all escaped relatively unharmed, although Torlot's deputy suffered minor injuries. On the same day at the Austrian gas company OMV in Haddah on the outskirts of Sanaa, a Yemeni security guard opened fire on those he was supposed to be guarding. As a result a French contractor was killed and his British colleague badly injured. The compound was quickly surrounded by Yemeni security forces who eventually disarmed the gunman.

Foreign Secretary *(FS)* William Hague commented on the diplomatic attack stating: "This morning's attack… highlights the risks our diplomats face working for Britain's interests abroad. I am full of admiration for the way our embassy is dealing with this difficult situation. This shameful attack on British diplomats will only redouble

Britain's determination to work with the government of Yemen to help address the challenges that country faces."

After the second attack, Foreign Secretary Hague informed me that he wanted to travel to The Yemen. The Joint Terrorism Analysis Centre *(JTAC - based in MI5's London HQ)* threat assessment for such a visit was Critical – meaning it had the highest level of threat attached to the visit. In other words, according to JTAC, Intelligence suggests that an attack is in the planning, and it is highly likely that an assassination attempt will be made. Nevertheless, by the first week in February 2011 Foreign Secretary Hague told me that his mind was made up, he wanted to travel to the Yemen!

A special RMV was convened at COBRA to consider the extremely high risk visit. All the main parties were present: the chair of RMV, the head of SO1, Sam Bait, senior representatives from MI5, MI6, GCHQ and Special Forces, the head of the F&CO protocol office, FS' PPS, British Ambassador Torlot, *(via video link from the Yemen)* and of course, me.

As head of the Foreign Secretary's protection team I was the person who would lead any operation to The Yemen.

I knew the Yemen. I had operated there on several previous occasions, so I was confident that the mission was doable if I received the highest degree of assistance from the bodies around the table. I told the Chair that I had designed an operational plan for the visit in which I'd limit the Foreign Secretary's exposure to six hours in-country and secure every aspect of his travel. In order to do this, I'd travel in advance to the Yemen and provide the committee with a detailed operational plans and the outcome of my negotiations with Yemeni authorities concerning their assistance prior to recommending whether the visit should take place. I travelled to Yemen the following day taking SO1's communications expert, Jim, a DS who I'd worked with on several occasions in the past, with me. To provide the worried officials at COBRA with up-to-date information on the operation I had Jim set up an encrypted live video and audio feed, back to SO1 HQ at the Yard for onward transmission to COBRA.

Having won the initial argument regarding the potential for such an operation to go ahead, I refined the plan in the Yemen which COBRA subsequently signed off somewhat hesitantly. It was undoubtedly a dangerous operation.

I now commenced my operational and tactical plan. I met with the Yemeni generals in charge of the special police and security police to gain assistance to line vulnerable sections of the route I proposed for the Foreign Secretary's visit to the British embassy and President Salah's Palace. My plan foresaw three mobile concentric security circles orbiting the Foreign Secretary. An outer shield of Yemeni Special Police and Special Forces, an intermediary body of trusted Yemeni protection officers who were assigned to Ambassador Torlot's protection team by the Yemenis and finally an inner close protective shell of SO1 officers who would shield the Foreign Secretary. This inner body would include an SO1 counter assault team *(CAT)* armed with H&K G36s.

Throughout, I would stay close to the Foreign Secretary in the principle personal protection role, backed up by one of my FS's protection team's top DS's, who would ride shotgun in the Foreign Secretary's vehicle. In my outer rim I'd also include an advance vehicle that would seek-out would-be assassins. I'd staff this both with SO1 and trusted Yemeni officers.

I'd tasked GCHQ, at COBRA, to provide me with constant live updates of any relevant sigint. As for the aircraft used by the FS, if he used one of the RAF's Queen's flight aircraft, I arranged for Yemeni Air Force security police, the Yemeni Army and British security staff from the Embassy supervised by one of my SO1 officers to secure it. The RAF crew would also stay on board throughout protecting its interior. I'd agreed with the general in-charge of Yemeni air defences that his personnel would deal with any aerial threats whilst the FS' aircraft was in Yemeni airspace. As for comms, SO1 officers' communications and those of our embassy's Yemeni police staff were to be patched through to me directly, through Jim, he also provide me with any critical up dates from other comms feeds.

In addition to SIS, and JTAC intelligence, I gained protective security intelligence on the local Yemeni scene from the Special Agent in charge *(SAC)* of the US Diplomatic Security Service *(DSS)* at the US embassy in Sana'a. Chuck was a good guy, it was through him that I secured the agreement of the US Navy to, in-extremis, medevac the Foreign Secretary and I to their fully-equipped hospital aboard an aircraft carrier attached to their nearby Sixth Fleet *(I requested this assistance from the Americans as I'd previously recced Sana'a's major hospitals and accessed that Yemen's medical facilities were incapable of dealing satisfactorily with major trauma)*.

I couldn't guarantee the missions success, but I'd done all I could to secure a favourable outcome. However, as British interests were clearly in al Qaeda's sights, many at COBRA, including Sam Bait and the RMV Chair, thought the visit unwise. I couldn't deny that it was a calculated gamble.

For my part I knew from my time in SIS, that al Qaeda in Yemen had assassination operations on the shelf, jobs which could be picked up, dusted off and executed at short notice. So my calculation of around the six hours on the ground for the Foreign Secretary was heavily predicated on the belief that those deadly pre-recce'd ops could not be deployed within this limited timeframe. Our lives would depend on my calculation.

My self-assurance in calling this mission, against resistance from many at COBRA was built on everything my life in the Branch and SIS had taught me. Thanks to my time on 'E' Squad I already possessed a relatively good understanding of Yemeni history and its political scene. 'C' Squad had revealed to me how extremist hierarchies tended to function, whilst my years in MI6 made me au fait with the relevant terrorist groups in the region and their capacity, and finally the years on 'A' Squad/SO1 had provided me with the understanding of how to mitigate such groups' deadly intentions.

The self-belief garnered by this experience and expertise gained, allowed me to cajole, direct, press, spoon feed, soothe, mollify or stand firm as was required to achieve this mission. My interlocutor's rank, role or position was immaterial. I knew that in such operations deficiencies in knowledge, capability and capacity could be fatal a situation that was more likely to occur as more and more experienced ex-Branch personnel retire to be replaced by inexperienced officers selected by less rigorous criteria. After all SO1 officers are tasked with protecting the nation's and the World's, primary political leaders.

The FS' visit was a complete success, it ran like clockwork from start to finish, as everyone around the COBRA table could only have hoped but many secretly doubted. It had been an expensive operation, especially considering the limited length of time the Foreign Secretary actually spent on the ground, but I believe it was worth every penny.

I had no faith in the conventional War on Terror. In my opinion such a war was nothing but overkill and, more importantly, only served to work as an excellent recruiting sergeant for jihadi terrorism. We could have dealt with 9/11 by massively increasing counter terrorist funding in the police, security & intelligence services, Special Forces and most importantly through Islamic theological deliberation with the fundamentalist on the meaning of Jihad. However, the cards had been dealt and two conventional wars later, I felt we now had to stay the course to prevent further terror. The Foreign Secretary's visit to Yemen had to be seen in this context as it carried a strong political message to the UK's friends and enemies alike. We were in the struggle for keeps. That's why I supported William Hague's desire to travel to the Yemen and that's why I used everything I could to make it happen.

I was working from a similar calculation when I authorised a comparable mission to Peshawar, Pakistan, the most dangerous part of a hazardous country where the Taliban and a plethora of other domestic Jihadi and religious-based terror organisations roam free.

When running ops in Pakistan one has to be rather permissive in terms of risk, as if not, one would never authorise a Minister to visit any other city than Islamabad and then only the diplomatic enclave.

I have led numerous operations in Pakistan and on this occasion I was tasked with leading the protection operation to secure the life of the Secretary of State for International Development, Andrew Mitchell *(later of Plebgate fame)*. Prior to the deployment Secretary of State Mitchell informed me that in addition to visiting Islamabad and various other cities he would like to visit the ultra-dangerous city of Peshawar and hold meetings with moderate politicians and civil society there. At the time, the British consulate in Peshawar had been closed and mothballed for over two years, as it was simply too dangerous for F&CO staff to work there.

The extremely heavily fortressed American consulate in Peshawar had remained open but even it had recently been attacked by Jihadi terrorists who almost managed to force their way into the structure in a sustained bomb and small arms attack. Moreover, Peshawar's particular dangers were well known to me, as I'd been there on a few previous occasions. So if I did agree to take the minister there,

I was conscious that he would be the first British cabinet minister to visit the city for several years and would therefore be a major target. Peshawar was simply considered by most, too dangerous to visit. Nonetheless I travelled the 120 miles with members of my Islamabad advance team to covertly recce our mothballed Consulate. Whilst there, as I often did in countries I visited the US Consulate in the city to speak to the United States Department of State Security Service Regional Security Officer *(DSS RSO)*, Arthur Williams. I often touch base with the DSS as they invariably had access to good intelligence on the localities in which they were stationed, Arthur was no exception. Arthur was extremely helpful, sharing amongst other things the DSS's findings concerning that recent Jihadi attack on the Consulate which still bore the scars left by bombs and bullets. Arthur's US Intel afforded me with an excellent insight into the local terror picture.

I was acutely aware that it was especially important for HM Secretaries of State for International Development to visit hard-to-reach places, as he/she often requires a view that is independent from that espoused by the host nation and even his/her own officials. So as I calculated the threat and concluded that allowing the SoS to visit Peshawar was a risk worth taking, I combined Arthur's US Intel with that which I'd previously gained from UK sources and formulated a stealthy operational plan, of short duration, to our mothballed Consulate.

The person I chose as 2ic for this mission was Tarik, an excellent Special Branch DS. We'd known of each other for many years but he'd only begun working for me when I returned to 'A' Squad as a DI. Tarik was a British Asian of East African/Pakistani heritage. A former medic in the British Army Tarik was a capable fellow and his excellent Indian sub-continental language skills were invaluable. We'd worked on several sub-continental Prot jobs together.

Even though Pakistani forces had been penetrated by terrorist groups, I'd used their specialist units on prot jobs, including Rangers, counter-terrorist commandos and the Frontier Corps, on many previous occasions. The mortality rate of these units was phenomenal. Each time I returned to Pakistan, I'd enquire after someone I'd worked with previously to be told that they'd been killed in the line of duty.

After requesting any threat sigint from both British and American agencies via my contacts at GCHQ and NSA, Tarik and I went to see the head of Pakistani Special Branch in Peshawar. He agreed to provide us with some officers to sure-up security and to provide us with their own up-to-the-minute threat intelligence. The chief also confirmed that the moment the British embassy staff in Islamabad sent out invitations to those the Minister wished to meet at the consulate, the terrorists would simultaneously be made aware of the visit. It's just the way it was, Peshawar leaked like a sieve. With this in mind, I made sure the embassy would only inform guests the night before the meeting.

On the day of the Peshawar op I sent Tarik and Dave, another of my officers, plus two members of the embassy's security staff ahead to open up the consulate, with the help of the local caretaker, and then secure it. In addition to our Glocks my SO1 team members also carried H&K G36's or MP5 A3s this would provide us with the capacity to at least have a chance of fighting off a potential ambush. The Heckler & Koch G36 was an excellent weapon system which I had been able to introduce when I formed the HTLI *(High Threat Low Infrastructure)* team in 'A' Squad/SO1 post discussions with ACSO Veness, shortly after my initial Iraq operations during and after the 2003 war fighting stage of operation 'Iraq Freedom'. As for me, on this operation, because I was travelling with the Minister as the Principal Protection Officer *(PPO)*,

I'd carry the MP5 Kurtz as its smaller frame would allow me to better manhandle the principal should we come under attack.

On this occasion I controlled the operation from my position in the principal's armoured vehicle. On other occasions I'd choose to do this from the back-up vehicle. For reasons of stealth, I decided we'd travel in a small convoy of three-vehicles to Peshawar. Tarik would return with us in a fourth vehicle.

Most importantly of all, I set a four-hour maximum window from arrival to leaving the consulate – this was a calculation I made based on various factors along with secret intelligence - but it was only a calculation. Anybody in the chain could have let the cat out of the bag regarding the actual date and time of the visit prior to my authorised timings *(the night before the meeting – albeit as additional security I made the embassy withhold the Consulate venue until the morning of the visit. The enemy might think we'd use one of the city's main 5 star hotels for the meet.).*

I'd use alternative routes in and out of Peshawar, but again there were only so many routes to the venue and back to Islamabad. I was not kidding myself, to achieve the op successfully and to return home unharmed, we'd have to be on our toes throughout the day.

On the day of the races the Pakistani SB informed us that terrorist sympathisers had got to hear of the visit but after consulting all the intelligence agencies, I decided to go ahead. The stealthy nature of our operation allowed us to travel to the Consulate, open it, stage some community meetings and return to the Embassy in Islamabad before the enemy could initiate an attack. The plan had come together and the Minister's visit had passed off without incident.

Unfortunately, as time ticks and the Branch recedes into history, those former Branch officers who possess the breadth of knowledge, personal contacts and fortitude to challenge senior ranks or to direct Principals of what is, or is not possible, will dwindle never to be replaced. In my opinion this does not bode well for the future.

Today, it is likely that these visits would either not take place at all or be undertaken in a less embracing manner. The fallout for senior UK VIPs will be that their visits to trouble spots may be compromised or curtailed. If nothing else, Ministerial visits inform politicians of the actual situation on the ground, foster personal contacts and helps shape UK government policy vis-à-vis nations across the world. An inability to achieve this safely will do the nation a disservice.

Chapter Twenty - Heads of State

Shortly before some parts of the Branch were swallowed up into the new Counter Terrorism Command *(CTC/SO15)*, my rotation out of protection was under consideration. Two potential roles had been earmarked, that of the Branch's man in either the German BKA in Berlin, the Dutch CRI in Den Haag, Netherlands or the Federal Police in Brussels, Belgium utilising either my German or Dutch language skills. The other option, thanks to my experience in 'C' & 'E' Squads, NPOIU and SIS was as head of 'C' Squad's Prosecutions Unit, dealing with breaches of the Official Secrets Act, arresting amongst others, spies.

But when the music stopped playing and my spiritual home the Metropolitan Police Special Branch, aka Specialist Operations 12 *(SO12)* was disbanded forever, on 3rd October 2006 at the stroke of Commissioner Ian Blair's pen, the days of rotation in the field of specialist political policing intelligence died.

It wouldn't take long for me to realise that I was fortunate to have been on 'A' Squad when it all ended. With very few exceptions the disbanding of MPSB hit all Branch officers very hard but at least those on 'A' Squad, now SO1, knew that their role was to be maintained whereas those on 'B', 'C', 'E', 'P' 'R' and 'S' squads were in turmoil. On these squads the work of whole sections would be cut, merged with other MPS units or simply halted. The powers that be hadn't thought this through at all, even though their actions, in my opinion, undermined the security of the United Kingdom.

The majority of 'B', 'C', 'E', 'S' and 'P' squads combined with the Anti-Terrorist Branch *(SO13)*, the Met's CID unit that investigated 'terrorist' offences nationally, to form the Counter-Terrorist Command *(SO15)*. Unfortunately, this collaboration was not a unifying of

Branches, but rather the takeover of the much larger rump of Special Branch by what was previously SO13. Therefore, much of 'B', 'C', 'E' and 'P's political intelligence gathering, monitoring and targeting work went by the wayside, in favour of the CID-centric ethos of 'bodies in the cell'. The long held secret intelligence gathering, assessment and collative philosophy of the Branch was effectively no more.

For the first time in 120 years the MPS no longer had the independent capacity to fully assess social cohesion, survey, analyse or pre-empt politically orientated criminality, extremism and terrorism, or to avert politically inspired public disorder in London or to assess the effect that political violence elsewhere in the UK and abroad might have on the capital. The fact that my efforts on September 17th 2001 to create a NSB to stave off this day had come to nought, had now hit full frontal. MPSB was no more.

Although I argued to *officially* keep 'A' Squad's intelligence gathering role in the change-over to SO1, I'd lose this battle. Prot would now major solely in protection, so along with other ex-Branch Protmen, I'd remain in the protection role, although I had to transform myself from a Special Branch 'A' Squad intelligence centric protection officer into an SO1 Specialist Protection operative.

Rebranded as the independent protection body SO1 *(Specialist Protection)* within the MPS's new Protection Command along with Royalty and Diplomatic Protection Group, the old SB ethos would be slowly transformed from within. Therefore, as time went on, new recruits to SO1 would no longer have even basic political knowledge about the people they were protecting. The gathering of secret intelligence was never even considered and unlike Special Branch officers many of these SO1 recruits were unacquainted with the use of secret intelligence in operations not to mention the geographical location of some of the countries they would operate in, yet alone their history, political tensions and leanings. It was also the case that officers, lacking knowledge of the political sphere and thus confidence in this area, were much less likely to challenge their principal's wishes, even in the interests of safety.

In my opinion, it was impossible to spin the Branch's demise as a positive outcome. I wasn't alone. Some months after the disbanding of the Branch I met with former Home Secretary Dr John Reid *(on whose watch the Branch was disbanded)*, to discuss his continuing personal protection package. To my surprise, Dr Reid proclaimed: "I was always against the disbanding of the Special Branch." Although I was dismayed, it was pointless saying anything. The damage had been done. All I could do was try to continue to do what I did best.

*

In 2008 I found myself in Beijing at the Olympic Games securing London House against terrorist attack. With the UK as the Games' successor country, London House was set to be one of the major attractions in Beijing over the period of the Games. Every UK dignitary, from the Prime Minister down, who visited Beijing during the Games would pass through its doors. London House was in fact a huge and famous restaurant on a beautiful lake near Shi–Chai-Hai Lotus market. When I first saw the facility, which sat on a 3,000m2 plot, with three weeks to go before the opening ceremony, I could immediately see it was wide open to an attack from any would-be terrorist. Nothing had been done.

A myriad of threats had been made against the Games, the most viable of which came from a Turkic-Chinese organisation known as the East Turkestan Islamic Movement *(ETIM)*. The ETIM were affiliated with Al-Qaeda and claimed to represent the non-ethnic Han-Chinese, Uighur people in their goal to establish, in their home region of Northwestern China, the fundamentalist Muslim state of 'East Turkistan' and to convert all citizens there to Islam. In 2007, ETIM militants had shot Chinese nationals in Pakistani Balochistan, in retaliation for the Beijing execution of an ETIM official earlier that year. Even more worryingly, ETIM had committed a number of atrocities in the run-up to the Olympics, including a series of bus bombings and an attack on paramilitary troops in Kashgar that killed seventeen officers. ETIM had since issued several videos in which they threatened to attack the Beijing summer Games.

The first problem was that the site was very large, it had several points of entry, was in a built-up area to which all-comers had access and it was situated on a major thoroughfare. These were ideal conditions from a commercial, optical and fashionable perspective, but from the point of view of security it could hardly have been worse.

Terrorists could easily drive a vehicle with explosives into the building or use it as a feeder, placing several smaller devices and weapons in cars, motorbikes or tuck-tucks parked around the facility's exterior and follow any initial attack with secondary gun and knife attacks on fleeing guests exiting the facility *(in March 2014, Uighur separatists would do just this - shooting and stabbing their way through a crowd of people near a railway station in Kunming, killing 29 and injuring more than 130)*. Such an attack would not necessarily be a suicide attack as the perpetrators could easily melt into the ever-present crowds or, in the ensuing panic, use numerous connecting avenues and streets to escape. The building was also vulnerable to sniper attack as it was overlooked by several high rise properties.

The site had been bought and paid for and it was too late to do anything about moving location. My only option was to toughen up security. That meant convincing the Chinese authorities – the police and the city of Beijing's council - as well as newly-elected London Mayor Boris Johnson's London Development Agency that my plans were necessary and doable. I would also have to explain that my official stamp of approval was going to come with a hefty price tag.

After negotiations with the Chinese owners of the site I immediately began the internal changes to the facility introducing airport-style search arches. I also surrounded the site with CCTV cameras and arc-lighting *(taking care to remove blind spots)* and created a command centre from where security could be run and the CCTV be monitored. I also agreed protocols with the Beijing Police for patrolling the external areas of the facility, citing the UK's participation at the time in two active wars in Afghanistan and Iraq that made us a particular target, adding that the ETIM were affiliated with some of those we were combating in those wars.

Like in the UK, the vast majority of Chinese police are unarmed. So I spoke to representatives of China's paramilitary police, the People's Armed Police *(PAP)* who agreed to provide armed protection for London House, with extra numbers on hand when high value principals came to visit, including Prime Minister Gordon Brown, ex-Prime Minister Tony Blair and any UK Cabinet Ministers. With some difficulty, I also managed to persuade PAP to deploy additional security such as anti-sniper positions in areas that were vulnerable to being observed from the high buildings surrounding London House.

Via my Chinese Security Police liaison, I approached the Chinese Internal Security Service to check out the residents in the high rise buildings that overlooked the site. I also *spoke* to the facilities and exhibition crews at London House who were setting London-themed adornments in the grounds, and persuaded them to place a few of their decorative structures in the potential line of fire from these high rise buildings. Having done all I could to foil a would-be sniper I turned to the issue of external security measures, which was where I hit a brick wall.

I met with the deputy area Commander of the Beijing Police and put to him my requirements for the facility's external security. "Parking has to be suspended near to the building's walls and I'd like permission to build a concrete buffer zone around the whole of the facility with chicanes at two extremely vulnerable points to slow down traffic and prevent trucks being driven straight through the facility's walls.

"I'd also like to put Hesco-bastion fortifications in front of the enormous historical wooden gate which leads directly into the facility's courtyard from the lake's shores. Such Hesco fortifications would help withstand certain types of direct attacks on the facility."

The Deputy Commander was having none of it. His proposal was simple, as there was no real terrorism in China, he would simply put police officers all around the facility at vulnerable times; if necessary two deep, and ward off any would be attackers that way. I pointed out that even if the police did manage to prevent an assassin in a VIED getting close to the building they probably wouldn't be able to prevent suicide bombers from exploding their device and that any blasts emanating from the roads surrounding the building would most probably destroy the facility. The Deputy Commander refused to accept this.

I asked the Deputy Commander if he could set up a meeting between myself, the Commissioner of Beijing police and the head of the PAP to iron this problem out. I knew I wouldn't get such a high-level meeting, but I felt that if I pushed for the top people, then they might send me somebody of sufficient seniority so they could make policy and not just follow orders. Later that day I received notice I'd be able meet with the Chief of Police for that quadrant of Beijing – an officer akin to an Assistant Commissioner in the MPS. Not to be outdone, the PAP said they'd also send a senior officer to the meeting.

To ensure I had the right amount of "firepower" available to me concerning countering IEDs, I'd spoken to the Military Section at our Embassy and asked if they had an explosives expert amongst their staff. The Colonel in-charge *(the British Military Attaché) said I was in luck, an EOD Major (Bomb disposal officer)* had recently arrived in Beijing to study Chinese at Beijing University. Although he wasn't technically a member of their staff, the Colonel was fairly sure that he'd be willing to help. Excellent, I thought. I got the officer's mobile number and gave him a call. We agreed to meet about an hour before my scheduled meeting with the Chinese at London House at a drinks stand about sixty metres from the entrance.

I had no doubt that with his knowledge he'd be able to fully explain what blasts actually do, and why I needed external fortifications to shore up the facility. I was also pretty sure that if the Chinese brought an EOD of their own, in order to rebut my requests, that their man's actual knowledge in the field couldn't match that of my Major's who'd serviced in Afghanistan, Iraq and Northern Ireland.

As time passed, I grew worried that he might not show up. In a city of twenty million people there were invariably always thousands of inhabitants around, no matter where one was, and the area surrounding London House seemed even more crowded. As I scanned the crowd for my EOD Major I noticed a local guy was watching me. If he was a member of a security police surveillance team, he'd need some retraining, I thought.

It was unlike a British Army officer to no-show bang on time, so after about ten minutes or so, I decided to call him. As I did, I noticed the Chinese guy who'd been watching me answer his mobile.

"You're not Steven are you?" I said, looking straight at him.

"Ya," he said in that rather cut-glass British Army officer's tone. I hung up, walked the several metres towards him and shook hands.

"I guess we were both looking for somebody else!" he quipped, as we both saw the funny part of our standoff.

Mistaken preconceptions continued to play a significant role as the day continued. As we went into meet the senior Chinese officers my interpreter overheard the Assistant Commissioner saying to his assistant that he had thought he was meeting with the British, not the Americans and despite reassurances that we were indeed British, the Assistant Commissioner still looked puzzled, so I made sure that I introduced Steven as a member of Her Royal Britannic Majesty's armed forces and one of our foremost experts in explosives and myself as Detective Inspector from Scotland Yard's Special Branch – practically every law enforcement officer worldwide is familiar with Scotland Yard.

The negotiations were difficult yet successful. It cost the British Government £200,000 in terms of fortifications, which I had to get made from scratch, eventually finding a firm outside the city that could handle the order in the required time.

By the time Prime Minister Gordon Brown arrived on an official visit and stopped by London House, I was confident he was as safe as he could possibly be inside that building. Unfortunately for Gordon, Tony Blair decided to drop in at the same time. Let's just say that by this time they were not the best of friends. Blair's charisma shone through as he stole the much-needed limelight from the new Prime Minister.

*

Of course, Blair didn't always get his own way. One memorable instance took place in the summer of 2003 at the annual Progressive Governance Summit on this occasion held in Kent, UK. Some twelve centre left heads of State/government and several hundred delegates attended the conference to discuss world issues from this left leaning perspective. Amongst those leaders who attended was SPD *(The German Labour Party)* leader and Chancellor of Germany at the time, Gerhard Schröder. I was in charge of the 'A' Squad team protecting Chancellor Schröder.

As a key attendee Schröder was scheduled to have a bilateral meeting in the margins of the summit with Prime Minister Tony Blair. As the time approached for the meeting, I was informed through my earpiece that the Prime Minister had excused himself from the leaders he had been conversing with and was making his way to the room where he and Chancellor Schröder were due to meet. As the meeting room was around a hundred and fifty metres away from our present location on the front lawn of the conference hotel, I imparted this information to Chancellor Schröder's PPS.

The Chancellor was enjoying an expensive glass of wine provided by the British taxpayer as he conversed with the leaders of Brazil, Sweden and Chile.

A voice squeaked through my earpiece. "The PM has arrived in the meeting room, Carlton."

I looked at Chancellor Schröder. He was savouring the last sips from his glass.

"The Chancellor's just finishing his drink." I radioed to the PM's protection team leader.

"Okay, I'll tell the PM." He responded. A few more minutes passed.

"Any ETA, Carlton?"

"I'm afraid not. I've told Schröder's PPS we're running late and Chancellor's acknowledged my nod. So I guess we'll be coming soon." I replied.

To reinforce the urgency I told Uli, Chancellor Schröder's BKA protection team leader that Prime Minister Blair had been waiting for the Chancellor for almost five minutes in the bilateral meeting room. Uli walked over to Chancellor Schröder and whispered in his ear.

I was acquainted with Schröder having protected him on several occasions in the past. From his position sitting down in one of the comfy seats he turned to look at me, clearly acknowledging my presence, then turning back towards the other leaders he'd been holding court with and suggested loudly, for my benefit, that they should perhaps share another bottle of Tony's excellent, expensive wine. I immediately radioed the PM's protection team leader to tell them that Schröder was standing them up.

Some minutes later, the PM returned to the front lawn gathering. Entering the fray, he glanced angrily towards Schröder, before engaging that winning Blair smile and fraternally joining a separate huddle of world leaders.

Threats to the PM's life could come from surprising angles. On behalf of 'A' Squad's Prime Ministerial protection team, I advanced several visits of PM Tony Blair to Iraq. On one of these operations PM Blair first stopped off in Kuwait. I'd accompanied the PM to Kuwait as it was the anniversary of Kuwait's liberation from Iraq, and there was an expectation of threat. I led the operation from the back-up vehicle behind the principal, having placed one of the PM's regular team members in the car with him. There was no doubt that the PM, one of the main architects of the Iraq war, was in danger of assassination.

Conscious of this threat, Kuwaiti Protection Service officers took no chances. Trained by the US Secret Service the Kuwaitis utilised large convoys with an integral CAT team, ambulance, police pilot and escort vehicles as well as motorcycle outriders, although the outriders were not well-used. Unlike the Met's Special Escort Group *(SEG)* the Kuwaiti motorcyclists did not attempt to ride ahead and halt traffic or to mark a clear route to keep the convoy moving. They seemed to be there to make the convoy look good.

In keeping with many overseas ops where full protection is afforded, the vehicles and drivers were provided by the local Kuwaiti police/protection agency. And they drove like maniacs through the narrow downtown streets of Kuwait City. They drove with such recklessness that I feared for the PM's life - not to mention the Kuwaiti pedestrians. I was told that this was a tactical measure to prevent the convoy being targeted by Rocket Propelled Grenades *(RPG)*.

At that moment we pulled up at a red traffic light.

"If that's the case then why are we stopping?" I asked.

The answer was due to a recent Royal Decree that forbade protection vehicles from travelling through red traffic lights - the decree was a result of an accident. I suggested to the head Kuwaiti protection officer that if we were going to stop at every traffic light we might as well travel at much slower speeds between them. They complied and after the operation was over, I offered the Kuwaitis the opportunity to gain training from the Met's Driving School in the use of motorcycle escort techniques.

*

In September 2010 Deputy Prime Minister (DPM) Nick Clegg attended the United Nations General Assembly *(UNGA)* in New York. At the time the DPM was representing the Prime Minister David Cameron as the UK's head of delegation. I was in New York for two reasons; firstly I was in charge of Foreign Secretary William Haigh's protection team and therefore I was attending UNGA in this capacity. Secondly, several other protected senior UK politicians were also attending UNGA and I was tasked with coordinating their protection operations as well. As head of the UK delegation, Clegg was afforded a large US protective security package for the duration of the conference. One evening, after sessions, Clegg said that he'd like to visit an old university friend who happened to live in New York. The large ten vehicle US/British convoy arrived at the friend's typical New York brownstone home taking up half of the neighbourhood. Alighting one of the massive black, smoked windowed Chevy Suburban protection SUV's we escorted Clegg to the friend's front door and he rang the bell. As he stood waiting I could plainly see Clegg's excitement. The door opened and the friend beheld the spectacle of his old university pal, Nick, silhouetted against the flashing blue and red lights of his large protection convoy consisting of six blacked out massive US 4x4 SUVs, two sedan's and two NYPD patrol vehicles manned by numerous US Secret Service, Department of State Security Service, Alcohol Tobacco & Firearms *(ATF)* and US Marshals Service Federal Agents, plus NYPD police officers and of course us - his team from Scotland Yard's SO1 Specialist Protection unit. Clegg could hardly contain his bursting pride as he greeted his friend, who asked, wide-eyed:

"Is this all for you?"

Nick knew he'd made it that night.

*

When John Prescott announced his intention to step down from the role of DPM towards the end of the Tony Blair's Labour government, I scheduled a meeting with him. As DPM he had received 24/7 'A' Squad personal protection which I was in charge of, amongst several other teams at the time. I therefore organised a meeting with the ex-DPM concerning his expectations as to the gradual phasing out of this personal protection package. We met in Prescott's office in the House of Commons. After some small talk, I got down to the issue at hand.

"What do you see happening to your protection now you are no longer the DPM?"

"Gone," replied the ex-DPM.

"Excuse me?"

"It'll go, hopefully immediately." He reiterated. "You're good guys and girls but I didn't want it in the first place and I don't need it now."

"So you thought you never needed protection?"

"That's right. Your guys were at greater threat up in Hull than I ever was. This whole protection thing was Tony's bloody way of keeping an eye on me. Not the other way round."

"What do you mean?"

"It was after this guy threw an egg at me and I decked him. Which I think was all set up by Sky TV any way. It was too much of a coincidence, they had it almost immediately. Tony wanted me to apologise for what I did and I told him he could go and jump. No way was I going to apologise. Then suddenly your guys turned up to protect me. So that's why I say that you weren't protecting me, but others from me."

"So you think we were part of the mechanism of keeping you in check and therefore, as it was during elections, securing your votes."

"I guess you could say that."

"I think that analysis was unfair," I ventured. "When you hit that guy back, I think that many normal citizens especially males and possibly those with a Northern bias, probably thought good on you, this is a proper guy who lives in the real world. I'll vote for him. In that one act I think you connected with a hard-to-reach segment of voters, normal everyday people especially in old labour strongholds. But maybe that was the problem for your spin-doctors as it only affirmed your traditional support. That's my humble opinion anyway."

A flash, a sparkle of the real politician momentarily shone in the ex-DPM's eyes, possibly this occurred as he considered the real reasons why he entered politics as a seaman all those years ago. We spoke for a while longer. He was a plain-speaking, good guy. Prescott was the only politician I've ever known who, when it actually came to it, didn't try to keep his personal protection. Personal protection can be very seductive. Principals don't need to think when receiving prot. Prot officers take care of everything, getting principals where they need to be without them even breaking sweat. So for many, losing prot can be devastating. It can also be the last visible sign of status or loss thereof.

*

As the 'A' Squad officer in charge of Home Secretary David Blunkett's protection team I was notified by 'C' Squad that the Diplomatic Protection Group *(DPG)*, the armed uniformed officers that guard government and diplomatic premises, had arrested an individual hammering on the gates of Downing Street with a sledge hammer. After his arrest the suspect was transported to Cannon Row police station from whence the Branch was called, due to the fact that the assailant stated that he wished to do the Home Secretary harm. Having established that the individual had previously been convicted of the USI *(unlawful sexual intercourse)* with a minor, and had been subject to chemical libido suppression to prevent future urges, we unearthed a pad highlighting the grounds for his attack. Documentary evidence left behind by the assailant reasoned that by hammering on Downing Street's gates, he would leave the DPG with no choice but to shoot him.

To make sure he'd be shot and not tasered, the suspect had subjected himself to long bouts of electrical shocks hoping in this way to build up resistance to the Taser should it be deployed. The suspect also considered the police use of CS spray. So in an attempt to withstand this weapon he wore builder's goggles and a makeshift respiratory mask. And finally, in an attempt to survive the gunshot wounds he hoped to sustain, the assailant tried to make homemade body armour *(bullet resistant jacket)*. To achieve this, the suspect wore several layers of clothing. The idea being that as Kevlar body armour is made up of layers and layers of Kevlar, why wouldn't multiple layers of clothing act in the same manner?

Hence, with the media's undoubted interest in him piqued, due to the location of the shooting, he would then give interviews to the press from his hospital bed berating the Home Secretary's authority to take away his human right to experience sexual urges for whomsoever he liked. Unfortunately, for the assailant the DPG didn't play ball and instead of shooting, tasering or spraying him, the quick thinking DPG officers simply asped *(used his extendable metal truncheon)* the man to the ground.

If it was at all required, the assailant's thoughts and actions provided 'A' Squad officers with another wake-up call. The assailant's warped logic and detailed yet flawed planning could just as easily have been directed in a traditional manner towards the Home Secretary – by carrying out a close quarter assassination attempt. The assailant was sectioned for psychiatric evaluation.

By summer 2005 David Blunkett had regained a ministerial role after the scandal that had caused him to resign the Home Secretary's position. Due to the residual threat caused by his actions as Home Secretary, Blunkett had retained his 'A' Squad personal protection team whilst out of office and it was assessed that he should also keep it in his new role as Secretary of State for works and pensions *(SoSWP)*. I was still in charge of Blunkett's team, in addition to those of several other high-ranking ministers. As one of the few senior blind politicians in the world, Blunkett had a world-wide profile and hence a higher vulnerability to attack. On a visit to Sannitch, Victoria Island, British Columbia, Canada, Blunkett was in a vehicle driven by one of my specialist protection drivers. I was also in the vehicle performing the role of principal protection officer *(PPO)* in addition to another close protection officer from the team. We were all en route to Sannitch Airport to catch a return flight to Vancouver. As we travelled along we were discussing favourite films and TV series, I asked Blunkett if he'd seen *Deadwood* and what he thought of it. Blunkett said he had and that the film and its songs were one of his favourites. I remarked that I did not mean the film, but the rugged TV show starring Ian MacShane as a brutal whore house owner in the pre-state South Dakota territory of the 1870's. Although he had not seen the programme, Blunkett said he would no doubt prefer the Doris Day musical and burst into a rendition of the 'Deadwood Stage'. It was infectious and as though the Welsh male boys' choir had landed in our vehicle. We all began singing at the top of our voices, 'Oh the Deadwood stage is travelling down the road.... Whip crack away, whip crack away, whip crack away!'

    We arrived in the airport environs still in good voice but in a split second, as we stopped the vehicle and alighted, we replaced our previous jovial countenance with the sober appearance and demeanour of a Scotland Yard Special Branch protection team escorting a senior British cabinet minister on government business.

    Waiting for us at the airport, in addition to the local police who we'd orchestrated earlier, stood the proverbial 'little old lady'. Ministerial and earnest, we guided the minister to the little old lady, who at 85 had a delighted smile of expectation on her face. She was introduced as the grandmother of one of the Canadian police officers who we had met on the previous day's recce. The officer explained that all her life his grandmother had wanted to meet a Scotland Yard Detective so when she heard that officers from Scotland Yard's Special Branch were in town, she just had to meet us. Meeting and shaking David Blunkett's hand was, comparatively for her, by-the-by.

*

For a period of two years, I ran former Prime Minister Sir John Major's protection team travelling to top locations all over the world. This was a 'Hollywood Prot'. In Texas in 2007, I was advancing Sir John's speaking tour. On arrival in the US I had asked the United States Department of State Security Service *(DSS)*, the US Federal Agency responsible for protecting foreign dignitaries, to assist me with the protection of the former PM. Unfortunately, the DSS had refused. In their analysis Sir John was too long out of office to warrant their protection, plus they had no intelligence to suggest that he was under any specific threat of assassination. I countered by stating that an absence of knowledge is not an absence of malice and that there was a potential for a transfer of terrorist activity to Sir John, as a British figurehead, not least as a result of our involvement with the United States in the ongoing wars in Afghanistan and Iraq. However, although the senior DSS officer sympathised and appreciated my arguments, their assessment stood. After all, he argued, any immediate attacks could be dealt with by me and my team. This was why, he said, the United States government was allowing us to carry firearms unsupervised throughout their territory; something he knew would never be countenanced in the UK. I had to accept his point.

The reason why I wanted DSS assistance was down to experience. When working in foreign lands it's always best, except when spying of course, to have the local Security Service/Law enforcement in tow. Then if anything untoward occurred the local Security Service or Law enforcement officers would generally know the procedures to perform and have instant authority to deal with any issues; whereas I wouldn't. Nevertheless, knowing that the DSS wouldn't budge, I thanked them for their help and resolved to try my luck with state and local law enforcement. Because Sir John's tour was scheduled to take in several Texan cities: Dallas, Fort Worth, San Antonio, Austin and Huston etc., I decided to advance the op with one of my DC's. Pete was a great guy who was good at his job and also good company. The first call I made was to the Texas Rangers – they were the state law enforcement body who had jurisdiction throughout the whole of Texas, so if I could get their assistance it should be plain sailing throughout the operation.

Time had been built into Sir John's programme to spend an afternoon with his old friend and ex-President George Bush senior, so as his son was presently the President of the United States I knew that the Rangers wouldn't want anything going wrong with our visit in the good old state of Texas, especially as it was the President's home state. Moreover, my goal was also helped by the fact that the Governor was a Republican like the President. So after contacting the Governor's office, it was the Lt Governor who contacted me to say that we could expect all the assistance we required from any state, county or city law enforcement bodies whilst we were in God's own country. All I'd needed to do was ask.

In terms of visiting the ex-President, that would be plain sailing. We'd already contacted US Secret Service, whose job it was to protect all Presidents for life, so this aspect of the job was in the bag. Wherever we'd visit President Bush, be it at his Texan ranch, the oilmen's club or in his office outside the city, I knew this could all be relatively easily organised with the Secret Service. That said, for sake of professionalism we'd recce all these venues to make sure we familiarised ourselves with them, so we'd be on the ball regardless of where the meet would take place.

To perform our recces in the various cities of Texas, my team were assigned several Texas Rangers and, thankfully their vehicles. Texas is a very large state, so we had to fly between some of the cities. I also had to stagger the earlier arrival of another of my officers to recce and wait in San Antonio area due to the sheer distances involved in moving between the Texan cities. In addition to cities we also visited some venues in 'county' areas such as those surrounding Dallas and Fort Worth. Dallas area Texas Ranger, Jesus Antonio Ramirez, took us to one of these counties where I met Sheriff Douglas B Alderman III. If you can picture J W Pepper from the James Bond movie *'Live and Let Die'*, then you're not far off picturing Sheriff Alderman III. Douglas was a good man and he was going to make sure that there'd be no problems in his county. Douglas assigned his relative to us - Nathaniel T - a chip off the old block. Nathaniel was one hell of a guy. As tall as he was wide, Nathaniel carried a revolver slung low off his hips balanced by old-style cylindrical handcuffs and ammunition pouches. His avuncular features, added to his larger than life appearance as did his constant habit of chewing tobacco and spitting it ever so often into an open Coca Cola can situated in the centre drinks console holder of his big American police cruiser. Nathaniel knew every nook and cranny of his county, and was keen to show us this, explaining where he thought any problems might well arise. At the conclusion of our recces late that evening Nathaniel suggested we go with him for something to eat and drink before heading back to our hotel some distance away in city of Dallas.

As we drove, Nathaniel got on the phone to his *'Darlin'*.

"Hey Darlin, you're on speaker."

"Okay," we heard his wife drawl.

"You ain't gonna believe who I got with me, Honey!"

"Who you got baby?" The female voice sounded only slightly inquisitive.

"It sounds like a joke, but it ain't," he teased.

"Well okay...."

"I got me a Mexican Texas Ranger."

"Yeah?" She was clearly underwhelmed.

"Yeah, an I got me two British Secret agents!" he played his trump card with glee.

"You got you *what*?!" She shrieked.

"I got me two British fellas from Scotland Yard."

"No Honey!" Excited now. "You sure you're tellin' me right?"

"That ain't all, Honey, one of them Scotland Yard agents is black!"

"He's what?"

"Yep, and he's in charge too!"

"Honey, my gawd, let me talk to him!"

"Alrightee." He turned to me, grinning. "Carlton, would ya speak to my darlin?"

I obliged.

"Darling, how are you?"

"Oh, well Sir, I'm real good. You really from Scotland Yard?"

"Yes I am. Please call me Carlton."

"I don't believe it! Scotland Yard? Oh my! Wait 'til I tell my girls!"

Nathaniel took control again.

"Okay darlin, we're gonna eat now."

Nathaniel hung up. He'd been bathing in the reflected glory of his two new Scotland Yard colleagues. In this slice of the ante-bellum south, which time seemed to have passed by, these *secret agents* from Scotland Yard were an unimaginable breed. We were making a splash in this rural county where even a Mexican Texas Ranger was an object of interest not to mention two British Scotland Yard secret agents, one of whom was black and in-charge.

On one of many visits to New York Sir John and I were staying in the 5-star $850 per night Four Seasons hotel in Manhattan. During our stay Sir John met General Colin Powell for lunch in one of the hotel's restaurants. Sir John, always a gentleman, introduced the former US Secretary of State and Chairman of the Joint Chiefs of Staff to me. In line with US convention General Powell, who had been out of office for more than a year, was not afforded US government personal protection. A fact that started a debate on Sir John's continued protection between me and one of my officers. I came down on the side of him still receiving it. As a Prime Minister one needs to make decisions that will follow him/her for the rest of their lives. If they thought that some years down the line they'd be jettisoned by the state – life and death decisions, such as committing British forces to war or to combatting terror etc., might be taken with the incumbent's future self-preservation in mind rather than the country's well-being.

*

Former US President Bill Clinton, a frequent visitor to the UK, also provided me with many fun (and worrisome) moments. As per agreement with the United States on every occasion that any former President visits the UK he receives 'A' Squad, latterly SO1 personal protection. On such occasions, the SO1 team works closely with the President's own US Secret Service *(USSS)* protection detail. During one such visit, whilst I was running the SO1 team, the President and I were talking about various issues as we walked in central London. Discussing Rwanda the President explained that "America had had no appetite for another African adventure post-Somalia." He also mentioned that the fact that he didn't call the actions there genocide was one of the major regrets of his presidency.

"I'm sorry I let it happen," he said referring to the Rwandan holocaust, where 800,000 civilians were massacred in less than a hundred days in 1994, whilst the world stood by. The President's apology was clearly heartfelt and real.

A larger than life character, President Clinton has mass appeal and an incredible capacity to raise funds for the causes he supports. One of his causes is the rejuvenation of Rwanda which is perhaps, in part, a result of this regret.

President Clinton has a legendary ability to draw people simply by his presence. An affable man, his homely and engaging manner excites individuals, which can be problematic for protection officers.

On one occasion we were shopping on an abnormally quiet Bond Street, in London's West End. Having purchased some jewellery the President exited the upmarket shop in one of Bond Street's grand shopping arcades. My team and the Secret Service had secured the shop by having myself and President's Secret Service protection team leader inside the shop with Clinton whilst several US agents and my officers were outside the shop's environs controlling the mall. Both sets of operatives were relatively unobtrusive so none of the seemingly up-market shoppers appeared to have noticed anything out of the ordinary. Clinton exited the shop and entered a street scene of utter tranquillity. Suddenly, the President spotted a good-looking couple with a young toddler in a stroller. Seemingly drawn to these picture postcard Londoners, the consummate politician couldn't stop himself from going over to the child and praising her beauty to the parents. It took a split second but the recognition streaked across the mother's face as the tall ageing, yet still Hollywood handsome, former US President, praised her child's looks.

"What a beautiful child you've got there." He beamed,

"It's Bill Clinton!" exclaimed the mother excitedly.

"It's President Bill Clinton!" Her partner stood in awe.

Suddenly, the street was full. People came from everywhere, pouring out of buildings to take pictures and shake the former President's hand. We were utterly mobbed but luckily by a crowd that clearly loved Bill Clinton. The President loved it, he looked rejuvenated and didn't want to go, despite our insistence. Like most in the performing arts, to the discomfort of Protmen, most politicians seem to live off the oxygen of the masses.

*

One evening in Monaco, Monte Carlo, I was discussing the Arsenal football team's selection with a former PM, when as is normally the case with Arsenal rivals, he said Arsenal hadn't fielded a single Englishman. At the time at least two of the team's regular players, Theo Walcott and Kieran Gibbs, were playing. I pointed out that we were fielding these players, whereupon the ex-PM rested his case. I retorted that both these guys were English born and breed, as I believed, were their parents. The only difference I could see with any other Englishmen was that both happened to be black, to be precise, mixed race. So I pointed this out. However, the former PM was having none of it, and negated my point saying they were West Indians. Using this criterion, I thought, perhaps the greatest of recent Englishmen, and the former PM's favourite, Sir Winston Churchill, was an American; Winston's mother being American born and breed.

For me it was interesting to note the difference between this former PM's perspective and that of both former US Secretary of State, General Colin Powell, and former US President Bill Clinton, both of whom instantly recognised my Britishness. Indeed, President Clinton signed and annotated his book to me with the words: 'Thanks for your service to your country'. Maybe when Brits of colour are universally seen by their fellow countrymen and women as truly English, Scottish, Welsh or Northern Irish, will real unity have been achieved in these isles. After all, former politician Michael Portillo, Radio and TV presenter Adrian Chiles and many other first generation mixed-nationality white men and women never have their English or Britishness questioned. It was perhaps this concept of national belonging that most motivated me to write this book.

Many BEM *(Black & Ethnic Minority)* Brits in the past, and indeed at present, are undertaking activities other than sport and entertainment to progress the wellbeing of this - our nation, although unfortunately all-too-often this goes unnoticed.

In the four years since I've written this memoir and fought to get it published, I have seen some changes in society that I would rather have not. Clearly the UK is a different Kingdom than I was born into. For the young me, it was not uncommon when visiting areas of Manchester to see signs proclaiming 'No Blacks, No Dogs and No Irish. Although many signs regularly omitted one, if not both of the latter categories. After all, England is a nation of dog lovers. However, slowly but surely such signs began to disappear as many decent politicians, trades unionists, political activists of all colours and creeds and simply descent normal people made it bad form to act in this manner and legislation, the Race Relations Act of 1965, forbade it.

The ex-Prime Minister I mentioned earlier was anything but a racist. Old fashioned, of his time or even misguided, but not a racist. Indeed, he and I got on well and I valued his wisdom. But hard fought battles can be easily overturned. Feelings of alienation, even in what one perceives to be one's own indigenous nation can lead to ill thoughts if not deeds. The inclusivity I sought for all citizens regardless of colour, creed or nationality has come under even greater attack as, Jihadis through terror, sought to divide and conquer us and self-serving politicians banged the drum of nationalism. So now, even Poles, who having once been feted as fellow RAF Battle of Britain heroes where seemingly overnight transformed by some Brexit campaign leaders, into EU freeloaders.

The dangers of derision and division I'd spent my career trying to supress were once again being uncapped and let out of the bottle, with as yet unknown and perhaps unintended consequences for our economy, our political influence our place in Europe, the world and indeed the very unity of our now, discordant united Kingdom. To my mind nothing embodied this more than the actions of one senior popularist Conservative politician. Seemingly imbued with anti-EU fervour and Prime Ministerial ambition, this politician even insulted the President of the United States apparently claiming that President Obama's race and cultural heritage precluded him from being a true staunch ally of the United Kingdom. I can imagine the incredulity of the angst ridden senior foreign office diplomats tasked with picking-up the pieces of this 'questionable statement' in the US corridors of power. Such diplomats, no doubt already fearing what withdrawal from the EU would do to the so called 'special relationship' and Britain's role as the

US' gateway to 'European' diplomacy, must have wondered how any British politicians with a degree political acumen could have uttered such a statement.

Post the EU referendum it seems that for a substantial number of my country men and women that the worm has turned. It would appear that patriotism in various guises, has now come to the fore, and that 'immigrants', visible or not, are left wondering whether they are seen as belonging to this 'new' traditional Britain.

Chapter Twenty-One - Dis-integration

The Special Branch of the 1980's was mostly cossetted from the type of crude societal racism that existed in the MPS in general. It was simply more enlightened. However, as MPSB's management and cadre began to change in the late 1990's due to the less than exacting recruitment processes, thanks to the Met's new corporate approach, racism began to take root.

In 2004 an 'A' Squad DCI, clearly jealous of the success of my counter-reconnaissance unit, made his thoughts known in a racist manner when he refused to endorse my promotion papers. At the time, this DCI who had recently failed his Superintendent's promotion process said to me, in the presence of another DCI, that he would not support my promotion application because: "There's no way you're going to be same rank as me." Previously, the DCI had told me that he had left the UK and joined a colonial police force because he saw "black people getting away with murder in the UK." When I tried to tell the DCI that the Commissioner *(at the time Sir John Stevens)* had directed me to reapply for promotion so the MPS could promote me this year, righting an injustice I'd suffered during the previous year's promotion process, the DCI simply rebutted my statement with an expletive.

The injustice the previous year, 2003, had occurred as I successfully reached the final stage of the promotion process. Inspectors seeking promotion, from throughout the Met, who reached this final stage were required to verbally inform the board *(a panel of senior officers)* why their activities over the past three years made them suitable for promotion to the rank of Chief Inspector. In my case, having recently returned to the police from SIS, it meant that I had to describe some of my less sensitive actions as an MI6 case officer.

Some weeks later, when I was informed that I'd failed the board, the Superintendent providing me with my board feedback said that the two Superintendents listening to my activities, simply didn't believe what I had done in SIS. As general duty Superintendents they just couldn't believe that any police officer performed Top Secret work in SIS. This was the case, even though I hadn't told them anything particularly *sensitive* or overly remarkable, as like practically all non-Special Branch officers, these senior officers were not vetted and hence were not permitted to hear secret intelligence. Nevertheless, according to the Superintendent providing me with the feedback, what I did say still appeared outlandish and frankly like something straight out of an Ian Fleming novel.

Clearly, institutionalised racism could have been a factor in the Superintendents' unwillingness to believe me, however, it was just as likely that these senior officers just couldn't grasp the Branch, its actions and contacts, not to mention the world-wide clandestine operations I performed in the Secret Intelligence Service. In fact during the promotion interview I knew my chances of passing the board were slipping away when after explaining some of my activities to prevent terrorism around the world, one of the Superintendents' said: "I hear what you 'say' you've done in MI6, but what have you done to prevent robberies and crimes that affect the police and public here in the MPS in London?"

So it was some months after being informed that I would not be promoted, that I attended one of the then Commissioner Sir John Stevens' obligatory question and answer sessions. The sessions were designed to tease out problems among MPS staff. Therefore, after hearing other MPS staff air their points and grievances in front of five hundred of their peers, I took the floor concerning my promotion attempt. I asked the Commissioner how it was possible that an individual who had spent his time successfully fighting terrorism around the world was dismissed by a promotion panel for not working on London-centric volume crime, such as burglary. I pointed out that I found this particularly galling as in his priorities for that year he had put 'preventing and combatting terrorism' as the Met's number one priority. The Commissioner, whom I knew due to the unique nature of my SIS secondment, addressed me immediately by name.

"Carlton, I know exactly what you did and what you do, nobody in the MPS, in fact the whole of the British Police Service has done more to keep London safe from international terrorism."

The Commissioner then turned to Bernhard Hogan-Howe *(who at the time was Assistant Commissioner (AC) for staffing and promotion)* and directed him to make sure that I was promoted in the coming year.

So it was I explained to Geoff, my DCI, that in line with the Commissioner's wishes, that AC Hogan-Howe's Superintendent Staff Officer had contacted me and asked me to immediately submit my promotion application. I had done as the AC requested and so that's what I'd passed to him, so he could annotate it and forward it up the chain as per protocol.

Even though I explained what had happened the previous year and that I was submitting my application at AC Hogan-Howe's direction, Geoff still refused to endorse my application.

"I don't give a fuck who's told you to submit your papers, as your line-manager I don't think you're capable of being a Chief Inspector." Was Geoff somewhat crude reply.

"That's interesting, Geoff," I retorted, "Just two months ago you wrote my annual PDR *(Personal Development Review)*, you gave me nearly all box *(level)* ones, with a few twos, these were by far the highest marks given to any officer regardless of rank in the unit."

"Yes, but that was before I failed my Superintendent's board."

"I'm sorry for you, Geoff, but that's not my problem."

Then, as though he'd suddenly grasped the significance of the PDR he'd given me he added:

"You deserved those marks, but I was assessing you as a DI."

I shook my head in amazement.

"Geoff, that's a ludicrous argument. It could be argued that the only way you can assess if somebody would be good at the next rank is if he performs well at the present rank. You went that step further though and you documented that I have excelled as a DI. Indeed, you even wrote that I was working beyond the level of the average DI. If that doesn't show potential for promotion, what will?"

It soon became clear that I was wasting my breath. I knew only too well that racism is not based on rationality. My first fight at school, aged five, was on account of my race. We were the only black family in the Northern mill town in which I was born and so I stood out. This led a fellow pupil to taunt me by calling me "Blackie." Even though I was only five-years-old and had yet to know what racism was, I knew that this was clearly an insult and so, after a few days of taunts, a fight ensued which led to us being brought before the headmaster:

"King, why were you fighting?"

"Because he called me 'Blackie', Sir."

"But you are Black, so you'd better get used to it," was the Headmaster's advice as he bent me over and administered two of the best to me, followed by my opponent.

Later, in the mid 60's, as previously mentioned, visits to the big city where punctuated by unwelcoming signs. In the 70s - which saw the popular rise of the National Front – racism raised its head as I was prevented from seeing my young white girlfriend during school hours, at the behest of her father albeit that this prohibition was achieved without race ever being mentioned. My school simply enacted new procedures to prevent sixth formers (me) and fifth formers (her), from fraternising whilst at school. When this didn't do the job her parents contacted the police! The Lancashire Constabulary desk sergeant explained that unless coercion was involved, as far as he knew a boy going out with a girl was not yet a crime Britain, regardless of the boy's colour. No further action was taken. In the end, my girlfriend's parents often resorted to keeping her at home where her mother beat her telling her she was a whore for bringing shame on the family. "No white boy will ever look at you again!" her mother would say.

When I joined the Met Black police officers were very, very, rare. During my probation as a uniformed constable at Rochester Row, one of the nick's sergeants radioed me and told me to meet him in the sergeants' office. When I arrived my reporting sergeant (effectively my boss) was also there. I knew something was amiss as my reporting sergeant looked sheepish. A decent man, he made it clear that he was only present because the other sergeant had requested his attendance and this was borne out by his pained expression. The other sergeant's demeanour couldn't have been more different, he was visibly triumphant. It was as if he'd finally achieved a difficult victory.

"I've been looking through your records of work, Carlton *(my stops, arrests, traffic reports etc.).*"

"Okay." I said gingerly.

Disingenuously, he suggested it was a matter of welfare. Making sure I got all the help I needed.

"I thought that was the job of my reporting sergeant?" I queried.

"All good supervisors should take a keen interest in all the nick's probationers," he retorted smugly.

By now my reporting sergeant's unease was palpable.

Looking earnest, the sergeant continued.

"Well, while doing these checks, something strange jumped out at me, something that I think requires an explanation."

"What's that?"

"Well, I noticed that you don't seem to stop and search many Black people!"

After gathering myself for a split second I asked the sergeant how he'd come to this deduction. As if to enforce his answer, he stood up and, hardly able to contain his glee, he explained that he'd randomly dip-sampled several officers' stop-and-search records against mine. In doing so he'd even been totally 'objective' by selecting both probationers and substantive officers. So now having done this work he could say with absolute authority that only 20% of my stop-and-searches were on Black people, whereas the nick's average was between 50% and 65%.

"So, do you have a reason for this massive disparity?" he inquired.

"Let me get this right, Sarge. I'm stopping 20% Blacks under the stop and search provisions?"

"Yes. That's right."

I looked straight into the sergeant's eyes. "It's worse than I thought."

"What's worse than you thought?"

I didn't answer his question.

"I'd like to go to the Chief Superintendent *(the officer in charge of the police station)* and seek his permission to report my actions to the folks at 10-12 Arlington Street."

"10-12 Arlington Street?" the sergeant repeated

"Yep. Arlington Street."

Arlington Street was on our patch. As I'd said the address I'd noticed some of the cockiness seeping from the sergeant's bearing.

"Why would we need to do that?" He asked.

The sergeant knew, as did we all, that 10-12 Arlington Street was the home of the Commission for Racial Equality *(CRE)*. Now sensing his unease, I happily provided him with my reasoning.

"I don't know the exact number, I'm sure you could do some more research to find out, but I think the ethnic make-up of our division *(Rochester Row police area)* is practically 98% white. The few Blacks that pass through our ground are generally making their way to and from work, generally from south of the river. So if I'm stopping such a high percentage of Black people, where there are hardly any, statisticians would no doubt say that many of these stops could only be racially biased and made without reasonable grounds to suspect an offence. Well, as you can imagine, Sarge, if that's the case and we are acting unlawfully, as a probationer I'd like to do all I can to prevent this. That's why I think its best that I bring my actions on stop and search to the attention of the CRE, as they might be able to assist me in getting this under control."

The sergeant immediately began to backtrack and we left the office a few minutes later. Nothing more was ever said about my stop and search regime. Interestingly, I noticed a subsequent dip in stops and searches performed by my relief also. Word had obviously got around.

Many years ago I was on protection with Bassam Abu Sharif *(Abu Umar)*. Bassam, the former leader of the Popular Front for the Liberation of Palestine *(PFLP)* and a target both for Mossad, whose previous attempt at assassination had left him horribly disfigured and ANO, was visiting the UK to discuss Palestinian matters with the F&CO, other British officials and various other contacts, followed by a visit to Eton to participate in an upper school debate with the Israeli Ambassador on the 'Arab/Israeli conflict. On several occasions we visited a plush apartment where Bassam's partner and young son were living. On this particular occasion Bassam was working on correspondence, whilst I waited in the living room with the GCS driver, Jim and Bassam's son. My 'A' Squad colleagues were downstairs in the back-up vehicle, with eyes on the unoccupied lead vehicle and the surrounding environs. Bassam's son was watching *Escape to Victory* - the football movie starring Sylvester Stallone, Michael Caine, Pelé and many of the world's greatest footballers. The movie, set in a WWII prisoner of war camp, revolved around a football match between the German captors and Allied prisoners who wished to utilise the match to escape. Whilst watching the movie, Jim, a cockney who'd probably been born during WWII said to Bassam's son that he shouldn't take the movie too seriously.

"It's a good film, but they've made a mistake putting Pelé in it. There weren't any coloureds fighting on our side. The Yanks had a couple, but there were none on ours."

Jim's comment took me back fifteen or so years to when I was a DJ compering in a packed working men's club of some 2,000 covers outside of Manchester. That night's top of the bill was popular northern comedian Bernard Manning. I'd just introduced Bernard onto the stage to rapturous applause – he put his hand out for me to shake as he informed the crowd how great a disc jockey–compere I was. As I put my hand out to meet his, he sharply withdrew his.

"You think I'd shake hands with you, you bastard." He said into the mic. "You see 'em on the fucking beaches, You see 'em in the fucking skies, You see 'em every fucking where, but where were they when Churchill fucking needed 'em in 1940? I don't know about never surrendering. It wasn't the fucking Germans we needed to be bothered about."

The crowd loved it. They roared with laughter. I was grateful for small mercies as he never said *Black bastard*. If he did, I might have decked him there and then. When he finally came off stage I collared him. His answer was pure Bernard.

"It's just show-business lad. You know the game."

What bothered me, as it did with Jim's comments, was that he and the crowd believed it. They had a complete lack of understanding regarding the participation of Black British and commonwealth citizens in the Second World War. Indeed, in all Britain's wars from the 1600's, if not before. Everybody in show-business knows you never take a comedian on when he's armed with a live microphone. You won't win. So I couldn't confront Bernard on that stage, but I could confront Jim.

"Actually Jim, my father was in the Merchant Marine on the Atlantic Convoys during the Second World War and the Merchant Navy was the service with one of the highest British loss rates. You should also know that there were many West Indians in the RAF and many Africans and West Indians also served and lost their lives for the Mother Country as they called it, in the Army and Navy. And if you're talking about the Second World War, India lost some three million dead in that conflict, three times as many as Britain and still a million more than the combined death toll of Britain's total losses in the First and Second World Wars combined."

It had always seemed strange to me that Australia, New Zealand, Canada, South African and even Polish participation and losses in WWII were always commented on by the media and the establishment in Britain, yet the sacrifice of others from the Commonwealth family seemed to be glossed over or forgotten. I wanted to change this so that the role of its BEM citizens in the UK's history would become more visible, otherwise the White majority community would continue to question how 'foreigners' can take out without putting in and the BEM community would continue to say that my forebears put in without any recognition or recompense. Worse still other BEMs who did not know the depth of their belonging would continue to say: 'There ain't no Black in the Union Jack' and actively work against the only homeland they'd ever really known – whilst professing to belong elsewhere.

It was the events and experiences described above that led to me to take up an idea I'd had when working at the Strategic Analysis Unit of the NPOIU. I created something I called "The Balance Theory", which would provide people with a counterweight to the belief that BEMs were new to Britain and were a drain on the nation's resources. I came to the conclusion that a good counterweight would be to identify BEM individuals in British and world history so that people would know, for example, that the great French and Russian novelists Alexandre Dumas and Alexander Pushkin were both Black (Dumas' father was born in Saint-Domingue (present-day Haiti) to a French nobleman and an enslaved African woman, while Pushkin's matrilineal great grandfather arrived in Russia as a slave from what is now Eritrea).

This ethnic identification of historical figures is important for many reasons not least because most people in the West, regardless of their ethnicity, automatically assume that such 'great' historical figures are White. Furthermore, our present educational system reinforces such assertions. Ethnic identification is also important as up to now most African and African-Caribbean people have been deprived of such positive Black role models by a slavery/colonial-induced ignorance of the past.

No less important though is the effect that such knowledge has on the majority White community. Like me, the majority community believes that it is important that all members of society pull their weight. Presently, because of the lack of the ethnic identification of historical and even present day figures of note - as well as the poor knowledge of BEM citizen's sacrifices for Queen and country - BEM citizens seem as though they have not participated in our nation's creation and maintenance. As this unbalanced ideology has been allowed to permeate, it has been easy for many in both the majority and minority communities to perceive BEM's as alien and marginalised from society's mores and traditions. Such alienation has led to the marginalisation of young BEM's, leading in some cases to a devil-may-care criminality - which is used by some as evidence to show how BEM's are a drain on the nation's resources.

I managed to pitch my Balance Theory to Foreign Office Minister Dr Kim Howells. I'd protected Kim on many occasions in various war zones and dangerous countries and we'd got on well. During an operation to Colombia he told me how shocked he was about the alienation of some Muslim youth of Pakistani heritage in Bradford - something he'd observed while visiting a university. I told him about my paper for the SAU, that it had warned against faith and de-facto faith schooling, entryism, radicalisation, religious bolstering and alienation in many religious communities. Although my paper pointed out that these concerns were not unique to Islam *(Northern Ireland and Scotland had shown how this could be a problem for Christianity)*, the trait within the Islamic community had world-wide significance. Judaism also reflected the same issues, especially in parts of London and Manchester, but it was Islam that was at the forefront of most politicians' and state functionaries' minds since 9/11. Dr Howells was keen to see a copy of my paper and asked who else had seen it. I told him that ACPO, the Security agencies and the Military; No.10, the Department for International Development *(DfID)* and the Home Office had been sent copies. I knew it had been read by Claire Short as Secretary of State for DfID at the time.

As we talked I explained how this created a sense of alienation among many BEMs and how radicals preyed upon this by giving young people the belonging they craved.

I explained how I believed that by propagating an inclusive history, where race is explicitly identified, would help to combat this. I provided the example of the significant number of 'West Indians' and other Black people who'd fought in all of Britain's wars since the 1680's, even serving on the Victory with Admiral Lord Nelson. In WWII the tiny British West Indian Islands, with a collective population less than that of Greater Manchester, sent up to 10,000 of its sons to Britain to serve in the RAF and even more of its sons and daughters into the Merchant and Royal Navies and the British Army. In its time of need the mother country called and these subjects answered in large numbers.

Even prior to the main influx of Anglo Saxons into Britain in the fifth century AD, Black and mixed-race people had settled in Britain for more than three hundred years as part and parcel of Rome's ruling elite. These Black British Romans were soldiers, merchants, domestics, politicians; one of these Black Romans was even the emperor of Rome itself. That particular Black emperor and general of the Roman armies was Emperor Septimus Severus. After military campaigns at and beyond Hadrian's Wall, Severus would later take ill and die in York, where he was buried in 211 AD.

I also mentioned the Black presence in Britain during the reign of Queen Elizabeth I in 1601, and after the American war of independence in the 1770's, through to the two world wars in the last century. Kim was enthusiastic and asked me to discuss the matter with him and the then Ambassador to Colombia, Haydon Warren-Gash and both men agreed that they could see the merit in my Balance Theory.

Ambassador Warren-Gash suggested that this would be something Prince Charles would be interested in progressing through the Prince's Trust. Kim told me to leave it with him and that on our return he'd contact those necessary to get it moving. As good as his word when we returned from Colombia, Venezuela and the USA, the Minister organised a meeting for me with Sir Tom Shebbeare, Director of Charities for HM Prince Charles at Clarence House. Unfortunately, Sir Tom didn't get it and I was eventually unable to get the idea off the ground.

In 2004, the racism I faced wasn't only from Geoff, some other senior ranks in 'A' Squad who could have helped didn't. So in the end I'd take Geoff and the MPS to tribunal. Still loyal I'd settle out-of-court to protect the high-level Top Secret intelligence I'd be forced to reveal in open court to prove beyond reasonable doubt that I was worthy of promotion to the rank of DCI. By this time many months later I decided never to seek promotion again, to continue doing my job to the best of my ability, but to leave the service the moment I could without losing too much pension. What I wouldn't do though was lessen my performance; my pride wouldn't allow this.

In the end, although more than five years had passed since the emergence of racism in the "new" version of Special Branch and SO1, the new recruitment policies and their dangerous and detrimental effect on operations added to my decision to leave. Some good people had joined SO1 but in the political and intelligence realm the unit's capacity had undoubtedly diminished. More importantly to me, some of the leadership level players in SO1 - DIs, DCIs and Detective Superintendents - were changing the protection ethos. SO1 officers were becoming weapon-orientated bodyguards, rather than intelligence-conversant protection officers. When the Branch disbanded, the joined-up nature of the Met's security/intelligence apparatus was shattered forever. This change, a retrograde and highly dangerous step, was a terminal blow to the Met's protective security professionalism.

Therefore, as I'd long vowed, the moment I became eligible for retirement and a nearly full pension, I quietly left the MPS in 2012, aged 55 and after 28 years of service. I was proud of my many achievements in the Branch as an intelligence officer, a UC, and a Prot man and in SIS as a Case Officer, but equally satisfying was that no innocents had died on my watch and I'd saved many lives.

No Branch man could ask for more.

Images

Baghdad 2003, during the war fighting stage. The author standing in front of a giant portrait of Saddam in his main Baghdad palace, soon to be CPA HQ.

Flying an RAF C130 during a light hearted moment on a mission to Afghanistan.

Leading President Bill Clinton's protection team in London with US Secret Service colleagues.

Downtown Tripoli. On operation in Gadhafi's Libya.

Leading the protection operation for former PM Tony Blair in Rwanda

The Author directs one of his officers and a colleague from HM Customs, whilst supervising the arrival of President Obama at Stansted Airport on board Air Force One.

Protecting former Prime Minister Sir John Major in ancient Petra, supported by colleagues from the Jordanian Security Service.

Commanding the protection operation to secure Dutch right wing anti-Islamic party leader, Geert Wilders, during his visit to the UK. Wilders was at extreme threat of assassination. Here the author, his team, Dutch protection colleagues and uniform police secure Wilders' departure under heavy media coverage and angry Islamic extremist demonstrators.

Wilders, who had previously been band from the UK took full advantage of his invitation by a lord of the realm to address peers and the British press in one of the reception rooms at house of Lords

No rest for the wicked. Co-ordinating logistics. My US bedroom in Baghdad during the invasion. Below: Danger everywhere. My accommodation in the ruined, old British embassy. It was way outside the Green zone.

Photo op. Outside the then new British Embassy in Kabul, Afghanistan whilst commanding a ministerial protection operation carrying my MP5 Kurtz machine gun and Glock 17 semi-automatic pistol. Like Iraq, seemingly every other month I'd be in Afghanistan. They'd become my second home.

With Chinese Police Colleagues from Beijing Security Police and the PAP (People's Armed Police) during the Beijing Olympics. I was charged with securing London House (LH), the UK's Olympic residence in Beijing. During my seven week stay in the country PM Brown, former PM Blair, Mayor Boris Johnson and many others would attend the facility. LH was a potential terrorist target as it staged aspects of the UK's Olympic handover ceremony. It's not all work. Below: On the Great Wall of China.

320

My view from a helo, on a raid to burn down a coca plantation with Colombian Narco Police, Search Bloc (Bloque de Búsqueda), near Bogota, Colombia.

On operation in the one of the main squares in Bogota, Colombia. Hostage taking was a concern in any part of Colombia.

Foreign Office Minister, Bill Rammel, and the British Ambassador to Afghanistan, Rosalind Marsdon, pictured with my joint MPSB and RMP team at the British Embassy in Kabul, Afghanistan. The RMP team was assigned to the Ambassador but were always supportive of MPSB operations. Rosalind would later become our Ambassador in Iraq also.

Glock hidden under my tunic, the US Navy fly me and a member of my advance team out of Bamiyan, Northern Afghanistan. Having arranged my op with New Zealand Special Forces, I'd return with a minister later that week.

On US ops. Outside the Whitehouse, Washington DC after discussions with US Secret Service, State Department Security Service, FBI and US Special Forces colleagues.

323

On ops in Singapore. One of my guys and I stayed in the lavish Shangri la Hotel's ultra-high end Valley Wing. We're pictured here with a local Security police colleague.

In Washington DC. A regular 1st world stomping ground along with Brussels, Paris and Berlin

Advancing a UK customs assistance programme aimed at reducing the finances gained by the Taliban from Heroin trafficking, north of Kabul. As the location was massively overlooked I arranged the assistance of Dutch Apache attack helicopters, in addition to UK military, to cover our position.

My team and I with Secretary of State David Blunkett and friends on Victoria Island, British Colombia, Canada.

One of my guys and I during the extremely dangerous occasion of the 2nd inauguration of President Karzhai in Kabul, Afghanistan, I'd also been present at the 1st inauguration, several years earlier.

Leading a protection operation in Afghanistan for the then Foreign Secretary, William Haigh. I'd run his protection team for some two years prior to finally retiring.

Arrival of HRH the Prince of Wales in Saudi Arabia on board the Queen's Flight.

328

Sheer opulence. Inside HRH Saudi Prince Mutaib's personal hotel, reserved solely for the Prince's chosen guests. The chandelier hangs six floors.

Whilst HRH Prince Charles was in the desert, I was one of very few guests in this 300 rooms 6 star establishment

PM Blair's visit to Kuwait, whilst on route to Iraq, on the 10th anniversary of Kuwait's liberation. This lead vehicle was being driven too fast by Kuwaiti Prot.

Above: My view out of a US Navy Special Forces helo of the Hindu Kush mountains. Spectacular.

On the red carpet at London House 2008 Olympics Games in Beijing

On ops in Seoul, South Korea

On a mission in Jamaica

In Canada on an protection operation
Join the Branch and see the world!
In my career ops were many and varied Intel and Prot, opulent and basic.
Monte Carlo, Syria, Russia, Ukraine, Beijing, Iraq, North & South Sudan,
Kenya, South Korea, Canada, USA, Colombia, Venezuela, Australia, Jamaica,
Afghanistan, Israel etc., etc., etc.

Check Point Charlie. At the time of my detention there, in the early 80's, this was the main border between communism and capitalism – East and West.

Colombian drugs tsar Pablo Escobar was so serious about killing President elect Gaviria that he blew up the above plane killing all on board.

Flying it.

On board a US Black Hawk with US Apache escorts I'd arranged with the Americans to fly our Ministers to and from BIAP when travelling to Central Baghdad. I considered travel by road on along *Route Irish* to be just too dangerous for Ministers.
(However, when I undertook pre-visit recces or travelled without a 'principal' I'd have to take my chances by road.)

Boarding an RAF Chinook in Basra with one of my top DS', whilst leading the protection operation for Armed Forces Minister, Adam Ingram

Leading another high risk protection operation (HTLI).
Organising the convoy, utilising British military support and private
security, to move the Secretary of State for Defence through Basra City,
in the British sector of Iraq

President Bill Clinton's captioned his book to me "Thanks for your service to your country".

Printed in Great Britain
by Amazon